Simplicity

Of

Scripture

A Bible Study Companion

Clifton Harper, MBS

Table of Contents

Old Testament

New Testament

All biblical quotes are from KJV 1611.

ISBN: 978-0-9903185-1-4

Kerusso Publications
2000 N. Pennsylvania Ave.
Mangum OK. 73554

Introduction

Simplicity of Scripture is not a complete concordance but rather a guide intended to aid the reader in understanding key elements in each book of the Bible and to see the thread of unity that runs through the Bible by revealing Christ in each book. God desires for all honest hearts to read and understand the Bible because He wants all men to seek Him, "But seek ye first the kingdom of God, and his righteousness; and all these things shall be added unto you." (Matt. 6:33). God wants man to seek Him because He wants all men to be saved, "The Lord is not slack concerning his promise, as some men count slackness; but is longsuffering to us-ward, not willing that any should perish, but that all should come to repentance." (2 Pet. 3:9). The Bible provides to mankind all that is necessary for him to have life and to have it more abundantly, "According as his divine power hath given unto us all things that pertain unto life and godliness, through the knowledge of him that hath called us to glory and virtue:" (2 Pet.1:3). Man needs nothing outside of the Bible to guide him or teach him. God has given His word to mankind for us to know it, understand it, obey it and live by it, "All scripture *is* given by inspiration of God, and *is* profitable for doctrine, for reproof, for correction, for instruction in righteousness:" (2 Tim. 3:16).

There is a theme that runs through the Bible from the beginning to the end and that theme is Redemption. God knew from before the foundation of the world that man would need to be saved and knew how He would bring salvation to mankind, "According as he hath chosen us in him before the foundation of the world, that we should be holy and without blame before him in love:" (Eph. 1:4), and, "Who verily was foreordained before the foundation of the world, but was manifest in these last times for you," (1 Pet. 1:20). Peter is telling us that Christ who was manifested in these last days was foreordained to do so that He might take away man's sins. Christ is the key to understanding how the story of the Bible unfolds. Through each book of the Bible the reader will be shown how Christ is mentioned and included in each book. From Genesis 1:1 to Revelation 22:21 the presence of Christ is sensed. The entire Bible focuses on Christ. A gentleman by the name of Dr. G. Campbell Morgan wrote, "The roads of the books of the Old Testament lead up to Him… He, the lonely and perfect Personality of the Gospel narratives, stands at the center, and all the highways meet in Him." As the reader moves through the pages of this book and studies form each book of the Bible it is hoped that that they will find Christ and ultimately find Him in life too.

This book is dedicated to one of the best friends I have had in this life and the one to come. He was my friend and my brother and a fellow minister in the Lord's church. Leon Jones has gone to be with the Lord however he will never be forgotten. He had a love for God, His word and for lost souls. He shared that love with me and taught and shared with me much of the knowledge he had learned and now I am sharing some of it with you in this book. Part of our jobs as Christians is to share the knowledge of God's word with others, 2 Tim. 2:2.

A Glimpse at the Bible

   The Bible is one compete story telling of mankind's origins, how he is to live and his eventual destiny. The Bible story contains knowledge of man's creator and the creator of all things which is God. The story also includes instructions for mankind from God, telling mankind what he must do to have eternal life in heaven with God when all time comes to an end. The Bible is broken into two parts or two great covenants also called testaments. One is the Old Testament and the other is the New Testament. The Old was designed to lead man and prepare man for the New. The Old was also the foundation upon which the New is built. Without the New the Old is a start that has no finish and without the old the New is a finish that has no starting point. The Old begins and the New completes. Following is a comparison between the Old and the New Testaments take note of the similarities:

OLD TESTAMENT	NEW TESTAMENT
The Old begins with God.	The New begins with Jesus Christ.
(Genesis 1:1)	(Matt. 1:1)
The Old introduces the first Adam.	The New reveals the second Adam.
(Genesis 2:20)	(1 Cor. 15:20; Rom. 5:14)
The Old is linked with Moses.	The New is linked with Christ.
(John 1:17)	(John 1:17)
The Old deals with Law.	The New deals with Grace.
(John 1:17)	(John 1:17)

The Old is a shadow.	The New is the real thing.
(Heb. 10:1)	(Heb. 10:1)
The Old points to Christ.	The New portrays Christ.
(Gal. 3:24)	(Heb. 12:2)
The Old prepares for the Messiah.	Then New delivers the Messiah.
(Isa. 7:14)	(Matt. 1:21)
The Old focuses on a nation.	The New focuses on a man.
(Gen. 35:11)	(Rev. 1:1)
The Old gathers at Sinai.	The New gathers around Calvary.
(Exodus 19:1, 2)	(John 12:32)
The Old recalls sins.	The New removes sins.
(Heb. 10:3)	(Heb. 10:17; Acts 2:38)
The Old deals with Israel.	The New deals with the Church.
(Gen. 35:10)	(Matt. 16:18)
The Old earthly Jerusalem.	The New heavenly Jerusalem.
(John 4:20)	(Rev. 21:2)
The New is contained in the Old.	The Old is explained by the New.
The New is concealed in the Old.	The Old is by the New revealed.
The New is foretold in the Old.	The Old is fulfilled by the New.

Important Dates of the Old Testament

Abraham's birth	2166 B.C.
Abraham comes to Canaan	2091 B.C.
Isaac's birth	2066 B.C.
Jacob's birth	2006 B.C.
Joseph's birth	1915 B.C.
Jacob's family moves to Egypt	1876 B.C.
Joseph's death	1805 B.C.
Moses' birth	1526 B.C.
The Exodus	1446 B.C.
Moses' death; Entrance into Canaan	1406 B.C.
Death of Joshua' Judges period begins	1385 B.C.
Saul crowned king	1050 B.C.
David crowned king	1010 B.C.
Solomon crowned king	970 B.C.
Solomon's temple begins	966 B.C.
Solomon's death: Divided Kingdom	931 B.C.
Northern Kingdom (Samaria) falls to Assyria	722 B.C.
Assyria (Nineveh) falls to Babylon	612 B.C.
Southern Kingdom (Jerusalem) falls to Babylon; Solomon's temple destroyed	586 B.C.

Babylon falls to Persia	539 B.C.
Exile ends;' 1st return of exiles under Zerubbabel	536 B.C.
Temple rebuilt	515 B.C.
2nd return of exiles under Ezra	458 B.C.
3rd return of exiles under Nehemiah	445 B.C.
Old Testament revelation ends	400 B.C.

Suggestions for Bible Study

Man first of all must have respect for the Bible and believe it is the inspired word of God. "All scripture *is* given by inspiration of God, and *is* profitable for doctrine, for reproof, for correction, for instruction in righteousness:" (2 Tim. 3:16). Not only must man believe the Bible is inspired of God he must study the word of God, "Study to shew thyself approved unto God, a workman that needeth not to be ashamed, rightly dividing the word of truth." 2 Tim.2:15).

Someone desiring to study must also find a quiet place to sit and reflect, meditate and pray about what they have read and studied. The prayer should be for wisdom to be able to discern and apply the truth as they have learned it. Their study should be from a good translation of the Bible known for its accuracy such as the KJV of 1611 or the American Standard of 1901 just to name two. The translation should be one taken form the earliest transcripts nearest the originals as possible. The student should also have a pencil or pen and be willing to make notes in the margins of their Bible and keep a notebook of their findings, perhaps some questions to ask and a list of their discoveries.

The student should also develop a systematic approach to their study so they are continually building on their previous study and thereby growing in their knowledge of the word of God. Part of their systematic study should include the following:

a. Who is doing the speaking?

b. Who is being addressed or spoken to?

c. What is the subject being discussed? (What is the context of the scripture?)

d. When was it written?

e. Are there any words that I do not know?

f. Are there any promises I need to claim?

g. Are there any commands I need to obey?

h. Does this apply to me today or for someone who lived under the Old Law?

i. What is God trying to say to me? (Remember God's word can be understood.)

Genesis

Summation

The Greek word for Genesis literally means "origin while the Hebrew word for Genesis means "in the beginning." The book of Genesis tells mankind of the beginning of everything with the exception of God who has no beginning and no end, "And he said unto me, It is done. I am Alpha and Omega, the beginning and the end. I will give unto him that is athirst of the fountain of the water of life freely." (Rev. 21:6), and, "And God said unto Moses, I AM THAT I AM: and he said, Thus shalt thou say unto the children of Israel, I AM hath sent me unto you." (Ex. 3:14). Contrary to what some believe, Genesis is a real historical anthology of real people from Adam to Joseph. Because Genesis is the first book and the beginning of all history it is also the foundation for the entire Bible. The book was written by Moses approximately 1450-1410 B.C. All of the events that take place in Genesis occur in a time frame that covers approximately half of the time encompassed in all of the Old Testament which is approximately 2500 years. Our Lord Himself affirmed the historical trustworthiness of Genesis, "For as in the days that were before the flood they were eating and drinking, marrying and giving in marriage, until the day that Noe entered into the ark, And knew not until the flood came, and took them all away; so shall also the coming of the Son of man be." (Matt. 24:38, 39), and (Luke 17:32, John 8:56ff).

Breakdown

A. Fellowship with God. (Generation) – Gen. 1-2

B. Fall from fellowship with God. (Degeneration) – Gen. 3

C. Fear of God. (Veneration) – Gen. 4-11

D. Faith in God. (Regeneration) – Gen. 12-50

Pivotal Word - Generation

Ten sections of the book are introduced by the words, "these are the generations of" (2:4; 5:1; 6:9; 10:1; 11:10; 11:27; 25:12; 25:19; 36:1;

37:2). In each of the generations the reader is able to observe God's divine process of selection and election, "According as he hath chosen us in him before the foundation of the world, that we should be holy and without blame before him in love:" (Eph. 1:4), of those who will accomplish His purposes.

Characters of Importance

Adam – The first man.

Noah – A righteous man in a wicked generation.

Abraham – Father of the faithful.

Isaac – The son of promise.

Jacob – The father of Israel.

Joseph – The most Christ-like figure in the Old Testament.

Important Verses

Gen. 1:1- Here the reader learns of creation.

Gen. 1:26-27- Man appears and is made in the image of God.

Gen. 2:7- This verse shows man becoming a living soul.

Gen. 2:24 – Man is introduced to God's marriage law.

Gen. 3:1-7 – Man is tempted and falls.

Gen. 3:15 – The Bible's first promise (prophecy) of a coming redeemer.

Gen. 4:9 – Man is shown that he is his brother's keeper.

Gen. 6:5-5 – Man has become an evil generation before God.

Gen. 12:1-3 – God chooses Abram.

Gen. 50:20 – God's providence is shown in the life of Joseph.

2

Major Themes

A. Creation – The absolute beginning of all life and the universe.

B. The Fall – The introduction of sin into man's existence.

C. Civilization – The start of nations and different languages.

D. Judgment – The Flood and the Tower of Babel, God's judgment.

Christ Revealed

1. Christ identified as:
   a. Part of the Godhead. – Gen. 1:26; 3:22; 11:7
   b. Angel of the Lord. – Gen. 16:7-14; 17:1-22; 22:11-18; 31:11-13

2. Christ typified by:
   "For the law having a shadow of good things to come, *and* not the very image of the things, can never with those sacrifices which they offered year by year continually make the comers thereunto perfect." (Heb. 10:1)
   a. Adam shown to be the opposite of Christ. (Rom. 5:12-21)
   b. Abel's offering characterized the Lamb of God. (John 1:29)
   c. Melchizedek is the representation of Christ as both a priest and king. (Ps. 110:4)
   d. Isaac's deliverance exemplified Christ's resurrection. (Heb. 11:17-19)

Prophecies of Christ

1. Gen. 3:15 – Seed of woman.
   a. Identity of the seed.
      (1) Seed of Satan – (lies, sin) John 8:44; Eph. 2:2
      (2) Seed of Woman – Gal. 4:4
   b. Enmity of the seed.
      (1) Between Satan and Eve.
      (2) Between their descendants.
   c. The consequences of the enmity.
      (1) Satan will bruise Christ's heel – minor wound.

(2) Christ will bruise Satan's head – mortal wound. Rom. 16:20;
1 Cor.15:24-28; John 12:31; 14:30; 16:11

2. Gen. 12:1-3 Seed of Abraham.
   a. This is repeated to Abraham five different times. – Gen 12:1-3;
      13:14-17; 15:1-21; 17:1-22; 22:15-18
   b. Retold to Isaac. – Gen. 26:2-5
   c. Retold to Jacob. – Gen. 35:11-13
   d. There are three parts of the covenant with Abraham:
      (1) His descendants would become a great nation.
      (2) His descendants would inherit Canaan.
      (3) His descendants would bless the world. - Gal. 3:8, 16, 28-29

3. Gen. 49:9-10 Seed of Judah.
   a. Judah would be the leader among the twelve tribes of Israel.
   b. This prediction was fulfilled 640 years later in King David.
   c. The Messiah would come from the tribe of Judah. – Rev. 5:5;
      Heb. 7:14
   d. Judah and the Kingdom
      (1) Ruler of the Kingdom – a Lion's whelp the king of beasts
      (2) Symbol of the Kingdom – the scepter a ruler's staff
      (3) Nature of the Kingdom – it is eternal, referenced "shall not
         depart."
      (4) Subjects of the Kingdom – people shall gather, obey.

Exodus

The word Exodus literally means "a way out, going out, departure." This title is given obviously in reference of the exodus of the Israelites (Hebrews) from the land of Egypt as promised in Genesis, "And he said unto Abram, Know of a surety that thy seed shall be a stranger in a land *that is* not theirs, and shall serve them; and they shall afflict them four hundred years; And also that nation, whom they shall serve, will I judge: and afterward shall they come out with great substance." (Gen. 15:13-14, also, Exodus 19:1). The time span of the book is approximately two years covering the time that Israel left Egypt and arrived at Mount Sinai. The book is the story of how Israel gains its freedom from Egypt and becomes a nation in its own right and having a covenant relationship with God sealed by the giving of the Law at Sinai and the building of the Tabernacle according to God's design. The book of Exodus was written by Moses during the time of the wilderness wanderings approximately 1450 – 1410 B.C. (Ex. 17:14; 24:4; 34:27). Jesus Himself recognized the book as one written by Moses when He cites Exodus 3:6, (Mark 12:26).

Breakdown

A. God Delivers His People – Ex. 1:1- 12:36
   Israel in Egypt: oppression and subjection

B. God Disciplines His People. – Ex. 12:37 – 18:27
   Israel's journey to Sinai: emancipation and education

C. God Directs His people. – Ex. 19:1 – 40:38
   Israel at Sinai: revelation and organization

Pivotal Word – Redemption

Israel's redemption is brought about for the purpose of future redemption, (Gen. 6:6; 13:13-15). Redemption is clearly seen throughout Exodus. The need of redemption is seen in the bondage (chapters 1-2). The way of redemption is in the blood of the lamb (chapter 12). The possibility of redemption is seen in the power and ability of God (chapter 14). The law of redemption is revealed in the covenant of God's divine will (chapters 19-24). The medium and expression of redemption is seen in the Tabernacle and its priestly institutions (chapters 25-40).

Characters of Importance

Moses – His call, character, conduct, courage. – Acts 7:22

Pharaoh of the Oppression – Ex. 1:8-11; 2:23
   Identity: Thutmose III (1482-1450 B.C.)

Pharaoh of the Exodus 5:1
   Identity: Amenhotep II (1450-1425 B.C.)
   This Pharaoh had his heart hardened, here are some details:
   (1) Ten times it is said that Pharaoh hardened his own heart.
     Ex. 7:13, 14, 22; 8:15, 19, 32; 9:7, 34, 35; 13:15
   (2) Ten times it is said that God hardened Pharaoh's heart.
     Ex. 4:21; 7:3; 9:12; 10:1, 20, 27; 11:10 14:4, 8, 17
   (3) Paul uses this as an example of God's sovereignty.
     Ex. 9:14-18

Important Verses

Ex. Chapter 2 - Moses' birth and protection.

Ex. Chapter 3 - The burning bush.

Ex. 7:14-11:10 - The ten plagues.

Ex. 12:1-36 - The Passover.

Ex. 14:1-22 - Miracles at the Red Sea.

Ex. Chapter 16 - Quail and manna.

Ex. 19:4-6 - God's covenant with Israel.

Ex. Chapter 20 - Ten Commandments.

Ex. 32:1-10 - The golden calf.

Ex. 33:12-23 - The manifestation of God (theophany).

Major Themes

A. Bondage and Deliverance.

B. Instruction and Discipline.

C. Reluctance and Rebellion.

D. The abiding presence of God.
     (1) A pillar of cloud and a pillar of fire. Ex. 13:21-22
     (2) "And he said, My presence shall go *with thee,* and I will give
         thee rest." (Ex. 33:14).

E. The revelation of the character of God.
     (1) God controls all history. Chapter 1
     (2) God is self-existent. – Ex. 3:14
     (3) God is the faithful redeemer. – Ex. 6:6; 13:15
     (4) God is judge. – Ex. 4:14; 20:5
     (5) God is sovereign of the covenant relationship. – Ex. 19:4-6
     (6) God is the transcendent one. – Ex. 33:20

Christ Revealed

1. The Passover. – Ex. 12:1-36, Christ is our Passover Lamb
    a. Without blemish. – 1 Pet. 1:19; 2:22-24
    b. Killed at a specific time. – John 2:4; 7:30; 8:20; 12:23, 27;
       13:1; 16:32; 17:1
    c. Bones are not to be broken. – John 19:36
    d. Blood accomplished deliverance. – John 1:29; Heb. 9:14;
       1 Pet. 1:18-19
    e. "Purge out therefore the old leaven, that ye may be a new lump,

as ye are unleavened. For even Christ our Passover is sacrificed for us:" (1 Cor. 5:7).

2. Manna in the wilderness. – Ex.16:1-36
   a. Manna (literally means "What is this?") It sustained Israel's life during their wanderings.
   b. Jesus is the true bread from heaven who sustains our spiritual life. – John 6:31-58

3. Water from solid rock. – Ex.17:1-7
   a. Israel needed water to survive in the desert.
   b. Christ, the rock, furnishes man with the water of life. John 4:14; 6:35; 7:38

4. The Mercy-Seat – Ark of the Covenant. – Ex. 25:10-22; 37:1-9
   a. The mercy-seat was where the blood of atonement was sprinkled. – Lev. 16:14, 19
   b. Christ is our mercy seat, our satisfaction or propitiation for sin today. – Rom. 3:25-26; Heb. 9:5; 1 John 2:1-2; 4:10

Leviticus

Summation

The title "Leviticus" comes from the Greek translation of the Old Testament (Septuagint) and literally means "pertaining to the Levites." Although the Levites are mentioned only once by name (25:32-33), their function is described throughout the book of Leviticus. Exodus contains God's moral law and Leviticus contains God's ceremonial law spoken from the Tabernacle. Leviticus is more than a handbook for the priests. Its laws concern all of Israel and their approach to God through sacrifices and special seasons and feasts. The book covers a span of time of one month and 20 days, (Ex. 40:17; Num. 10:11). Moses wrote Leviticus in approximately 1444 B.C. Moses' authorship is acknowledged in Mark 1:44; Lev. 13:49; Luke 2:22; Lev. 12:2-6. Twenty of the twenty-seven chapters start with the phrase, "then the Lord spoke to Moses saying..." In the New Testament Leviticus is referred to at least 90 times and the book of Hebrews is a good companion to it.

Breakdown

A. The Call to Pardon. – Lev. 1-10
    (The Way of Access to God: Sacrifice)
    (1) Presentation of sacrifices. – Lev. 1-7
    (2) Mediation of priests. Chapters 8-10

B. The call to purity. – Lev. 11-27
    (The way of living for God: Sanctification)
    (1) The laws of purity. – Lev. 11-16
    (2) The laws of holiness. – Lev. 17-27

Pivotal Word - Priest

Leviticus is a priestly book filled with commands concerning sacrifices. "Priests" is found about 189 times; "holy" about 87 times;

"blood" about 86 times; "atonement" about 45 times; and "sacrifices" about 42 times.

Characters of Importance

Moses – The great law giver and leader. – John 1:17; 7:19

Aaron – The brother of Moses and a descendent of Levi who became Moses' assistant and the first High Priest.

The Priests – the perpetual priesthood came only from the tribe of Levi. 29:9; 40:12-15; Num. 25:13

Important Verses

Lev. 10:1-3 – The sin of Nadab and Abihu. God accepts no substitutes.

Lev. Chapter 16 – The Day of Atonement.

Lev. 17:11 – Atonement by blood.

Lev. Chapter 18 – God's standards for sexual relationships.

Lev. 19:2 – "You shall be holy, for I the Lord your God am holy."

Lev. 19:18 – "You shall love your neighbor as yourself."

Lev. Chapter 20 – Discipline and the death penalty.

Lev. 26:3, 14 – The "If… But" conditions of obedience.

Major Themes

A. Holiness of God. – 19:2; 20:7, 26; 21:8

B. Sinfulness of man. – 11:44-45

C. God's Grace and Blood Atonement – Chapter 16

D. God's Provision of worship. Chapters 1-7
   (1) Man must approach God through the priests.

10

      (2) There are five fundamental offerings. Burnt, grain, peace, sin, and trespass.

      (3) In today's world Christians are priests and have access to God through Christ. – 1 Pet. 2:5, 9; 1 Tim. 2:5

E. Remembering God. Chapters 23, 25

      (1) The Sabbath, the Sabbatical year, the Year of Jubilee.

      (2) There are seven fundamental feasts. Passover, Unleavened Bread, First fruits, Pentecost, Trumpets, Atonement, and Tabernacles.

Christ Revealed

1. Christ is our High Priest. – Lev. 16:2-3; Heb. 3:1; 7:26-28; 8:1

2. Our Scapegoat is Christ. – Lev. 16:8, 10, 20-22; Isa. 53:5-6; 2 Cor. 5:21; Heb. 9:28; 1 Pet. 2:24

3. Christ is our Mercy Seat. – Lev. 16:13-15; Heb. 9:1-5; 1 John 2:1-2

4. Our blood atonement in Christ. – Lev. 17:11; Heb. 9:11-14, 22; Matt. 26:28; 1 John 1:7; Eph. 1:7

5. Our first fruits is Christ. – Lev. 23:9-14; 1 Cor. 15:20

Numbers

Summation

The Hebrew title is "in the wilderness" and it is taken from the first verse of the book. The Greek Septuagint title is "Arithmoi" or "numbers" because of the prominence of the census mentioned in chapters 1-4 and 26. Numbers reveals the molding of the nation of Israel by our loving and longsuffering of God. Israel however rebelled and suffered from unbelief and had to pay a high price by wondering in the wilderness for 40 years, "as to you–your carcasses do fall in this wilderness, and your children shall wander in the wilderness forty years, and bear your whoredoms until your carcasses be wasted in the wilderness;" (Num. 14:32, 33). For 40 years God providentially cares for Israel, a people numbering between 2-3 million. During the 40 years God trains a new generation. He takes a multitude of former slaves and farmers and molds them into a nation and an army ready to conquer the Promised Land. The first and last verses of the book tell us Moses was the author in 1444 B.C., (Num. 1:1; 36:13). The book covers 38 years of Israel's journeys from Mount Sinai to Kadesh-Barnea to the plains of Moab across the Jordan River from Jericho.

Breakdown

A. Preparation at Sinai. – Num. 1:1-10:10
    Encampment and census.

B. Pilgrimage to Kadesh-Barnea. – Num. 10:11-12:16
    Marching and Murmuring.

C. Waiting at Kadesh-Barnea. –Num. 13:1-20:13
    Wilderness wanderings.

D. Movement to Plains of Moab. – Num. 20:14 – 36:13
    Instructions for possessing and dividing Canaan

Pivotal Word – Wander

Although the word "wander" appears only once in the book, (Num. 32:13), the book of Numbers is filled with Israel's wilderness wanderings. Israel is in need of direction and guidance and this is predominantly demonstrated in the book.

Characters of Importance

Moses – the leader.

Miriam – Moses' sister who was smitten with leprosy for rebelling against Moses and then healed by God. – Num. 12.

Caleb and Joshua – the only two of the original generation who entered Canaan because of their favorable report, Num. 13:30; 14:30; 26:65; 32:12.

Korah, Dathan, and Abiram – Three men who led a rebellion against Moses and Aaron, – Num. 16; Jude 11.

Balaam – The prophet hired by Balak king of Moab to curse Israel, but instead Balaam blessed Israel, – Num. 22-24; 2 Pet. 2:15; Rev. 2:14.

Important Verses

Num. 1:45-46 – The first census (603,550) and the second census (601,730), – Num. 26:51.

Num. 6:24-26 – "The Lord bless you and keep you."

Num. 11:23 – "Is the Lord's power limited?"

Num. 12:3 – The humility of Moses.

Num. 13:30 – The positive report of Joshua and Caleb.

Num. 20:1-13 – The sin of Moses.

Num. 21:6-9 – The brazen serpent.

Num. 22:21-30 – Balaam's talking donkey.

Num. 25:1-9 – Israel worships Baal, – 1 Cor. 105-13.

Major Themes

A. Principles of leadership.
   (1) From God (Divine). – Num. 9:15-23.
   (2) From Moses (Spiritual). – Num. 11:10-12; 14:13-19.
   (3) From Caleb and Joshua (Bold). – Num. 14:6-9.

B. Principles of Following.
   (1) Man takes a risk when he rebels against God's appointed
       leaders. – Num. 12, 14, 16
   (2) Man typically does not know what type of leader he needs.
       Num. 14:4
   (3) The people of god must walk by faith in order to move
       forward. – 2 Cor. 5:7
   (4) Strength is in the size of a man's faith, not in his numbers.
       Num. 17:20; Deut. 7:7
   (5) God's people need to not be fearful and have a good self
       -image. – Num. 13:33
   (6) There were three kinds of followers among Israel just as there
       are in today's world.
       a. People living in yesterday or the past. - Those who longed to
          return to Egypt. – Num. 14:4
       b. Those who live in the present. – Those who complain about
          their present state. – Num. 11:1
       c. Those who see the big picture, who look to the future. –
          Those who see the vision of the Promised Land.
          Num. 13:30

<u>Christ Revealed</u>

1. The Passover Lamb whose bones were not broken. – Num. 9:12; 1
    Cor. 5:7; John 19:32-36

2. The sacrifice offered outside the camp. – Num. 19:3;
    Heb. 13:11-13

3. The one lifted up. (Bronze Serpent) – Num. 21:6-9; John 3:14-15;
    12:32-33

4. The star from Jacob and the scepter from Israel. – Num. 24:17;
    Matt. 2:2; Rev. 22:16

Deuteronomy

Summation

The name "Deuteronomy" like other titles has a meaning too. The meaning is "second law-giving." The book however is not the second in order but a repeat of the first law that is found in the book of Exodus, Leviticus, and Numbers. The book is written in a manner suggesting a sermon. Moses is the preacher that delivers the message to Israel in his last days just before Israel's entrance into Canaan, "beyond the Jordan, in the land of Moab, hath Moses begun to explain this law, saying:" (Deut. 1:5). During Moses' repeating of the Law, he also reminds Israel's new generation of God's power, and His love. God's love for Israel is demonstrated in all three tenses of time, Past (Deut. Chapters 1-4), Present (Deut. Chapters 5-26), Future (Deut. Chapters 27-34). Moses wrote Deuteronomy during the last months of his life in approximately the year of 1406 B.C. Moses is identified as the author in the following verses: 1:1, 5; 4:44; 31:24-26. There are some theologians who believe that chapter 34 was probably written by Joshua. The book of Deuteronomy was quoted by Christ more than any other Old Testament book. Some of the more notable quotes are the following: Christ's temptation (Matt. 22:37), Christ's teaching on marriage and divorce (Matt. 19:8), Christ's summarizing the Law (Matt. 22:37). Deuteronomy is quoted or referenced over 80 times in 17 of the New Testament books.

Breakdown

A. Remembrance of Israel's wanderings – Deut. 1:1-4:43
   1st Sermon

B. Looking back at God's commands – Deut. 4:44-26:19
   2nd Sermon

C. Determination to keep the Covenant – Deut. 27:1-30:20
   3rd Sermon

D. Moses' last days – Deut. 31:1- 34:12
   Conclusion

Pivotal Word - Command

The word "command" and varying forms of the word are found 109 times in Deuteronomy. Deuteronomy is overflowing with strong encouragement for Israel to obey God's commandments some examples are: "And it cometh to pass in the fortieth year, in the eleventh month, on the first day of the month that Moses spake unto the children of Israel according unto all that the Lord had given him in commandment unto them;" (Deut. 1:3), and "'Now these are the commandments, the statutes, and the judgments, which the Lord your God commanded to teach you, that ye might do them in the land whither ye go to possess it. That thou mightiest fear the Lord thy God, to keep all his statutes and his commandments, which I command thee, thou, and thy son, and thy son's son, all the days of thy life, and that thy days may be prolonged." (Deut. 6:1, 2).

Characters of Importance

Moses – A preacher and a prophet.
   A. Moses' voice. – Deut. Chapters 1-33
      (1) His sermons to Israel. – Deut. Chapters 1-30
      (2) His charge to Joshua. – Deut. Chapter 31
      (3) His song and blessings. – Deut. Chapters 32-33

   B. Moses' Vision. – Deut. 34:1-4; Heb. 11:27
   C. Moses' Victory. – Deut. 34:5-6; Jude 9
   D. Moses' Vigor. – Deut. 34. 7
      (1) He was a Prince in Egypt. (40 years) – Ex. 2:14;
          Acts 7:23
      (2) He was a shepherd in Midian. (40 years) –Acts 7:29-30
      (3) He lead Israel in the wilderness. (40 Years) – Ex. 7:7;
          Deut. 31:2

   E. Moses' Veneration. – Deut. 34:8-9; Num. 12:3

F. Moses' Virtue. – Deut. 34:10; 5:4; Ex. 33:11; Num. 12:8

G. Moses' Value. – Deut. 34:11-12; Luke 9:30ff

Important Verses

Deut. 5:6-21 – The Ten Commandments.

Deut. 6:4-9 – The Shema.

Deut. 7:6-8 – Israel chosen by God.

Deut. 10:12-13 – Basic requirements.

Deut. 18:15-19 –The prophet like Moses.

Deut. 29:29 – "The secret things belong to the Lord our God..."

Deut. 30:11-14 – Reception of the Word. – Rom. 10:6-8

Deut. 30:15-20 – The two ways. – Matt. 7:13-14

Major Themes

A. The relationship of Israel with God. – Deut. 7:6-11
   (1) His Choice. Vs. 6:7
   (2) His love. Vs. 8
   (3) His faithfulness. Vs. 9-11

B. How Israel responds to God. They must:
   (1) Remember. – Deut. 4:9; 8:11-20
   (2) Love God. – Deut. 6:5; Matt. 22:37
   (3) Worship God. – Deut. 6:13-15; Matt. 4:10
   (4) Obey God. – Deut. 10:12-13

Christ Revealed

Christ: He is the great prophet. – Deut. 18:15-19; Acts 7:37

1. Prophet from God. – Luke 7:16; 24:19; John 4:19

2. He is a prophet like Moses. – Heb. 3:1-5
   Some similarities listed: Both of their births were threatened.
   Both were deliverers.
   Both rejected.
   Both demonstrated miracles.
   Both were mediators.
   Both were God's spokesman.
   Both associated with baptisms that
   delivered from bondage.
   (1 Cor. 10:2; Gal. 3:27)

3. A prophet who speaks for and from God. – John 8:28; 12:48-50; 17:8

4. A prophet to be listened to and obeyed. – Acts 3:19-26

The Pentateuch in Perspective

The first five books of the Bible, Genesis, Exodus, Leviticus, Numbers and Deuteronomy are collectively called the Pentateuch. Together they form a unique perspective penned by the author Moses that teaches man his origin, God's sovereignty, God's love for man, God's providence, God's faithfulness, and God's righteousness. Together the books of the Pentateuch form a foundation for the rest of the Bible and some believe that in essence it is the Bible in miniature.

1. Moses is the author without question.
   a. Witness of the Pentateuch. – Ex. 17:14; 24:4; 34:27; Lev. "the Lord spoke to Moses" (38 times), Num. 33:1-2; Deut. 31:9-11
   b. Witness of other Old Testament books. – Josh. 1:8; 8:31-32; 1 Kings 2:3; 2 Kings 14:6; 21:8; Ezra 6:18; Neh. 13:1; Dan. 9:11-13; Mal. 4:4
   c. The witness of New Testament books. – Matt. 19:8; Mark 12:26; Luke 20:28; John 5:46-47; 7:19; Acts 3:22; Rom. 10:5; 1 Cor. 9:9; 2 Cor. 3:15; 2 Tim. 3:8; Heb. 12:21
   d. The witness of internal evidence found in the Pentateuch.
      (1) Eyewitness details of the Exodus.
      (2) Intimate knowledge of Egypt.
      (3) The unity of the five books speaks to a single author.

2. Looking at Moses.
   a. Genesis – Moses, the great historian.
   b. Exodus – Moses, the great deliverer.
   c. Leviticus – Moses, the great lawgiver.
   d. Numbers – Moses, the great leader.
   e. Deuteronomy – Moses, the great prophet-preacher.

3. Perspective on Content
   a. Genesis – (historical) Adam to Joseph
   b. Exodus – (redemptive) bondage and exodus
   c. Leviticus – (legislative) Tabernacle, Law, priests

d. Numbers – (instructive) Sinai to Jordan

e. Deuteronomy – (sermonic) preaching of the Law

4. Perspective from man's need.
   a. Genesis – ruin – through the sin of man. – Gen. Chapter 3
   b. Exodus – redemption – by blood and power. – Ex. 6:6
   c. Leviticus – Communion – on the ground of atonement.
      Lev. Chapter 16
   d. Numbers – direction – guidance by the will of God. – Num. 9:16
   e. Deuteronomy – Destination – through the faithfulness of God.
      Deut. 7:9

5. Perspective from God's Grace.
   a. Genesis – Divine sovereignty – in creation and election.
   b. Exodus – Divine power – by blood and power. – Ex. 6:6
   c. Leviticus – Divine holiness – in separation and sanctification.
   d. Numbers – Divine goodness and severity – in judging and
               caring.
   e. Deuteronomy – Divine faithfulness – in discipline and
               destination.

Joshua

Summation

Joshua picks up where Deuteronomy leaves off. Moses led Israel to the banks of the Jordan to a location just east of the city of Jericho. At this point in time Joshua becomes their new leader and will ultimately lead Israel into the Promised Land. Moses' symbol of authority was a staff and Joshua's symbol would be a spear. The book of Joshua covers a time span of approximately twenty years (1406-1385 B.C.). During the two decades the land of Canaan is conquered, divided, and settled by the twelve tribes, two and half tribes are east of Jordan and the other nine and half tribes are west of the Jordan. The main character and author is Joshua from whom the book gets its title. The author is eyewitness to the things that he writes about as noted, "And Joshua wrote these words in the book of the law of God, and took a great stone, and set it up there under an oak, that was by the sanctuary of the Lord." (Josh. 24:26) and, Josh. 5:1-6. The account of Joshua's death, Josh. 24:29-33, is believed to have been added by another author. In the New Testament Joshua is mentioned twice, Acts 7:45; Heb. 4:8.

Breakdown

A. Entering Canaan – Josh. Chapters 1-5

B. Conquering Canaan – Josh. Chapters 6-12

C. Settling Canaan – Josh. Chapters 13-24

Pivotal Word - Possess

Twenty times in the book of Joshua "possess" or "possession" occurs. Canaan was the Promised Land and had been since the days of Abraham, now it was time to possess the land. (Josh. 1:11)

Characters of Importance

Joshua – A strong leader of faith, full of courage, obedient and devoted to the word of God. He assisted Moses (Ex. 24:13; 33:11), and he was later commissioned by Moses (Num. 27:18-23; Deut. 31:23).

Caleb – Both Caleb and Joshua were the only two of the original generation to inherit a portion of Canaan. (Josh. 14:6-15)

Rahab – Rahab was a harlot in the city of Jericho. She believed in God from what she had heard about Israel and God. Because of her belief she hid two spies of Israel and was thus spared when Jericho was conquered. (Josh. 2:1, 18; 6:25; Heb. 11:31)

Achan – A man who learned the tragic consequences of sin. (Josh. Chapter 7; 22:20)

Important Verses

Josh. 1:9 – Be strong and courageous!

Josh. 2:10-11 – Rahab's rumor.

Josh. 3:14-17 – Crossing Jordan.

Josh. 4:6-7 – Twelve memorial stones.

Josh. 6:20 – The walls of Jericho fell flat.

Josh. 10:12-15 – Joshua's long day.

Josh. 23:4-5 – Pre-millennialism refuted – the land promised fulfilled.

Josh. 23:9-10 – God fights for His people. (Lev. 26:7-8)

Josh. 24:15 – Joshua's noble choice.

Josh. 24:31-32 – Joshua and Joseph.

Major Themes

A. The importance of reading and heeding the word of God. – Josh. 1:8; 8:32-35; 23:6-7; 24:26-27

B. Courageous leadership. – Josh. 1:6-7, 9, 18; Deut. 31:6-7, 23

C. Understanding that God's way will work.
   (1) At Jordan. – Josh. 3:3-4
   (2) At Jericho. – Josh. 6:1-5; Heb. 11:30
   (3) At Ai. – Josh. 7:11-12

D. Canaan as a type of Heaven.
   (1) Canaan was "rest." – Lev. 26:6; Deut. 6:10-11; Heb. 3:16-4:11
   (2) Canaan had "abundance." – Ex. 3:8; Rev. 22:1-4
   (3) Canaan meant "victory." – Josh. 23:9-10; Deut. 7:1-2; Rev. 2:10; 22:14

E. God's holiness and His wisdom demonstrated in the extermination of the Canaanites. – Josh. 23:12-13; Deut. 7:1-6; Num. 33:55 Lev. 18:24-25

F. Victory and triumph of faith. – Josh. 11:23; 1 John 5:4; 2 Cor. 5:7

Christ Revealed

1. The Lord is the Captain of the Host of the Lord. – Josh. 5:13-15
   a. Some believe this to be a pre-incarnate appearance (called a theophany) of the Lord Jesus Christ.
   b. Some examples:
      (1) The Lord appeared to Abraham as a traveler. – Gen. 18:2-3
      (2) The Lord appeared to Jacob as a wrestler. – Gen. 32:24
      (3) The Lord appeared to Moses as a fire. – Ex. 3:2
      (4) the Lord appeared to Joshua as a soldier. – Josh. 5:14

2. Cities of Refuge.
   a. Place of safety and security.
   b. Jesus is our refuge. – Heb. 6:18; Ps. 46:1-3

3. Jesus and Joshua are similar.
   a. In name – Joshua is the Hebrew name for Jesus.
      "The Lord is Salvation."
   b. In authority – Divinely appointed by God.
   c. In function – Leader of God's people.
   d. In purpose – To lead God's people to their inheritance.

Judges

Summation

The name Judges is derived from the valiant and courageous leaders (judges) that God brought forth to deliver Israel from her enemies, "Nevertheless the Lord raised up judges, which delivered them out of the hand of these that spoiled them." (Judges 2:16). The historic events taking place in the book of Judges covers a time from approximately 1385-1050 B.C. Another time reference could be compared to the time of completion of the conquest to the beginning of the monarchy, Judges 11:26. These were dark days in Israel's history. Apostasy was the order of the day, "In those days there was no king in Israel: every man did that which was right in his own eyes." (Judges 21:25). The book tells of six major oppressions that came upon Israel from the surrounding Canaanite tribes. Twelve judges were raised up by God to help deliver Israel. Jewish tradition says that Samuel was the author of Judges though we cannot be sure. Judges was written after the death of Samson, Judges 16:30-32, after the crowning of King Saul, Judges 17:6, and before the reign of King David, 1 Chron. 11:5. Therefore, the book was written between 1050-1000 B. C. An excellent summary of the book can be found in Judges 2:11-19.

Breakdown

A. Prologue to the Judges (Introduction) – Judges Chapters 1 -2

B. Narrative of the Judges (Historical) – Judges Chapters 3 - 16

C. Epilogue to the Judges (Conclusive) – Judges Chapters 17 -21

Pivotal Word – Evil

"And the children of Israel did evil in the sight of the Lord, and served Baalim," (Judges 2:11). See also, 3:7, 12; 4:1; 6:1; 10:6; 13:1. Spiritual decline results because of Israel's persistent wickedness and unfaithfulness. The hand of the Lord was against them for evil, Judges 2:15.

<u>Characters of Importance</u>

Judges – Twelve great leaders who provided the necessary leadership in times of crisis.
   A. Military leader (warrior) – to deliver people from their enemies. – Judges 2:18; 3:9; 3:15
   B. Judicial leader (judge) – to hear court cases. – Judges 4:4-5
   C. Spiritual leader (priest and prophet) – to speak to the people the commandments of the Lord. – Judges 2:17.

Deborah – The only woman judge over Israel. – Judges 4:4-5; 5:7

Gideon – the reluctant leader whose fear turned to faith.
   A. Gideon's call. – Judges 6:1-40
   B. Gideon's conquest over Midian. – Judges 7:1-25
   (32,000 – 10,000 – 300)

Jephthah – The judge who learned the danger of making rash vows or promises. – Judges 11:29-40

Samson – The mighty judge who fought the Philistines.
   Judges Chapters 13- 16

<u>Important Verses</u>

Judges 2:10 – One generation from extinction.

Judges 2:11 – 19 – The sin cycle of Judges.

Judges 5:2 – Leaders and followers.

Judges 8:23 – The Lord is the only true ruler.

Judges 9:7-15 – Jotham's fable.

Judges 17:6 – "In those days there was no king in Israel; every man did
what was right in his own eyes."

Judges 21:25 – A summary of the book of Judges.

Major Themes

A. The progressive nature of sin: failure to drive out the Canaanites,
military alliances, intermarriage, idolatry, apostasy. James 1:13-
15; Rom. 6:16; John 8:34

B. The repetitive sin cycle. Judges 2:11-18; 3:7-9, 12-15; 4:1-6; 6:1`-
11; 10:6ff; 13:1-5
(1) Apostasy (leaving the Lord) - Sin   - Rebellion
(2) Oppression (punishment from the Lord) - Suffering   -
Retribution
(3) Penitence (Cry unto the Lord) - Supplication - Repentance
(4) Deliverance (Help from the Lord) - Salvation - Rest

Christ Revealed

1. Christ as the Angel of the Lord.
a. Judges 2:1-5 – Appearance at Bochim (weepers).
b. Judges 5:23 – Meroz cursed for not helping in battle.
c. Judges 6:11-24 – The call of Gideon.
d. Judges 13:3-22 – The announcement of Samson's birth.

2. Christ as the true Judge. Judges 11:27; 8:23
a. Sent by God to deliver from sin. – Matt. 1:21; Luke 19:10
b. Sent by God to provide spiritual strength. – Phil. 4:13;
2 Cor. 12:9
c. Sent by God to build morale. – 2 Cor. 3:4-5; 10:17
d. Sent by God to lead to victory. – Rom. 8:37; 1 Cor. 15:57
e. Sent by God to execute judgment. – John 5:22; Acts 17:31

Ruth

Summation

The book of Ruth dates to a time during the time frame of the Judges, Ruth 1:1, approximately the latter part of the twelfth century. It was probably written by an unknown author during the reign of David, 1000 B.C. Added proof of this is evidenced by the linage of Ruth only going to David, Ruth 4:17. One reason for the book is to account for the inclusion of a non-Israelite in the royal linage of the Messiah, a Moabitess, Ruth 4:17-22; Matt. 1:1-6. The story of the book of Ruth portrays a beautiful love story of two women, Naomi and Ruth, both of whom have lost their husbands in death. The story focuses on Ruth, Naomi's daughter-in-law, and her subsequent marriage to Boaz, a relative of Ruth's deceased husband. Ruth is the only book in the Bible totally dedicated to a woman and gives a glimpse of Hebrew family life.

Breakdown

A. Ruth's resolve: Her noble choice. – Ruth Chapter 1

B. Ruth's response: Her lowly service. – Ruth Chapter 2

C. Ruth's request: Her tender appeal. – Ruth Chapter 3

D. Ruth's reward: Her marital joys. – Ruth Chapter 4

Pivotal Word - Redeem

More than a dozen times some form of the word "redeem" is found, Ruth 2:20; 3:13; 4:4, 6-7, 14. Redeem means to buy, purchase, rescue, or save. Ruth is one of the most instructive books in the Old Testament concerning the redemptive work of Christ.

Characters of Importance

Elimelech – (my God is king) Naomi's husband.

Naomi – (pleasant, lovely) (cf. 1:20-21)

Mahlon – (puny) Naomi's son and Ruth's first husband. – Ruth 4:10

Chilion – (pining) Naomi's son.

Orpah – (turning back) Naomi's daughter-in-law.

Ruth – (friendship) Naomi's daughter-in-law.

Boaz – Kinsman of Elimelech, Ruth 2:1, who became Ruth's second husband.

Obed – (servant) Ruth's son, Naomi's grandson, and King David's grandfather.

Important Verses

Ruth 1:16-17 – Ruth's commitment and allegiance.

Ruth 2:11 – Ruth's loyalty to Naomi.

Ruth 3:11 – Ruth a woman of excellence.

Ruth 3:13 – "… then will I do the part of a kinsman to thee…"

Ruth 4:10 – Levirate marriage law. – Deut. 25:5-10

Ruth 4:14 – "Blessed be the Lord, which hath not left thee this day without a kinsman …"

Ruth 4:17 – Ruth was the great grandmother of David.

Major Themes

A. Social barriers needed to be removed. (racial, cultural, social, religious, economic) – James 2:1, 8-9

B. God's grace is far reaching. Gentiles can be believers.
   Deut. 10:17-18; Acts 10:34-35; Rom. 1:16; 2:11

C. God at work in our lives.
   1. God's providence. – Ruth 2:3
   2. God's protection. – Ruth 2:12
   3. God's plan. – Ruth 4:14

D. Demonstration of good family relations.
   1. Naomi's love for her daughters-in –law. – Ruth 1:8-9
   2. Ruth's love for her mother-in-law. – Ruth 1:16-17; 2:11; 4:15

Christ Revealed

Christ: The kinsman-redeemer – Ruth 3:9, 13; 4:10, 14, 17

1. Christ had the right to redeem. (blood relative) Rom. 1:3; Gal. 4:4; Heb. 2:14

2. Christ had the will to redeem. (sacrificial love) John 10:11, 15, 17-18

3. Christ had the price to redeem. (precious blood) 1 Pet. 1:18-19; Heb. 9:14

4. Christ had the power to redeem. (forgiveness) Eph. 1:7; Col. 1:14

I Samuel

Summation

In the Hebrew Bible the books of I and II Samuel are considered a single book as well as the books of Kings and Chronicles. The Septuagint from the third century B.C. referred to I and II Samuel and I and II Kings the First, Second, Third and Fourth books of the Kingdoms. The time frame of I Samuel covers about 100 years of history (1050-950 B.C.). During this time a transition was taking place from the Judges (theocracy) to the Kings (monarchy). I Samuel was probably written sometime between 930 and 722 B.C. Samuel is considered to be the author of the earliest chapters, "Then Samuel told the people the manner of the kingdom, and wrote *it* in a book, and laid *it* up before the LORD. And Samuel sent all the people away, every man to his house." (I Sam. 10:25). Samuel's death is recorded in I Sam. 25:1. There are other men who could be considered as authors too such as Nathan and Gad, "Now the acts of David the king, first and last, behold, they *are* written in the book of Samuel the seer, and in the book of Nathan the prophet, and in the book of Gad the seer," (I Chron. 29:29). Unique to Samuel is that he was the last of the judges and the first of the prophets. Samuel certainly was an important figure in the Old Testament, (Jer. 15:1; Ps. 99:6). Samuel is mentioned three times in the New Testament, (Acts 3:24; 13:20; Heb. 11:32). I Samuel is dominated by three personalities: Samuel, his birth around 1100 B. C., his childhood and ministry; Saul, his rise and fall as the first king; and David, his growing power and influence.

Breakdown

A. Eli and Samuel (sadness). – I Sam. Chapters 1 – 7

B. Samuel and Saul (strength). – I Sam. Chapters 8 – 15

C. Saul and David (struggles). – I Sam. Chapters 16 - 31

<u>Pivotal Word</u> – Kingdom

I Samuel tells the reader about the beginning of the monarchy. The people demanded a king to be like other nations, "And said unto him, Behold, thou art old, and thy sons walk not in thy ways: now make us a king to judge us like all the nations." (I Sam. 8:5), see also I Sam. 10:24. Saul's kingdom was established by the Lord and taken away by the Lord, (10:1; 28:17). The words "king" and "kingdom" are very prevalent in the book. King is used some 80 times and kingdom is used 11 times.

<u>Characters of Importance</u>

Hannah – The godly mother of Samuel who prayed for a son and dedicated him to the Lord. – I Sam. 1:27-28

Samuel – Samuel means "name of God." He served as prophet, priest, and judge. – I Sam. 1:20; 2:21, 26; (cf. Luke 2:52)

Eli – The priest and judge under whom Samuel served. He met a tragic death because of his disgraceful sons. – I Sam. 2:12, 25; 3:13; 4:11, 18

Saul – The first king of Israel. – I Sam. 9:1, 2

Jonathan – Son of Saul and beloved companion of David. I Sam. 18:1-4

David – The shepherd lad anointed king by Samuel. – I Sam 16:12, 13

Goliath – The champion of the Philistines. – I Sam. 17:4-7 Goliath stood 9 feet and 9 inches tall, and his armor weighed 125 pounds.

<u>Important Verses</u>

<u>I Sam. 1:11</u> – Hannah's prayer for a son.

<u>I Sam. 3:1</u> – "and word of the Lord was precious in those days…"

I Sam. 3:10-11 – Samuel's call and obedient response.

I Sam. 8:5-7 – The demand for a king. Key verse in I Samuel.

I Sam. 13:14 – David, a man after God's own heart. – Acts 7:46; 13:22

I Sam. 15:22-23 – "Behold, to obey is better than sacrifice."

I Sam. 16:7 – "The Lord looketh on the heart."

I Sam. 18:7 – "Saul hath slain his thousands, and David his ten thousands."

I Sam. 31:4 – Saul's death on Mt. Gilboa.

Major Themes

A. The strong emphasis on prayer (mentioned 30 times in the book). i.e. I Sam. 1:11; 8:6; 12:23

B. Permissive parents lead to undisciplined children.
   1. Eli – Hophni and Phinehas. – I Sam. 3:13
   2. Samuel – Joel and Abiah. – I Sam. 7:15 - 8:5

C. The downfall of a great leader – Saul. We are show three sins:
   1. His sinful offering. – I Sam. Chapter 13
   2. His partial obedience. – I Sam. Chapter 15
   3. His visit to the witch at Endor. – I Sam. Chapter 28

D. A lesson on courage and faith – David and Goliath. – I Sam. 17:37, 42, 49-51

E. Insight into the "spirit of the Lord."
   1. David – I Sam. 16:13
   2. Saul – I Sam. 10:6, 9-10; 11:6; 16:14
   3. Messengers – I Sam. 19:20

F. The first school for training prophets – God's spokesman. I Sam 10:5-12; 19:20, 21-24; II Kings 2:3, 5 15

34

Christ Revealed

Christ: The anointed one.

1. I Sam. 2:10, 35, is the first mention of the Messiah (Hebrew for "anointed") in the Bible.

2. The anointing of David was a type of the anointing of Christ. David was anointed three times.
    a. Privately by Samuel. – I Sam. 16:12-13
    b. As king over Judah. – II Sam. 2:4
    c. As king over Israel. – II Sam. 5:3

3. Christ – Christos in Greek, Messiah in Hebrew, literally "the anointed one."
    a. Scriptures:
        (1) Psalm 2:2
        (2) Matt. 1:1
        (3) Luke 4:18
        (4) John 1:41
        (5) Acts 10:38

    b. His significance:
        (1) Christ was selected of God.
        (2) Christ was approved of God.
        (3) Christ was blessed of God.
        (4) Christ was empowered of God.
        (5) Christ was exalted of God.

II Samuel

I and II Samuel were considered to be one book in the Hebrew Bible, reference I Samuel for a more complete explanation. II Samuel is considered the book of David. The entire book centers exclusively on David's life and his reign that lasted from 1010 – 970 B.C. "And the days that David reigned over Israel *were* forty years: seven years reigned he in Hebron, and thirty and three years reigned he in Jerusalem." (I Kings 2:11), see also, II Sam. 2:11; I Chron. 26:31. The book of II Samuel ends just before the death of David as I Kings 1:1 – 2:12 tell of David's last days. The high points of David's reign as recorded in the book include the following: David made Jerusalem the religious and political center for Israel; David became known for his great victories in combat; David sinned with Bathsheba; David had family problems and he numbered the people. II Samuel tells the complete story of David from his rise to his fall. David was a man after God's own heart.

Breakdown

II Sam. 5:5 is a good outline of the book geographically.

A. David – King over Judah at Hebron. – II Sam. Chapters 1 – 4

B. David – King over Israel at Jerusalem. – II Sam. Chapters 5 – 24

II Samuel divides David's reign: His victories II Sam. 1:10, his vices II Sam. 11 – 24.

Pivotal Word – Established

David brought the twelve tribes together to form one Kingdom, (Judah and Israel). David also understood that his dynasty was one that was established by the Lord, II Sam. 3:1; 5:1 -5, 10-12; 7:16, 24, 26. "Established" means to be firm, prepared, directed.

36

Characters of Importance

David – The greatest king of Israel. The Biblical account of David is
recorded in:" I Sam. 16-31; II Sam. 1-24; I Kings 1:1-2:12;
I Chron. 12-29; (cf. I Kings 15:4-5)

Bathsheba – The wife of Uriah the Hittite with whom David had an
adulterous affair, II Sam. 11:1-13. She later became
David's wife and the mother of Solomon,
I Kings 1:11; 2:13.

Uriah – The husband of Bathsheba whom David had killed by having
him pressed to the heat of the battle, II Sam. 11:14-27.

Nathan – The prophet of God who revealed God's covenant to David,
II Sam. 7:1-17, and who also pointed out David's sin with
Bathsheba, II Sam. 12:1-7.

Absalom – David's rebellious son. II Sam. Chapters 14-18

David's Mighty Men – An elite group of thirty brave warriors who
helped David become king, II Sam. 23:8-39;
I Chron.1:10.

Important Verses

II Sam. 5:5 – David's forty year reign.

II Sam. 7:12-13 – God's covenant with David. (Prophecy of the
church).

II Sam. 12:7, 13 – David's guilt and confession.

II Sam. 18:5, 32-33 – David's concern and grief for Absalom.

II Sam. 22:2-3 – The Song of David.

II Sam. 24:24 – "… neither will I offer burnt offerings unto the Lord
my God of that which doth cost me nothing…"
Gen. 22:2; II Chron. 3:1

Major Themes

A. The impartiality of the Bible in describing David's shameful sins
as well as his valiant virtues.

B. The lasting lessons from David's sins of adultery and murder:
1. The conquering power of sin. – Rom. 6:16-18
2. The progressive nature of sin. – James 1:13-15
3. The deceptive nature of sin. – Heb. 3:13
4. The destructive power of sin. – Isa. 59:1-2
5. The inevitable consequences of sin. – Num. 32:23; Ga. 6:7-8
6. The blessed forgiveness of sin. – Ps. 51; 32:1-2; Rom. 4:6-8

Christ Revealed

Christ, the Eternal King, is in the Davidic Covenant of II Sam. 7:8-16:

1. Promises which occur during David's life. – II Sam. 7:8-11
   a. Will make David a great name. Vs. 9; 8:13
   b. Will give more land. Vs. 10; 8:1-3
   c. David will be given rest from his enemies. Vs.11: I Ki. 4:24;5:4

2. Promises to follow David's death. – II Sam. 7:12-16
   a. Eternal see (Christ) vs. 12-13. David would always have a male
   descendant in his lineage. God maintained the Messianic line for
   ten centuries until Christ, the son of David was born (Matt. 1:1).
   b. Eternal Kingdom (church) Vs. 14-16. Christ rules and reigns
   through His Kingdom, the church, which will endure forever
   (Dan. 2:44; Col. 1:13; I Cor. 15:24-28).

3. The promises fulfilled in Christ.
   a. Luke 1:30-33 – Gabriel's announcement of the birth of Jesus.
   b. Acts 2:29-31 – Peter quotes David (Ps. 16:8-11) as speaking of
   the Messiah.

I Kings

Summation

In the Hebrew canon the books of I and II Kings were originally counted as one book. The title of I and II Kings expresses their content, the record of the kings of Israel and Judah from Solomon to the downfall of the monarchy. The Jewish monarchy lasted for a time totaling almost 500 years, 1050-586 B.C. Three kings reigned over the United Kingdom; Saul, David, Solomon. Each reigned for 40 years, 1050-931 B. C. The Divided Kingdom, 931-722 B.C. and Judah alone, 722-586 B.C. finished out the days of the kings. It is thought that Jeremiah authored I and II Kings prior to the Babylonian exile around 600 B.C. The author obviously had access to material that was used to write the books, "And the rest of the acts of Solomon, and all that he did, and his wisdom, *are* they not written in the book of the acts of Solomon?" (I Kings 11:41), and, "And the rest of the acts of Jeroboam, how he warred, and how he reigned, behold, they *are* written in the book of the chronicles of the kings of Israel." (I Kings 14:19), also, "Now the rest of the acts of Rehoboam, and all that he did, *are* they not written in the book of the chronicles of the kings of Judah?" (I Kings 14:29), and, Isaiah 36-39 is almost verbatim in II Kings 18-20. The theme and purpose of the book is twofold: First it is to demonstrate that the national welfare of Israel was directly related to her faithfulness to God's covenant, and it showed how each successive king dealt with God in his covenant responsibilities.

Breakdown

A. The United Kingdom. – I Kings Chapters 1-11
    (Solomon's Splendor, Success, and Spiritual Decline)

B. The Divided Kingdom. – I Kings Chapter 12-22
    (Revolts, Reigns, and Reforms)

Pivotal Word – Glory

Solomon's glorious reign is especially emphasized during the first half of I Kings, I Kings 2:12; 5:4; 10:23. Israel reached the height of her splendor during Solomon's reign, I Kings 4:20-25. Our Lord paid tribute to Solomon's glory, "And yet I say unto you, That even Solomon in all his glory was not arrayed like one of these." (Matt. 6:29), also, Matt. 12:42.

Characters of Importance

Solomon – The son of David and Bathsheba and the third king of the monarchy.
1. His wisdom – I Kings 3:9-15; 4:29-34
2. His work – Temple (chapters 5-8), His own house I Kings 7:1-12, Navy, I Kings 9:26-28
3. His wealth – I Kings 10:14-29 (800,000 ounces of gold a year)
4. His waywardness – I Kings 11:1-6

Elijah –The prophet of God who violently opposed Baal worship in Israel. – I Kings 17:1-19:21; II Kings 2:1-11

Ahab and Jezebel – The wicked king and queen of Israel who advanced Baal worship in Israel. I Kings 16:30; 21:23; II Kings 9:10, 30-37

Important Verses

I Kings 2:1-2 – "…Be thou strong therefore, and shew thyself a man."

I Kings 6:1 – This is a key verse to dating the major events of the Old Testament. This verse establishes the date of the Exodus at approximately 1446 B. C.

I Kings 9:1-9 – God's covenant with Solomon.

I Kings 10:6-7 –The Queen of Sheba's impressions of Solomon.

I Kings 11:36 – David's "lamp" in Jerusalem. (cf. 15:4)

I Kings 13:21 – This specific "name" prophecy was fulfilled 300 years later when Josiah became king. – II Kings 23:15-20

Major Themes

A. A clear picture of the spiritual concept of God. – I Kings 5:5; 8:27; Acts 7:47-50; 17:24

B. Spiritual success is measured by loyalty to God. – I Kings 9:4-7; 11:11; Matt. 6:25-33, Vs. 29

C. Some special lessons from Elijah. Specifically "Jehovah is God."
   1. The power of Prayer. – I Kings 17:1; 18:41-46; James 5:16-18
   2. The duty of decision. – I Kings 18:21, 39; Josh. 24:15
   3. The danger of depression. – I Kings 19:4, 10, 17

Christ Revealed

Christ, the Glorious King, is typified in Solomon. Look at the contrasts:

1. His glory. – I Kings 3:12-13; John 1:14; 2:11

2. His fame. – I Kings 10:6-7; Matt. 4:24; John 21:25

3. His wealth. – I Kings 10:23; II Cor. 8:9

4. His wisdom. – I Kings 4:30; I Cor. 1:24, 30

5. His peaceful reign. – I Kings. 5:4; John 14:27; Isa. 9:6

6. His building of the temple. – I Kings 5:5; John 2:19-22

II Kings

Summation

The second book of Kings contains about 300 years of history inclusive of Israel and Judah from Ahab to the Babylonian captivity. The first half of the book gives a detailed account of Elisha's ministry and the second half records events leading up to the fall of Samaria and the captivity of Israel (722 B.C.), also the fall of Jerusalem and captivity of Judah (588 B.C.). There were 19 kings in Israel, none good, while Judah also had 19 kings and one queen, eight of who were good. The writing prophets who ministered during this time (pre-exile) included in Israel: Jonah, Amos, and Hosea; and in Judah: Joel, Obadiah, Isaiah, Micah, Nahum, Zephaniah, Jeremiah, and Habakkuk.

Breakdown

A. The divided kingdom. – II Kings chapters 1-17

B. The surviving kingdom of Judah. – II Kings 18-25

Pivotal Word – Apostasy

As in the book of Judges, the people of God "did evil in the sight of the Lord." This phrase is found over 20 times, (15:9, 18, 24, and 28). The kings often led the people into apostasy.

Characters of Importance

Elisha – Working for at least 50 years, (850-800 B.C.) Elisha a prophet of God performed many benevolent miracles.
  1. Elisha' ministry – II Kings 4:1-8:15 – widow's oil, Shunammite woman, Naaman the leper, the Syrians, etc.

  2. His death. – II Kings 13:20-21

42

Athaliah – She is the wicked daughter of Ahab and Jezebel who
usurped the throne of Judah by killing all the royal
offspring with the exception of Jehoash, – II Kings 11:1-16.

Hezekiah – One of the best kings to serve Judah.
1. His faith. – II Kings 18:3-7
2. His illness. – II Kings 20:1-11
3. His acts. – II Kings 20:20; II Chron. 32:32

Josiah – One of the youngest and best kings to serve Judah.
1. He repaired the Temple. – II Kings 22:1-7
2. He recovered the Law. – II Kings 22:8-20
3. He renewed the covenant. – II Kings 23:1-3
4. He reformed the nation. – II Kings 23:4-30, vs. 29 records
his death at Megiddo by Pharaoh Neco of Egypt.

Important Verses

II Kings 2:1, 11– Elijah's translation. (cf. Gen. 5:24; Heb. 11:5
concerning Enoch's translation.)

II Kings 4:34-35 – The resurrection of the Shunammite woman's son.

II Kings 5:14 – Naaman cleansed of leprosy.

II Kings 6:17 – "… I pray thee, open his eyes that he may see…"

II Kings 21:9 – The wicked king, Manasseh.

II Kings 22:8 – "… I have found the book of the law in the house of
the Lord."

II Kings 25:9-10 – The destruction of Jerusalem, the Temple, and the
city walls.

Major Themes

A. No one hides from God, all lives are in the "sight of the Lord."
Heb. 4:13

1. Some men do evil. – II Kings 21:2, 6, 15, 16, 20
2. Some men do good. – II Kings 20:3, 22:2
3. God holds all men accountable. – Eccl. 12:14; Rom. 14:12;
   II Cor. 5:10

B. God's anger and His wrath are kindled when man rebels against
   Him. – Rom. 11:22
   1. God's anger – II Kings 13:3; 17:18; 23:26; 24:20
   2. God's wrath – II Kings 22:13, 17; 23:26

C. When God speaks or gives commandments His word is
   authoritative and must be obeyed. – II Kings 20:4, 16, 19; 22:18

D. Sin has consequences. Israel learns this, II Kings 17:6, 23. Judah
   also learns this too, II Kings 23:27; 24:2; 25:21. – Rom. 6:23

E. We all must "…set thine house in order, for thou shalt die and not
   live." (II Kings 20:1). – Heb. 9:27

Christ Revealed

Christ: The Eternal Lamp (light)

1. David's lamp in Jerusalem:
   a. II Kings 8:19; I Kings 11:36; 15:4; II Sam. 21:17; II Chron. 21:7
   b. Lamp or light referred to David's offspring, his descendants, or
      his posterity.
   c. God made a promise that David's family would never be
      eradicated or extinguished. God would ensure that there would
      always be a perpetual light from David's house in Jerusalem.
      II Sam. 7:12-15

2. Christ is the Eternal Lamp of David and thus fulfilled God's
   covenant with David. – Ps. 132:11-17

3. Christ the eternal lamp.
   a. Christ is the "light of men." John 1:4
   b. Christ is the "true light." John 1:9; I John 2:8

44

c. Christ is the "light of the world." John 8:12; 9:5

d. Christ bids men to become "Sons of light." John 12:35-36

The Kings of Israel
Reference Chart

Israel's monarchy began with Saul who was the disobedient king, 1050-1010 B.C. Israel was consolidated and solidified under the rule of David who was the man (king) after God's own heart, 1010-970 B.C. The "united kingdom" lasted for about 120 years.

The kingdom divided when Solomon died. The tribes to the north, ten of them, were known as Israel and the tribes to the south, two of them, were known as Judah. The two kingdoms lasted until they were each conquered. Israel endured from 931 until 722 B.C. the time that Assyria conquered Samaria, the capital of the northern kingdom of Israel. Judah endured from 931 until 586 B.C. the time that Babylon conquered Jerusalem, the capital of Judah.

The Kings of Israel

King	Date	Scripture
1. Jeroboam	(931-910)	I Kings 12:25-14:20
2. Nadab	(910-909)	I Kings 15:25-31
3. Baasha	(909-886)	I Kings 15:32-16:7
4. Elah	(886-885)	I Kings 16:8-14
5. Zimri	(885)	I Kings 16:15-20
6. Omri	(885-874)	I Kings 16:21-28
7. Ahab	(874-853)	I Kings 16:29-22:40

8. Ahaziah	(853-852)	I Kings 22:51 II Kings 1:18
9. Jehoram	(852-841)	II Kings 2:1-8:15
10. Jehu	(841-814)	II Kings 9:1-10:36
11. Jehoahas	(814-798)	II Kings 13:1-9
12. Jehoash	(798-782)	II Kings 13:10-25 II Chron. 22:10-23:15
13. Jeroboam II	(794-753)	II Kings 14:23-29
14. Zechariah	(753)	II Kings 15:8-12
15. Shallum	(752)	II Kings 15:13-15
16. Menahem	(752-742)	II Kings 15:16-22
17. Pekahiah	(742-740)	II Kings 15:23-26
18. Pekah	(752-732)	II Kings 15:27-31
19. Hoshea	(732-722)	II Kings 17:1-41

The Kings of Judah

1. Rehoboam   (931-913)   I Kings 14:21-31
   II Chron. 10:1-12:16

2. Abijam   (913-911)   I Kings 15:1-8
   II Chron. 13:1-22

3. Asa   (911-870)   I Kings 15:9-24
   II Chron. 14:1-16:14

4. Jehoshaphat   (873-848)   I Kings 22:41-50
   II Chron. 17:1-20:37

5. Jehoram   (848-841)   I Kings 8:16-24
   II Chron. 21:1-20

6. Ahaziah   (841)   II Kings 8:25-29
   II Chron. 22:1-9

7. Athaliah (queen) (841-835)   II Kings 11:1-6
   II Chron. 22:10-23:15

8. Jehoash   (835-796)   II Kings 11:17-12:21
   II Chron. 23:16-24:27

9. Amaziah   (796-767)   II Kings 14:1-22
   II Chron. 25:1-28

10. Azariah   (790-739)   II Kings 15:1-7
    II Chron. 26:1-23

11. Jotham   (750-731)   II Kings 15:32-38
    II Chron. 27:1-9

12. Ahaz   (731-715)   II Kings 16:1-20
    II Chron. 28:1-27

13. Hezekiah	(715-686)	II Kings 18:1-20:21 II Chron. 29:1-32:33
14. Manasseh	(695-642)	II Kings 21:1018 II Chron. 33:1-20
15. Amon	(642-640)	II Kings 21:19-26 II Chron. 33:21-25
16. Josiah	(640-609)	II Kings 22:1-23:30 II Chron. 34:1-35:27
17. Jehoahaz	(609)	II Kings 23:31-33 II Chron. 36:1-4
18. Jehoiakim	(609-597)	II Kings 23:34-24:7 II Chron. 36:5-8
19. Jehoiachin	(597)	II Kings 24:8-16 II Chron. 36:9-10
20. Zedekiah	(597-586)	II Kings 24:17-25:21 II Chron. 36:11-21

I and II Chronicles

The author of I and II Chronicles is thought to be Ezra between 450 and 425 B.C. The Hebrew title for these two books is "the words of the days." Both books were considered one volume until they were divided in 180 B.C. The Chronicles repeat the history of Israel from the time of the creation until the Babylonian exile and return, 539 B.C. Well over half the information contained in the Chronicles is mentioned by other Old Testament books primarily Genesis, Samuel and Kings. Other Old Testament books provide the facts of history from man's point of view however uniquely different from that the Chronicles shows the reader God's viewpoint about the facts. It is apparent that the author's main intent is to show through genealogies and history how God preserved the Messianic line for some 3500 years. In keeping in line with this train of thought the author purposely omits the kings of Israel and focuses on the royal tribe of Judah, Gen. 49:9-10. The Chronicles were among the last Old Testament books to be written and were compiled after the exile to help the Jews appreciate their spiritual heritage. The author obviously had access to several sources for the writing of the Chronicles, "Now the acts of David the king, first and last, behold, they *are* written in the book of Samuel the seer, and in the book of Nathan the prophet, and in the book of Gad the seer," (I Chron. 29:29), see also, "Now the rest of the acts of Solomon, first and last, *are* they not written in the book of Nathan the prophet, and in the prophecy of Ahijah the Shilonite, and in the visions of Iddo the seer against Jeroboam the son of Nebat?" (II Chron. 9:29). Please note also the following: II Chron. 12:15; 20:34; 32:32; 33:19. There have been some who have called the Chronicles the "miniature Old Testament."

Breakdown

A. Adam to King Saul – I Chron. Chapters 1-9

B. King Saul's Reign – I Chron. Chapter 10

C. King David's Reign – I Chron. Chapters 11-29

D. King Solomon's Reign – II Chron. Chapters 1-9

E. Kings of Judah – II Chron. Chapters 10-36:21

F. The Decree of Cyrus – II Chron. 36: 22-23

 Pivotal Word – Worship

   While the other historical books have emphasized wars, Chronicles stresses worship. To illustrate this look at the following: the house of worship (Temple), the servants of worship (priesthood), the sanctity of worship (God's holiness), the authority of worship (God's law), and the purity and pardon of worship (sacrifices). I Chron. 16:29; II Chron. 7:3; 29:28-30.

Characters of Importance

Adam, Abraham, Isaac, and Jacob – The great patriarchs of Israel.
I Chron. Chapter 1

The Twelve Tribes of Israel – The descendants of Jacob who inherited Canaan. – I Chron. Chapters 4-8

Saul, David, and Solomon – The three great kings of the monarchy. Attention is focused on David (his covenant and dynasty) and Solomon (his temple and fame). – I Chron. Chapter 9 and II Chron. Chapter 9

The Kings of Judah. – II Chron. Chapters 10-36
1. Judah, and especially the house of David, was the only valid line for the coming Messiah. – Gen. 49:9-10; II Sam. 7:12-13; I Chron. 17:11-14
2. Israel, the ten northern tribes, had no valid king ruling over them by God's authority.

51

Important Verses

I Chron. 12:18 – "... For thy God helpeth thee..."

I Chron. 17:11-14 – God's covenant with David.

I Chron. 21:1 – Satan prompted David's census.

I Chron. 28:20 – David's charge to Solomon.

I Chron. 29:10-19 – David's prayer of praise.

II Chron. 7:14 – God's requirements for blessing; humility, prayer, devotion, and repentance.

II Chron. 16:9 – God's all-seeing eye.

II Chron. 36:20-21 – The prediction of the duration of the Babylonian captivity (cf. Jer. 25:11) which was written 150 years earlier.

II Chron. 36:22-23 – The Decree of Cyrus king of Persia in 538 B.C. allowing the exiles to return to Jerusalem.

Major Themes

A. Spiritual purity.
    1. Purity of race demonstrated in the genealogical tables. I Chron. Chapters 1-9
    2. Purity of worship as seen in the Temple: its preservation, restoration, and observations. – II Chron. Chapters 2-7

B. Spiritual Revival.
    1. Asa – II Chron. 14:2-4; 15:12-15
    2. Jehoshaphat – II Chron. 17:3-4, 7-9; 19:4; 20:20
    3. Jehoash – II Chron. 24:2-4
    4. Hezekiah – II Chron. 30:26; 31:20-21
    5. Josiah – II Chron. 34:31-33; 35:18

C. Spiritual Faithfulness.
   1. God's faithfulness to His promises and covenants.
   2. Man's unfaithfulness to God. Note the cycle: following and
      forsaking. – II Chron. 12:5, 14; 15:2; 23-26 (Jehoash, Amaziah,
      Uzziah)
   3. "Seek the Lord" is a key phrase found over 20 times.
      II Chron. 15:2, 4, 12, 13, 15
   4. Seeking, believing, obeying, serving, and loving the Lord are
      absolutely essential to a vibrant faith, a vital religion, and a
      victorious life. – II Chron. 7:14

Christ Revealed

Christ: The promised ruler. – II Chron. 7:18

1. Guaranteed by the genealogies. – I Chron. Chapters 1-9
   a. They revealed the process of God's divine election and eternal
      purpose for 3500 years of Israel's history. (cf. Eph. 1:3-14; 3:11)
   b. The genealogy of Christ was convincing proof that He was the
      Promised One of God. – Matt. 1:1-17 (from Abraham to Christ
      on Joseph's side) Luke 3:23-38 (from Adam to Christ on Mary's
      side)
   c. Nothing in the history of the human race parallels the sacred and
      secure genealogy of Christ, the Son of God and the Son of Man.

2. Confirmed by the Covenants.
   a. With Abraham. - Gen. 12:3
   b. With Isaac. - Gen. 26:2-5
   c. With Jacob. - Gen 35: 11-13
   d. With David. - I Chron. 17:7-14
   e. With Solomon. - II Chron. 7:12-18

Ezra

Summation

The book of Ezra begins with the Decree of Cyrus (538 B.C.) that allowed the Jews in Babylonian exile to return to Jerusalem, "Now in the first year of Cyrus king of Persia, that the word of the LORD *spoken* by the mouth of Jeremiah might be accomplished, the LORD stirred up the spirit of Cyrus king of Persia, that he made a proclamation throughout all his kingdom, and *put it* also in writing, saying, Thus saith Cyrus king of Persia, All the kingdoms of the earth hath the LORD God of heaven given me; and he hath charged me to build him an house in Jerusalem, which *is* in Judah. Who *is there* among you of all his people? The LORD his God *be* with him, and let him go up." (II Chron. 36:22-23), also, Ezra 1:1-4. The Jews had been in captivity in Babylon for seventy years, Jer. 25:11, when Persia conquered Babylon and released the captive Jews. The book of Ezra records two returns of the Jews one under Zerubbabel and one under Ezra respectively. The time frame is approximately 80 years, 539-458 B.C. Ezra is the author and tells of the reforms and the revivals of the Jews once they are back in Jerusalem.

Breakdown

A. Return under Zerubbabel. – Ezra Chapters 1-6
    1. Return of the Jews. – Ezra Chapters 1-2
    2. Re-erection of the Altar. – Ezra Chapter 3:1-7
    3. Rebuilding of the Temple. – Ezra Chapter 3:8-6:15
    4. Restoration of the Temple worship. – Ezra Chapter 6:16-22

B. Return under Ezra. – Ezra Chapters 7-10
    1. Respect for the word of God. – Ezra Chapters 7-9
    2. Repentance and reform through the word of God. –
       Ezra Chapter 10
    Note: between 516-458 B.C. a lapse of 58 years exists between Ezra Chapter 6 and 7. At the point of time the book of Esther fits nicely.

Pivotal Word – Rebuild

There is some form of the word "rebuild" found 16 times in the book of Ezra, (1:3, 5; 5:2-3, 17; 6:7). The main focus of the rebuilding effort is the Temple. The rebuilding effort takes some 20 years, 535-515 B.C. (cf. 3:8 and 6:15).

Characters of Importance

Zerubbabel – (descended of Babylon) Also called Sheshbazzar (1:8; 5:16). He led the first return of 50,000 exiles and supervised the construction of the second temple, often called Zerubbabel's Temple.

Ezra – (helper) The priest and scribe who led the second return of exiles to Jerusalem, and who was responsible for the spiritual revival among the people, 7:1, 6.

Four Persian Kings:
1. Cyrus (538-530) – Ezra 1:1-4; 6:3-5 His decree allowed the Jews to return.
2. Darius I (632-486) – Ezra 6:1, 11-12 His decree allowed work on the Temple to resume.
3. Xerxes I (Ahasuerus – 486-465) – Ezra 4:6 Esther's husband.
4. Artaxerxes I (464-423) – Ezra 4:7-23; 7:11-28 He supported the Jews in Ezra's time.

Two prophets of God: - Haggai and Zechariah whose prophecies encouraged the rebuilding of the Temple. Ezra 5:1-2; 6:14; Haggai 1:9, 14-15; Zech. 1:1-6

Important Verses

Ezra 1:1-4 – The Decree of Cyrus (538 B.C.) (cf. 6:3-5 for more details of this decree).

Ezra 2:64-65 – Nearly 50,000 returned with Zerubbabel.

Ezra 3:12-13 – Emotion over the Temple. (cf. Haggai 2:3)

Ezra 6:15 – The Temple completed in 20 years.

Ezra 7:10 – The key verse of the book.

Ezra 9:5-15 – Ezra's prayer of confession for the people.

Ezra 10:3 – A difficult covenant.

Major Themes

A. The word of the Lord is powerful and has a place.
    1. Teaching the word. – Ezra 7:10; (cf. Neh. 8:1-8)
        a. Study. – II Tim. 2:15
        b. Practice. – I Tim. 4:16
        c. Teach. – II Tim. 2:2
    2. Respect the word. – Ezra 9:4; 10:3, 9 "trembling"
    3. Obey the word. – Ezra 10:4-5, 10-12

B. God's ruling hand and His providence in history shown through King Cyrus of Persia. – Ezra 1:1-4; 8:22
    1. Raised up by God. – Isa. 44:28; 45:1, 12-13
       Isaiah wrote these prophesies 150 years before Cyrus lived.
    2. Stirred up by God. – Ezra 1:1; Jer. 25:12
    3. Spoken through by God. – Ezra:2-4

Christ Revealed

1. Zerubbabel – An ancestor of Christ.
    a. He was the "prince of Judah" (1:8) and as such was a forerunner of Jesus the "Prince of Peace."
    b. He is listed in the lineage of Christ. – Matt. 1:13

2. Ezra – a type of Christ.
    a. Priest of God. – Ezra 7:1; Heb. 4:14-16
    b. Scribe of the Law. – Ezra 7:6; Matt. 22:34-40

c. teacher of the word. – Ezra 7:10; Matt. 22:16; John 3:2

d. Preacher of repentance. – Ezra 10:3, 11; Mark 1:15

Nehemiah

Summation

In the Latin Vulgate from the 4th and 5th century the books of Ezra and Nehemiah were treated as one book. The date of Nehemiah is firmly set in the book itself as being in the "twentieth year of King Artaxerxes," Neh. 1:1, 2:1, around 445 B.C. With the book of Nehemiah the books of history in the Bible end. Nehemiah served as governor of Judah for two different terms, one for twelve years mentioned in, Neh. 5:14 and another term after his return back from Persia where he had been for a short time, Neh. 13:6. A total of three returns from exile are recorded one with Zerubbabel (536 B.C.) that focused on leadership and the rebuilding of the Temple. The second return by Ezra (458 B.C.) focused on spiritual leadership and the teaching of the word of God and the third return by Nehemiah (445 B.C.) focused on civil leadership and reconstructing the walls of Jerusalem. Zerubbabel and Ezra worked to restore religious and spiritual freedom in Judah while Nehemiah's efforts pertained mostly to social and political freedom in the land. During the time of Nehemiah the prophet Malachi was active. He encouraged the people not to neglect true worship and to be faithful to God.

Breakdown

A. The walls of Jerusalem to be rebuilt. – Neh. Chapters 1-6
   1. Concern for the work. – Neh. Chapter 1
   2. A call goes out to work. – Neh. Chapter 2
   3. People cooperate in the work. – Neh. Chapter 3
   4. Some criticism of the work. – Neh. Chapters 4:1-6:14
   5. The work is completed. – Neh. Chapter 6:15-19

B. The revival of the people. – Neh. Chapters 7-13
   1. The registration of the people. – Neh. Chapter 7

2. The renewing of the Covenant. – Neh. Chapters 8-10

3. Reformation of the people. – Neh. Chapters 11-13

Pivotal Word - Wall

Nehemiah had an obsession with rebuilding the walls of Jerusalem. Rebuilding the walls is mentioned 33 times, Neh. 1:3; 2:17; 6:15; 7:1; 12:27. The walls were originally destroyed by Nebuchadnezzar in 586 B.C., Ezra 4:6-23. For about 100 years the Jews had been back in Jerusalem (539-445) and the walls were still in a state of deconstruction.

Characters of Importance

Nehemiah – (the Lord has comforted)
>   a. Nehemiah was the cup bearer to King Artaxerxes of Persia – Neh. 1:11; 2:1. His job was to guarantee that the king's wine was free of poison and served as a close confidant and advisor.

Ezra – A priest and a scribe. He worked to bring about a spiritual revival among the people through his preaching, Neh. Chapter 8, and through his praying, Neh. Chapter 9.

Sanballat, Tobiah, and Geshem – These men were Nehemiah's enemies that worked against the building of the walls, Neh. 2:10, 19; 4:1; 6:1-3.

Important Verses

Neh. - 2:17-20 – "… Let us rise up and build…"

Neh. – 4:6 – "… for the people had a mind to work."

Neh. – 6:3 – Nehemiah's noble refusal to leave his work.

Neh. – 6:15-16 – The completion of the wall.

Neh. – 8:1-8 – Ezra's exposition of the word of God.

Neh. – 9:33 – God's faithfulness and man's wickedness.

Neh. – 13:23-25 – Mixed marriages and the language of Ashdod.

Major Themes

In the book of Nehemiah there are demonstrations of leadership and following that the church today can actively pursue to help it to grow and build.

A. The practices of Nehemiah.
1. He agonized over the situation. – Neh. 1:4-11
2. He visualized the goal. – Neh. 2:5, 12
3. He studied the situation. – Neh. 2:11-16
4. He organized the people. – Neh. 2:17-20
5. He oversaw all the work. – Neh. 4:1-6, 14-23; 5:16
6. He realized the victory. – Neh. 6:15-16

B. The people's response.
1. They prepared themselves to work. – Neh. 2:18; 4:6
2. They had a spirit to pray. – Neh. 4:9
3. They had an eye to watch. – Neh. 4:9
4. They had a hand to fight. – Neh. 4:17-20
5. They had a backbone to endure. – Neh. 4:21-23; 6:15-16
6. They had a heart to give. – Neh. 7:70-72

Christ Revealed – Nehemiah characterizes Christ.

1. Nehemiah had a compassionate heart. – Neh. 1:4; Matt. 9:36

2. Nehemiah was a humble servant. – Neh. 2:1-8; Phil. 2:5-11

3. Nehemiah was courageous in the face of opposition. – Neh. 4:14; Mark 8:31

4. Nehemiah was an energetic worker. – Neh. 4:23; John 9:4

5. Nehemiah was prayerful and dependent upon God. – Neh. 1:5-11; 2:4, 8, 12, 18, 20; 4:15, 20; 6:9, 16; Mark 1:35; Luke 6:12-13

Esther

The book of Esther pertains to a time between the third and twelfth years of King Ahasuerus, Xerxes, 483-471; (cf. Esther 1:3 and 3:7). Please recall as mentioned previously in Ezra, the events taking place in Esther occur between Ezra chapter 6 and 7. The book of Esther focuses on the plight of the Jews who remained in Persia after the Babylonian captivity. Something unique to the book of Esther is that it doesn't mention God by name and it is not quoted in the New Testament. The purpose of the book is very evident, it shows how Esther was providentially selected as queen in the Persian court and was able to use her influence to providentially deliver her people, the Jews from annihilation, Esther 4:14. It is unknown who the author exactly is though Mordecai is a possibility, Esther 9:20. What we do know about the author is that he was a Persian Jew of the mid fifth century B.C. who wrote the book shortly after the events took place.

Breakdown

A. Queen Vashti's refusal. – Esther Chapter 1

B. Esther is selected queen. – Esther Chapters 2-3

C. Esther's influence. – Esther Chapters 4-5

D. Esther's appeal. – Esther Chapters 6-7

E. Esther's victory. – Esther Chapters 8-10

Pivotal Word - Queen

"Queen" is the prominent word that is found some 25 times in Esther. As queen, Esther occupied a position of royalty, Esther 1:19; 2:17, which helped her gain favor, Ester 4:8; 5:8; 7:3; 8:5, and received any request "even to half of the Kingdom," Esther 5:3, 6; 7:2.

Characters of Importance

Ahasuerus (Hebrew), Xerxes (Greek) – the King of Persia from 486-465 B.C. – Esther 1:1; 8:9; 9:30

Vashti – the Persian queen who lost her position because she refused "to display her beauty." – Esther 1:11-12

Esther – The beautiful, young, virgin, Jewish girl selected as queen to replace Vashti. Her Persian name, Esther, meant "star." Her Hebrew name, Hadassah, meant "myrtle." – Esther 2:7

Mordecai – Esther's cousin, Esther 2:7, who was her guardian, Esther 2:15, and advisor Esther 2:20. He was appointed a position second to the King, Esther 9:4; 10:3.

Haman – The man over all the princes of Persia who conspired to destroy the Jews, Esther 3:1; 5:11; 3:8-9; 7:6.

Important Verses

Esther 1:12 – Vashti's noble refusal.

Esther 2:17 – Esther selected as queen.

Esther 3:8-9 – Haman's decree to kill the Jews.

Esther 4:14 – The key verse of the book.

Esther 7:10 – Haman is hanged.

Esther 8:11 – The decree of King Ahasuerus.

Esther 9:29-32 – The feast of Purim established.

Major Themes

A. There is an obvious absence of God by name while the Persian King is mentioned nearly 200 times.

B. God's presence established by providence.
    1. God's power, protection, preservation and providence are shown in the following verses and events.
      a. Vashti's removal. – Esther 1:12
      b. Esther's selection. – Esther 2:17
      c. Mordecai's discovery of the plot against Ahasuerus. – Esther 2:22
      d. Esther's favor and audience with the King. – Esther 5:1-2
      e. Ahasuerus' indebtedness to Mordecai. – Esther 6:1-2
      f. Haman's evil scheme foiled. – Esther 6:13; 7:10
      g. Miraculous delivery of the Jews. – Esther 8:16-17
      h. Divine retribution on the Persians. – Esther 9:5; 10:3
      i. Mordecai's promotion and fame. – Esther 9:4; 10:3
    2. Esther clearly shows evidence of God's providence at work. Gen. 50:20; Rom. 8:28

C. The problem of racial prejudice. – Esther 3:13; Acts 10:34-35; Gal. 3:28

D. The Feast of Purim is instituted. – Esther 3:7; 9:20-32

Christ Revealed

Christ our Savior is characterized by Esther.

1. Their presentation. – Both came at the right time. – Esther – 4:14; Rom. 5:6

2. Salvation – Both knew their purpose. – Esther 4:14, 16; Matt. 1:21

3. Intercession – Both were willing to plead for their people. Esther 4:8; 7:3; Heb. 7:25

4. Being exalted. – Both came from humble circumstances and were exalted to positions of power and authority. Esther 2:17; 9:29; Matt. 28:18; Col. 2:10

Job

Summation

The author of the book of Job is still unknown. It is a book that, though it is written in poetical form, describes real events and is acknowledged by other biblical writers, Ezek. 14:14, 20; James 5:11. The book is a story of Job, a character from whom the book draws its' name, and dates to a time during the patriarchal age around 2100 B.C. The book may have been written just shortly after the events recorded in the book took place and if that were true it would make Job the earliest Old Testament book. However it could have been written during the days of David and Solomon around 1000 B.C. when other poetical literature was written such as the Psalms, Proverbs, Ecclesiastes and Song of Solomon. The book of Job fits nicely in the days of the patriarchs because of the following reasons: Job's age, Job 42:16; Job's wealth is measured in livestock, Job 1:3; Job served as priest for his family, Job 1:5; there is never any mention of Mosaic Law, or of Israel. As the story of Job unfolds it deals with the age old question, "Why do the righteous suffer?" Job's family and friends try to help him resolve his dilemma and even Job's own faith does some deep soul-searching. Job eventually learns, when God speaks to him, that it is more important to know who is in control than why the events of life happen.

Breakdown

A. The circumstances. – Job 1:1-5

B. The calamities. – Job 1:6-2:10

C. Those trying to comfort. – Job 2:11-13

D. Conversations. – Job 3:1-41:34
   1. With his three friends. – Job 3:1-31:40
   2. With Elihu. – Job 32:1-37:24
   3. With God. – Job 38:1-41:34

E.   His confessions. – Job 42:1-6

F.   His compensations. – Job 42:7-17

<u>Pivotal Word</u> - Righteousness

There is some form of the word righteous that appears 38 times in the book of Job: "right" (18), "righteous" (12), and "righteousness" (8).   Job and his friends try to reconcile being right with God and suffering pain. Job's friends imply that if he were righteous he would not suffer, Job 8:6.   Job instead argues that he is righteous, Job 34:5, and God has wronged him. The fact is: even the righteous suffer.

<u>Characters of Importance</u>

Job – A morally pure man, Job 1:1, 8; 2:3, very wealthy, Job 1:3; 29:25; 31:25, and a resident of Uz, the land southeast of the Dead Sea, also called Edom, Lam. 4:21.

Job's wife – Her observation is humanistic and fatalistic. – Job 2:9-10.

Eliphaz, Bildad, and Zophar – these three men were friends of Job who tried to "sympathize with him and comfort him." Job 2:11; 16:1-4; 32:3; 42:7.

Elihu – A young man who listened to Job's conversations with his friends and then was compelled to speak his opinions, Job 32:1-10.

<u>Important Verses</u>

<u>Job 1:9</u> – "Doth Job fear God for nought?"

<u>Job 1:20-22</u> – Job's response to his trials.

<u>Job 2:4</u> – "… skin for skin…"

<u>Job 2:10</u> – "… In all this did not Job sin with his lips."

<u>Job 9:2</u> – "… but how should man be just with God?"

Job 14:14 – "If a man die, shall he live again..."

Job 19:25 – "For I know that my Redeemer liveth..."

Job 23:10 – "... I shall come forth as gold"

Job 38:1-4 – God reprimands Job.

Job 40:3-5 – Job's wise silence.

Job 42:1-6 – Job's repentance and confession.

Job 42:12 – "So the Lord blessed the latter end of Job more than his beginning..."

Major Themes

A. The universal problem of human suffering.
   Why do the righteous suffer?
   1. Reasons suggested in the book of Job.
      a. Man's character is tested when he suffers. – Job 1:6-12; James 1:2
      b. Suffering is due to personal sin. – Job 4:7-9; 8:6; John 5:14
      c. By suffering the sufferer is purified. – Job 23:10
      d. Suffering chastens, disciplines and educates. – Job 33:19-30
      e. All suffering is certainly not punishment from God. (cf. John 9:1ff; James 1:13)
   2. Man's response:
      a. Job's wife – "God is unfair." – Job 2:9
      b. Job's friends – "God is punishing you." – Job 11:6
      c. Elihu – "God is enlightening you." – Job 33:30
      d. Job – "God has wronged me." – Job 34:5
   3. God's response:
      a. God allows people to suffer for their good or benefit.
      b. The benefit of trials and suffering is taught throughout scripture. Ps. 119:67-71; Rom. 8:18; II Cor. 4:16-18; I Pet. 1:6-7
      c. Job understood that his sufferings were in the will of God, Job

66

23:14, and that ultimate good would result from his trials, Job
23:10. (cf. Rom. 8:28).

    d. There are some things in man's experiences that he is not able
to understand. Man does not need to know all things and
certainly does not need to know why God allows some things
to happen to man. The important thing to know is that God is
in control of our lives and that He loves us and that all things
will turn out for good for them that love God, Rom. 8:28.

B. Job is a wonderful example of endurance though his patience is
lacking.

    1. Job was very impatient.
      a. He cursed the day of his birth. – Job 3:1-3
      b. His desire to live faded. – Job 6:6-7
      c. He became bitter. – Job 10:1
      d. He complained to God. – Job 7:11-16; 23:2; 33:13
      e. He challenged God. – Job 9:34; 10:2ff; 13:3; 23:3ff; 31:35ff;
        40:2
    2. Job had endurance. He was steadfast and that helped to enable
him to remain faithful to God in the midst of pain and suffering.
– Job 1:22; 2:10; James 5:11

C. Self-righteousness is a folly and man needs to completely trust
God.

    1. Job's greatest problem was his self-righteousness. – Job 9:2;
      10:7; 13:18; 27:5-6; 31:6; 32:1-2; 33:9; 34:5; 40:8
    2. Job was guilty of other sins:
      a. Pride – Job 33:17; 35:12
      b. Rebellion – Job 23:2; 34:37
      c. Ignorance – Job 34:35; 35:16; 38:2
    3. Job finally learned to trust God. – Job 42:1-6
    4. Job was approved of by God. – Job 1:8; 2:3; 42:7-8 "My
Servant."

D. Satan is always active. – Job 1:6-2:10
    1. Satan is alive and well. – Matt. 4:1-11; I Pet. 5:8

2. Satan is determined to bring about man's destruction. –
   I Pet. 5:8
3. God limits the power of Satan. – Job 1:12; 2:6; I Cor. 10:13

E. God is sovereign.
   1. God's sovereignty is seen in His creative power. – Job 26:7-14
   2. God's sovereignty is seen in His knowledge and wisdom. –
      Job 38:1ff
   3. God's sovereignty is seen in His divine control. – Job 42:2
   4. God's sovereignty is seen in His providential care. –
      Job 42:10-12

Christ Revealed

1. Christ our Righteousness. – Job 4:17; 9:2; 25:4
   a. Job and his friends raise one of life's greatest questions.
   b. In the New Testament the answer is revealed. – Matt. 5:20;
      Rom. 3:21-28; II Cor. 5:21; Phil. 3:9; Titus 3:5

2. Christ is our mediator. – Job 9:32-33; 16:19
   a. Mediator, arbitrator, one who understands both God and man.
   b. Christ is our mediator before God. – Rom. 8:34; I Tim. 2:5;
      Heb. 7:25; 9:24; I John 2:2

3. Christ is our Redeemer. – Job 19:25-27
   a. Job's glimpse of the resurrection gave him hope for future
      vindication.
   b. The Christian has this glorious hope of immortality because
      Christ has conquered death and He has redeemed us by His
      blood. – I Cor. 15:19-22; Eph. 1:7

Psalms

Summation

In Hebrew the title for the Psalms is "The Book of Praises." The Psalms was used as a Jewish hymnal or psalter. The book of Psalms is the longest book in the Bible with a total of 150 chapters 73 of which are assigned to David, 12 to Asaph, 10 to sons of Korah, 2 to Solomon, 1 to Ethan, 1 to Heman, 1 to Moses and 50 of them are anonymous. It took a period of 1,000 years, from the time of Moses to the return from their exile, to write all the Psalms. Most of the Psalms however, were written during the time of David and Solomon, about 1000 B.C. Unique to the Psalms the reader is given insight to man talking to God and about God. The Psalms therefore come from the human experience and they reveal the heart, the inner emotions of man such as grief, sorrow, fear, doubt, joy, hope, care, anxiety and so forth. The writers of the Psalms always expressed himself in the presence of the living God with an awareness of God's goodness and grace. The Psalms have often been referred to as the "heart of the Bible."

Breakdown

The book of Psalms can easily be divided into five sections that we will call books. These sections are primarily by the author.

A. Book One – Psalms 1-41

B. Book Two – Psalms 42-72

C. Book Three – Psalms 73-89

D. Book Four – Psalms 90-106

E. Book Five – Psalms 107-150

<u>Pivotal Word</u>

Praise is a word that is found some 165 times in the Psalms in varying forms: "praise" (122), "praises" (30), and "praised" (5). The Psalms were mostly sung rather than just read therefore the word "sing" appears some (84) times. The key element of praise is found in all 150 of the Psalms with the exception for Psalm 88.

<u>Characters of Importance</u>

David – David is the second and by many considered the greatest king of Israel.
  a. Many of the Psalms are directly associated with events in the life of David. Ps. 3, 5, 7, 16-18, 23, 30, 34, 51, 52, 54, 56, 57, 59, 60, 142.
  b. David wrote 73 of the Psalms that are found mostly in Book One and Book Two.

Solomon – The son of David and full of wisdom. He was the third king of Israel.
  a. Solomon was a prolific writer of proverbs and songs. – I Kings 4:32
  b. Two of the psalms are accredited to Solomon: – Ps. 72 and 127

Asaph
  a. Asaph was an outstanding musician in David's time, and he was appointed chief musician in the Temple. – I Chron. 15:19; 16:4-5; Ezra 2:41
  b. Asaph wrote twelve of the psalms: - Ps. 50, 73-83.

Sons of Korah
  a. Korah was the great-grandson of Levi who led a rebellion against Moses and Aaron in the wilderness. – Num. 16:1-3
  b. The descendants of Korah were singers in the Temple. – II Chron. 20:19

c. Ten psalms are attributed to the sons of Korah: - Ps. 42, 44-49, 84, 87-88.

Moses – The author of Ps. 90, making it the oldest psalm in the collection.

Important Verses

Psalm 1 – The contrast of the righteous and wicked.

Psalm 8 – The majesty of God.

Psalm 19 – The revelation of God.

Psalm 22 – The psalm of Calvary.

Psalm 23 – The Shepherd psalm.

Psalm 32 – The psalm of forgiveness.

Psalm 46 – The psalm of trust.

Psalm 51 – The psalm of penitence.

Psalm 88 – The saddest psalm.

Psalm 90 – The oldest psalm.

Psalm 105-106 – The history of Israel.

Psalm 117 – The shortest psalm.

Psalm 119 – The longest psalm.

Psalm 139 – The attributes of God.

Psalm 150 – The psalm of praise.

Major Themes

A. There are different types of psalms.
    1. Royal psalm. – Ps. 2, 21, 45, 72, 110, 132
    2. Historical psalms. – Ps. 78, 81, 105, 106
    3. Thanksgiving psalms. – Ps. 30, 34, 62, 116
    4. Lament psalms. – Ps. 3, 5-7, 44, 74, 79-80
    5. Praise psalms. Ps. 8, 136, 146-150
    6. Penitential psalms. – Ps. 32, 51
    7. Imprecatory psalms. – Ps. 7, 35, 55, 58, 69, 109, 137

    In each of the psalms there are some commonalities worthy of note:
    a. The writer demonstrates a boldness and the willingness to openly praise and pray to God.
    b. The writer exhibits a belief in a God who he knew would and could do something on the behalf of His own.
    c. Worship and adoration of God is continually portrayed.

B. God has a presence in the psalms.
    1. God is active.
        a. God creates. – Ps. 104
        b. God saves and delivers. – Ps. 18, 32
        c. God reigns. – Ps. 93
        d. God elects. – Ps. 89, 105
        e. God reveals. – Ps. 19, 119
        f. God judges. Ps. 67, 75
    2. God's nature.
        a. God is holy. – Ps. 99
        b. God is righteous. – Ps. 119
        c. God is faithful and loving. – Ps. 103
        d. God is one. – Ps. 50:1; 71:22; 78:41; 89:18
        e. God is a spirit. – Ps. 139

C. The New Testament quotes and refers to the Psalms.
    1. The psalms are quoted by Jesus. – Matt. 13:35 (Ps. 78:2),

Matt. 21:42 (Ps. 118:22), Matt. 22:42-45 (Ps. 110:1),
Matt. 27:46 (Ps. 22:1).
2. The Apostles also quoted the psalms. – John 2:17 (Ps. 69:9),
Acts 1:20 (Ps. 69:25; 109:8), Acts 4:11 and I Pet. 2:7
(Ps. 118:22)
3. Psalms is the most quoted Old Testament book in the New
Testament especially notice Heb. 1-3 and Rom. 3:10-18.
4. Of special significance is the fact that the early church of the
1st century used the psalms in their worship, Eph. 5:19;
Col. 3:16.
   a. In the Old Testament in the Temple worship with psalms
      were often sung with instrumental accompaniment, Ps. 150;
      I Chron. 25:1-8
   b. When Jewish worship shifted from the Temple to the
      synagogue musical instruments were forbidden.
   c. The worship of the early church was patterned after
      synagogue worship and not Temple worship.
   d. There is no binding example, command, or inference that the
      early church used instrumental music with the psalms or
      anything other than just singing.

Christ Revealed

Christ was aware that the psalms spoke of Him. – Luke 24:44
Christ quoted the psalms more than any other Old Testament book.

1. Messianic psalms cited in the New Testament and applied to
   Christ:
   a. Ps. 2 – Acts 4:25-28; 13:33; Heb. 1:5; 5:5
   b. Ps. 16 – Acts 2:24-31; 13:35-37
   c. Ps. 22 – Matt. 27:35-46; John 19:23-25; Heb. 2:12
   d. Ps. 45 – Heb. 1:8-9
   e. Ps. 89 – Acts 2:30
   f. Ps. 110 – Matt. 22:43-45; Acts 2:33-35; Heb. 1:3; 5:6-10; 6:20;
      7:24

2. Different scriptures in the psalms that the New Testament applies to Christ:
   a. Christ's manhood. – Ps. 8:4-5 (Heb. 2:6-8)
   b. Christ's Son of God. – Ps. 2:7 (Heb. 1:5)
   c. Christ's deity. – Ps. 45:6 (Heb. 1:8)
   d. Christ's holiness. – Ps. 45:7 (Heb. 1:9)
   e. Christ's priesthood. – Ps. 110:4 (Heb. 5:6)
   f. Christ's kingship. – Ps. 2:6 (Rev. 19:16)
   g. Christ's conquest. – Ps. 110:5-6 (Rom. 2:5)
   h. Christ's eternity. – Ps. 102:25-26 (Heb. 1:10-11)
   i. Christ's universal sovereignty. – Ps. 72:8, 11; 103:19
      (I Tim. 6:15)
   j. Christ's obedience. – Ps. 40:6-8 (Heb. 10:5-7)
   k. Christ's zeal. – Ps. 69:9 (John 2:17)
   l. Christ's sufferings. – Ps. 69:9 (Rom. 15:3)
   m. Christ's betrayal. – Ps. 41:9 (John 13:18)
   n. Christ's death. – Ps. 22:1-18 (Matt. 27:35-46)
   o. Christ's resurrection. – Ps. 16:8-10 (Acts 2:25-28, 31; 13:35)
   p. Christ's ascension. – Ps. 68:18 (Eph. 4:8)
   q. Christ's coming again to judge. – Ps. 96:13 (II Thess. 1:7-9)

3. The psalms show Christ in many roles:
   a. King. – Ps. 2:6
   b. Son of God. – Ps. 2:7
   c. Prophet. – Ps. 22:22
   d. Priest. – Ps. 110:4
   e. Suffering Savior. – Ps. 22:1-18

Proverbs

Summation

Proverbs means, comparison, parallel, or similar. The Hebrew title for this book is "The Proverbs of Solomon." We are aware that the major contributor of the book of Proverbs was Solomon, Prov. 1:1; 10:1; 25:1; I Kings 4:32; Eccl. 12:9. The book of Proverbs contains wise sayings or maxims taken from everyday life intended to serve as practical guidelines for a successful life. All of the proverbs were written and compiled together between the time of Solomon and Hezekiah (950-700 B.C.). Proverbs could be called a book of comparisons such as, rich and poor, wise and foolish, righteous and wicked, industrious and lazy, obedient and rebellious, virtues and vices, God's way and man's way. There are three major points that the book of Proverbs makes very apparent as the reader progresses through the book, they are the following: 1. It is wise and practical to live a godly life. 2. It is foolishness and impractical to live an ungodly life. 3. Living godly is a blessed and rewarded decision both here and now and in the future.

Breakdown

Proverbs can be broken down into sections by subject and author.

A. Proverbs of Solomon. (Wisdom) – Prov. Chapters 1-9

B. Proverbs of Solomon. (Conduct) – Prov. 10-22:16

C. Proverbs of the wise. (Relationships) – Prov. 22:17-24:34

D. Proverbs of Solomon. (Transcribed by Hezekiah's men) – Prov. 25-29

E. Proverbs of Agur and Lemuel. – Prov. 30-31

Pivotal Word – Wisdom

There are three basic ways that wisdom is spoken of in the book of Proverbs and they are: "Wisdom" some 54 times in 53 verses. This pertains to a sound understanding and judgment of the basic issues of life and godliness. "Understanding" some 54 times in 53 verses. The ability to discern truth, values and priorities. "Sound Wisdom" some 3 times in 6 verses. This is applying divine principles to daily life.

Characters of Importance

Solomon – The wise son of David and the third king of Israel.
　　　　　a. Solomon authored the majority of the proverbs in the
　　　　　　　book of Proverbs. – Prov. 1:1; 10:1; 25:1
　　　　　b. Solomon was endowed with wisdom from God. –
　　　　　　　I Kings 3:5-15
　　　　　c. Solomon was famous for his wisdom, and he authored
　　　　　　　3,000 proverbs and 1,005 songs. – I Kings 4:29-34

Hezekiah's men – A committee was appointed by King Hezekiah
　　　　　　　some 250 years after Solomon's time. This
　　　　　　　committee's job was to take more of Solomon's
　　　　　　　proverbs and incorporate them into a collection. It is
　　　　　　　probable that King Solomon's writings were preserved
　　　　　　　in the royal archives of Israel, Prov. 25:1.

Agur and Lemuel – Two unknown men who authored the last two
　　　　　　　chapters in Proverbs, Prov. 30:1; 31:1.

Important Verses

Prov. 1:7 – "The fear of the Lord is the beginning of knowledge..."

Prov. 3:5 – "Trust in the Lord with all thine heart..."

Prov. 6:16-19 – Seven things the Lord hates.

Prov. 14:34 – "Righteousness exalteth a nation..."

Prov. 22:6 – "Train up a child in the way he should go…"

Prov. 23:7 – "For as he thinketh in his heart, so is he…"

Prov. 29:18 – "Where there is no vision, the people perish…"

Prov. 31:10 – "Who can find a virtuous woman? …"

Major Themes

A. God and man. – Prov. 3:1-7; 22:4

B. Wisdom. – Prov. 1:1-7; 4:5-9

C. The Fool. – Prov. 26:1-12

D. The sluggard. – Prov. 6:6-11; 26:13-16

E. The friend. – Prov. 17:17; 18:24

F. Words. – Prov. 15:1; 18:21; 25:11; 26:22

G. Life and death. – Prov. 10:16-17; 11:19; 27:1

H. The family.

> 1. Father and mother. – Prov. 6:20; 15:20; 19:26; 20:20
> 2. Good wife. – Prov. 12:4; 18:22; 19:13-14; 31:10-31
> 3. Bad wife. – Prov. 19:13; 21:9, 19; 27:15-16
> 4. Faithfulness in marriage. – Prov. 5:18-19; 6:26-32
> 5. Children. – Prov. 10:1; 17:25; 22:6; 23:22
> 6. Discipline. – Prov. 13:24; 22:15; 23:13; 29:15, 17

Christ Revealed

1. Christ, the Eternal One. – Prov. 8:22-26

2. Christ, the Creator. – Prov. 8:27-29

3. Christ, the Delight of God. – Prov. 8:30-31

4. Christ, the Wisdom from God. – Prov. 8:22-31
   a. This passage of scripture some believe to be referring to the character of wisdom and not to Christ. (cf. Prov. 8:1, 12)
   b. Think of this when making your decision, Christ is the wisdom of God personified. – I Cor. 1:24, 30; Col. 2:2-3

5. Christ, the Son of God. – Prov. 30:4
   a. Christ dwells in the presence of God. – Prov. 30:4 (a); John 3:13; Eph. 4:8-10
   b. Christ was intricate in the creation. – Prov. 30:4 (b); John 1:1-4
   c. Christ is God's Son, and His name is Christ! – Prov. 3-:4 (c); Phil. 2:9-11; Rev. 19:11-16

Ecclesiastes

The title Ecclesiastes means "preacher" or "one who convenes and speaks at an assembly." The book of Ecclesiastes was written by Solomon during his reign as king (970-932 B.C.). Evidence within the book itself identifies Solomon as the author such as: He was the son of David, and king in Jerusalem, Eccl. 1:1. He was wise, Eccl 1:16, wealthy, Eccl. 2:7 and worldly, Eccl. 2:3, a great builder, Prov. 2:4-6, and authored many proverbs, Prov. 12:9. In the New Testament Ecclesiastes is alluded to several times, Matt. 6:7 (Eccl. 5:2); Luke 12:20 (Eccl. 6:2); John 3:8 (Eccl. 11:5); II Cor. 5:10 (Eccl. 12:14). As with all things there are some who feel the need to criticize something they don't exactly agree with. Some have called the book of Ecclesiastes "too pessimistic." God has used Solomon's forty year quest to demonstrate what is meaningful and meaningless in life. God has used the approach of someone preaching to us, hence the title, to teach us some of life's most important lessons.

Breakdown

A. The preacher's introduction. (problem stated) – Eccl. 1:1-3

B. The preacher's sermon. (experiments conducted) – Eccl. 1:4-12:12

C. The preacher's conclusion. (solution proposed) – Eccl. 12:13-14

Pivotal Word – Vanity

The word "vanity" appears 33 times in 28 verses. Vanity means empty, fleeting, worthless, of no value, futile, useless. This word "vanity" was used by Solomon to describe his life "under the sun." This expression is found in 27 verses and is used to describe his natural life and all of his worldly pursuits. Solomon discovered in his worldly quest for satisfaction and happiness that all his efforts resulted in "vanity", Eccl. 1:2; 12:8, when God is not included.

Characters of Importance

Solomon – The preacher. Eccl. 1:1-2, 12; 7:27; 12:8-10

1. Solomon asked and received wisdom from God. – I Kings 3:5-15; James 1:5

2. Solomon learned truth through his experience. – Eccl. 7:27-29

3. Solomon shared knowledge with the people. – Eccl. 12:9a

4. Solomon was able to discover truth by studying and research. – Eccl. 12:9b; II Tim. 2:15

5. Solomon wrote down and taught acceptable words of truth. – Eccl. 12:10; Prov. 10:32; 22:20-21; Gal. 1:9-10

Important Verses

Eccl. 1:9 – "… there is nothing new under the sun."

Eccl. 3:1-8 – A time for everything.

Eccl. 5:10 – Money does not satisfy.

Eccl. 7:29 – "… God made men upright…"

Eccl. 8:11 – Punishment for sin may not be immediate.

Eccl. 11:9 – Be responsible in your youth.

Eccl. 12:1 – "Remember also your creator in the days of your youth."

Eccl. 12:7 – The body and spirit at death.

Eccl. 12:13 – "… fear God and keep His commandments…"

Major Themes

A. The vanity of knowledge and wisdom. – Eccl. 1:16-18; 12:12

B. The vanity of pleasure. – Eccl. 2:1-3, 10; I John 2:15-17

C. The vanity of wealth. – Eccl. 2:7-11; 10:19; Luke 12:15;
    I Tim. 6:6-10

D. The vanity of power, fame, and great accomplishments. – Eccl.
    2:12-23; Matt. 20:26

E. The vanity of false worship and mere religion. – Eccl. 5:1-7;
    I Kings 11:4-6; Matt. 15:8-9; 23:25-28

F. The vanity of life without God.
    1. Remember God. – Eccl. 12:1; Ps. 42:1-2; Matt. 6:33
    2. Reverence God. – Eccl. 12:13; 3:14; 5:7; 7:18; 8:12-13
    3. Respect God. – Eccl. 12:14; 3:17; 11:9; Rom. 2:16; II Cor. 5:10

Christ Revealed

Christ the preacher. – Eccl. 1:1; Mark 1:14

Christ the son of David. – Eccl. 1:1; Matt. 1:1

Christ the King. – Eccl. 1:1; I Tim. 6:15; Rev. 19:16

Christ the Creator. – Eccl. 12:1; John 1:1-3; Col. 1:16

Christ the Shepherd. – Eccl. 12:11; Heb. 13:20

Song of Solomon

The title and author are revealed in the first verse of the book, "The song of songs, which *is* Solomon's." (Song 1:1). In the Latin Vulgate the book was called "Canticles which means "song." This book is also called "The Song of Songs" perhaps to indicate that these are the best of the ones written by Solomon. Solomon wrote many songs and proverbs as revealed by scripture, "And he spake three thousand proverbs: and his songs were a thousand and five." (I Kings 4:32). The book is considered by some to be very difficult to understand and have suggested various interpretations such as: Allegorical, Historical and Typical. For the purpose of this study an approach aligning with historical and typical is suggested. This approach then suggests that the story literally depicts the love of Solomon for his Shulammite bride and her deep affection for him. However, this couple typically represents God's love for his people, and also foreshadows the mutual love of Christ and His Bride, the Church. The content of the story deals frankly with love, courtship, and marriage. The rabbis taught that no Jew should read the Song of Solomon until he had reached the age of thirty, an age considered in their culture to be one of maturity.

Breakdown

A. A marriage in the making, courtship. – Song Chapters 1-3

B. A marriage consummated, a wedding. – Song Chapter 4

C. A marriage in trouble, problems. – Song Chapters 5-6

D. A marriage that has matured, true love. – Song Chapters 7-8

Pivotal Word – Beloved

The term "beloved" is used 33 times in 27 verses. It is used to describe one another, the groom and the bride. Other forms of the word "love" appear 26 times in 23 verses. The lovers, Song 5:1, are lovesick, Eccl 2:5; 5:8, for each other. The book's pivotal word epitomizes the theme of love. This love is: pure, sensuous, youthful, blind, extravagant, and passionate.

Characters of Importance

Solomon
   a. Solomon is mentioned by his name. – Song 1:1, 5; 3:7, 9, 11; 8:11-12
   b. Solomon had many wives, which did not please God. I Kings 11:3-6

Shulammite woman.
   a. The woman was what we would call a country girl from Shunem near Jezreel, (Josh. 19:18), which was not far from Lebanon. Song 4:8; 6:13
   b. She was the "special" one among all of Solomon's wives (harem), Song 6:8-9, and she may have been his only true love.

Daughters of Jerusalem.
   a. This was a description used of Solomon's wives (harem). – Song 1:3-5
   b. The Daughters of Jerusalem serve as the chorus in the "song" and they extol the beauty of the Shulammite woman. – Song 5:9; 6:9b-10

Important Verses

Song 2:1 – "I am the rose of Sharon, and the lily of the valleys."

Song 2:4 – "… And his banner over me was love."

Song 2:15 – "… the little foxes, that spoil the vines."

Song 4:7 – "Thou art all fair, my love; there is no spot in thee"

Song 6:3 – "I am my beloved's, and my beloved is mine…"

<u>Song 6:7</u> – The qualities of true love.

<u>Major Themes</u>

The principles of marital love can be found in Eph. 5:21-33.

A. Mutual possession. – Song 2:16; 6:3
   1. The husband and wife belong to each other.
   2. The two shall become one. – Eph. 5:31

B. Mutual admiration.
   1. Take notice of the affectionate terms the lovers use: my darling, my dove, my perfect one, my beloved, my friend.
   2. Our words, actions and even our attitudes demonstrate our love.

C. Mutual Submission.
   1. The only problem that arises in this story is the refusal to submit by the wife. Her husband submits to her instead and later the wife regrets her action and the two are reconciled to each other. Song 5:2-6:7
   2. Submission to each other is based on reverence for God and mutual respect. – Eph. 5:21ff

D. Mutual attraction and satisfaction.
   1. The husband is for his wife. – Song 4:1-15; 7:1-10
   2. The wife is for her husband. – Song 5:10-16
   3. Physical love is shown in its rightful place, within the bounds of marriage. The author talks of the intimacies yet he is not obscene or vulgar. – Prov. 5:18-19; I Cor. 7:1-5; Heb. 13:4

E. Mutual affection. – Song 8:6-7; Prov. 6:30-35; I Cor. 13:1-7
   1. To have true love is to have a treasured possession.
   2. True love is as strong as death.
   3. Jealousy has no place in true love.
   4. True love cannot be quenched.
   5. No one can buy true love.

<u>Christ Revealed</u>

Christ is characterized by the Bridegroom in the Song of Solomon.

1. Marriage has always been a means of illustrating God's relationship with His people. – Jer. 3:1-20; Hosea Chapters 1-3

2. The Bridegroom is Christ and the church is His bride.
   a. Eph. 5:21-33; Rev. 19:7; 21:2, 9; 22:17
   b. The principles of Divine love as seen in the Divine marriage: Fidelity, Faithfulness, Forgiveness, Sacrifice, Submission, and Service.

Writing Prophets Timeline

Prophets before the exile 9th thru 7th century B.C.

Prophet	Approx. Date	Nation	World Power
Obadiah	840	Edom	
Joel	835	Judah	
Jonah	780-750	Nineveh	
Amos	760-750	Israel	
Hosea	760-710	Israel	Assyria
Isaiah	740-680	Judah	722 B.C. Israel falls to Assyria
Micah	730-700	Judah	701 B.C. Assyria invades Judah
Jeremiah	627-585	Judah	
Nahum	650-612	Nineveh	
Zephaniah	625	Judah	

Prophets of Exile 6th century B.C.

Prophet	Approx. Date	Nation	World Power
Habakkuk	607	Judah	Babylonia 612 B.C. Assyria falls to Babylonia
Daniel	605-536	Judah	605 B.C. Judah falls to Babylonia 1st Deportation 597 B.C. 2nd Deportation
Ezekiel	597-570	Judah	586 B.C. Jerusalem falls to Babylonia 3rd Deportation
Lamentations	585	Judah	
Haggai	520	Judah	Persia 539 B.C. Babylonia falls to Persia 538 B.C. Decree of Cyrus freeing the Jewish exiles
Zechariah	520-518	Judah	536 B.C. 1st return-Zerubbabel 458 B.C. 2nd return-Ezra
Malachi	450-400	Judah	445 B.C. 3rd return-Nehemiah

A comparison can be made with the chart showing the Kings on to determine who was king during a particular prophet's ministry.

Isaiah

Isaiah began his work in 740 B.C. according to Isa. 6:1. Isaiah served at least 40 years in Judah during the 8th century and Isa. 1:1 confirms Isaiah as the author of this book. Isaiah told of the constant threat of overthrow and exile for the Southern Kingdom and many of the historic events of his day are recorded in II Kings chapters 15-20 and II Chron. 26-32. There is a liberal view of Isaiah that suggests that Isaiah was actually written by two perhaps even three different authors. As a result of this liberal idea they try to divide the book of Isaiah by content and authorship in this manner: Isa. Chapters 1-39 and Isa. Chapters 40-66. The strongest argument against this liberal approach is quoted by Isaiah himself, "The vision of Isaiah the son of Amoz..." (Isa. 1:1). Also adding to the authorship of Isaiah is the New Testament use of the book. Isaiah is quoted by name 22 times in the New Testament. The most conclusive New Testament quotation is John 12:38-41 where verse 38 quotes Isa. 53:1 and verse 40 quotes Isa. 6:10. The famous Dead Sea Scroll of Isaiah that was discovered in 1947 dates approximately 150-100 B.C. This makes it over 1,000 years older than the oldest dated manuscript previously known and it is the only complete copy of a book of the Old Testament yet discovered. The text of this scroll has proved to be essentially identical with our standard Hebrew Bible of today. Isaiah presents the doctrine of Christ more than any other Old Testament book and for this reason Isaiah has been called the Messianic Prophet.

Breakdown

A. Condemning prophecies. – Isa. Chapters 1-39
   1. The sins of Israel. – Isa. Chapters 1-12
   2. The oracles of nations. – Isa. 13-23
   3. The judgments and deliverances. – Isa. 24-29

B. Consolation in prophecies. – Isa. 40-66
    1. Deliverance: God. – Isa. 40-48
    2. Deliverer: Servant-Messiah. – Isa. 49-57
    3. Delivered: Israel. – Isa. 58-66

Pivotal Word – Salvation

    "Salvation" is a word that appears 28 times in 26 verses in Isaiah. "Salvation" is not only the pivotal word, it is the main theme of the book and helps to demonstrate that God is the salvation of His people, Isa. 12:2-3.

Characters of Importance

Isaiah – He is the Messianic Prophet.
    1. Isaiah's background.
        a. His name means "Jehovah is Salvation."
        b. Isaiah's wife was a "prophetess." – Isa. 8:3
        c. Isaiah had two sons:
            1. Shearjashub – "a remnant shall return" – Isa. 7:3.
            2. Maher-shalal-hash-baz- "swift is the booty, speedy is the prey" – Isa. 8:1-4.
    2. Isaiah's work.
        a. Isaiah was called. - Isa. 6:1-13
        b. Isaiah's ministry in the court of Kings. – Isa. 1:1
    3. Isaiah's character.
        a. Isaiah was courageous in proclaiming a message that was not popular.
        b. Isaiah had great knowledge of his world and unsurpassed literacy.
        c. Isaiah greatly respected the holiness of God.
        d. Unlike the other prophets God greatly honored him by revealing more about the Messiah.
        e. Isaiah is quoted more often by name in the New Testament than any other prophet.

Important Verses

Isa. 1:18 – The cleansing of sin.

Isa. 6:8 – "Here am I; send me."

Isa 28:16 – Christ the cornerstone.

Isa. 40:8 – The eternal nature of the word of God.

Isa 40:31 – New strength comes from God.

Isa. 44:28; 45:1ff – This specific "name" prophesy was fulfilled 150
years later when Cyrus became king of Persia and
released the captive Jews. – II Chron. 36:22-23;
Ezra 1:1-4

Isa. 53:1-10 – Prophecy of our Lord and Savior Jesus Christ.

Isa. 55:6-11 –The invitation to salvation.

Isa. 59:1-2– The separating power of sin.

Major Themes

A. The tragedy follows rebellion and disobedience. – Isa. 1:2-3

B. The certainty of impending judgment and captivity. – Isa. 5:1-7

C. The returning faithful remnant of Israel and Judah from exile.
– Isa. 10:21-22; 11:11, 16; 48:20-22

D. God is holy. – Isa. 6:3 the phrase, "Holy One of Israel" is used 26
times in Isaiah.

E. The prophecy concerning the establishment of the church, God's
eternal kingdom. – Isa. 2:2-4; Micah 4:1-3
1. The time is predicted. "Last Days"
2. The place is specified. "Jerusalem"
3. The Messiah. – Isa. 42:1-12; 49; 50:4-6; 52:13-53:12

F. The concept of servitude in Isaiah is threefold.
    1. The Hebrew nation. – Isa. 41:8: 42:19; 44:21
    2. The faithful remnant. – Isa. 43:1-10; 45:4; 48:20
    3. The Messiah. – Isa. 42:1-12; 49; 50:4-6; 52:13-53:12

Christ Revealed

1. The Branch of the Lord. – Isa. 4:2; 11:1; 53:2; Jer. 23:5; 33:15; Zech. 3:8; 6:12

2. The Virgin-born Immanuel. – Isa. 7:14; Matt. 1:23

3. A four-fold description of Christ is given in Isa. 9:6.
    1. Wonderful Counselor. – Isa. 28:29
    2. Mighty God. – Isa. 10:21
    3. Eternal Father. – Isa.63:16; 64:8
    4. Prince of Peace. – Isa. 26:3; John 14:27; 16:33; Eph. 2:13-18

4. He is the root of Jesse. – Isa. 11:1; Acts 13:22-23

5. He is the Cornerstone. – Isa. 28:16; Ps. 118:22; Rom. 9:33; Eph. 2:20; I Pet. 2:6

6. Another four-fold description of Christ is given in Isa. 33:22.
    1. Judge. – Isa. 2:4; 11:4
    2. Lawgiver. – James 4:12
    3. King. – I Tim. 6:15
    4. Savior. – Matt. 1:21

7. Christ is God's Servant. – Isa. 42:1-4; Matt. 12:15-21

8. Christ is the Suffering Servant and the Smitten Lamb. – Isa. 52:13-53:12; Acts 8:28-35
    1. His preeminence. – Isa. 52:13-15
    2. His person. – Isa. 53:1-3
    3. His passion. – Isa. 53:4-6
    4. His passivity. – Isa. 53:7-9
    5. His portion. – Isa. 53:10-12

9. Christ our Redeemer. – Isa. 59:20; Rom. 11:26

10. The Messiah's Ministry. – Isa. 61:1-2; Luke 4:16-21

11. Judge. – Isa. 63:1-6; Rev. 14:18-20; 19:13-15

Jeremiah and Lamentations

Summation

Jeremiah prophesied from 627-585 B.C., Jer. 1:2-3; 25:3, for over forty years in Judah, during and after the fall, and in Egypt. Nahum, Zephaniah and Habakkuk perhaps knew Jeremiah as they were contemporaries of Jeremiah. The biblical record of Jeremiah's day is found in II Kings 22-25 and also in II Chron. 34-36. Jeremiah also wrote the book of Lamentations which he penned after the fall of Judah. Lamentations means "to cry aloud." The reader will soon discover that the book of Jeremiah is not written in chronological order. Jeremiah wrote the book while lamenting the destruction of Jerusalem. Daniel and the exiles found comfort in Jeremiah's book, (Dan. 9:2; Jer. 25:11-12; 29:10. In the New Testament Jeremiah is referenced several times, Matt. 2:17-18 (Jer. 31:15); Matt 16:14; 29:9 (Zech. 11:12-13; Jer. 18:1-4; 19:1-3); Heb. 8:8-12 (Jer. 31:31-34. Jeremiah is known as the "weeping prophet" because he had to deliver a very sad message of doom to a sinful and disobedient people, Jer. 9:1; Lam. 1:16. The theme of Jeremiah is found in the Lord's words to Pashhur the priest in Jer. 20:4-6, it is the captivity of Judah by Babylon.

Breakdown

A. Jeremiah's reluctance to his call: – Jer. Chapter 1

B. Jeremiah's courage in his ministry: – Jer. Chapters 2-45

C. Jeremiah's oracles (teaching), condemnations: – Jer. 46-51

D. Jeremiah's retrospect and conclusion: – Jer. 52

E. Jeremiah's lamenting and compassion: – Lam. 1-5

Some form of the word "weep: is found 16 times in Jeremiah and Lamentations as Jeremiah weeps because of the sinful condition of Judah and ultimately because of her destruction and desolations, Jer. 9:1, 18; 13:17; 14:17; 31:16; Lam. 1:2, 16; 2:11, 18; 3:48-51.

Characters of Importance

Jeremiah – Known as the weeping prophet.

 A. Jeremiah's background.
  1. His name means, "Jehovah exalts or establishes."
  2. Jeremiah was the son of Hilkiah the priest, and he was from Anathoth, a small village about three miles north of Jerusalem, Jer. 1:1.
  3. Jeremiah never married as he was forbidden to marry, attend funerals, or to attend joyous occasions, Jer. 16:1-9.

 B. Jeremiah's work.
  1. Jeremiah was called. – Jer. 1:5-10
  2. Jeremiah was commissioned to prophesy. – Jer. 1:14-19; (cf. 37:17)
  3. Jeremiah was commissioned to write. – Jer. 36:1-32
  4. Jeremiah's conflict with false prophets. – Jer. 5:31; 6:13-14; 23:25-32; 27:9-10.

 C. Jeremiah's character.
  1. Jeremiah was very compassionate. – Jer. 4:19; 9:1
  2. Jeremiah was courageous. – Jer. 11:21; 15:20; 26:8; 38:6
  3. Jeremiah had convictions. – Jer. 7:1-11; 20:9

Important Verses

Jer. 2:13 – Broken cisterns that hold no water.

Jer. 5:1 – The search for a just man.

Jer. 6:16 – "… ask for the old paths…"

Jer. 8:12 – "… nay, they were not at all ashamed, neither could they
blush…"

Jer. 8:20 – "Harvest is past, summer is ended, and we are not saved."

Jer. 9:23-24 – The true ground for boasting.

Jer. 10:23 – Man cannot direct his own steps.

Jer. 20:9 – "… his word was in mine heart as a burning fire shut up in
my bones…"

Jer. 25:11-12 –The duration of the Babylonian captivity.

Lam. 1:12 – "Is it nothing to you, all ye that pass by? …"

Lam. 3:22-26 – "… the Lord is my portion..."

Major Themes

A. God's judgment.
    1. The reason – Judah was stubborn and rebellious. – Jer. 3:17;
       4:17; 5:23; 7:24; 9:14; 11:8; 13:10; 16:12; 18:12; 23:17.
    2. The result – Judah provoked God's anger. – Jer. 11:17; 25:6-7;
       32:29-32; 44:3.
    3. The outcome – Babylon would come down from the north and
       lead Judah captive. – Jer. 1:14; 4:6-7; 5:6; 6:22-26; 13:20; 20:4

B. The signs of Jeremiah and symbolic acts.
    1. Sign of the waistband. – Jer. 13:1-11 (Judah is worthless).
    2. Sign of the jugs of wine. – Jer. 13:12-14
       (Drunkenness = punishment).
    3. Sign of the unmarried prophet. – Jer. 16:1-4 (Warning of
       captivity).
    4. Sign of the potter and clay. – Jer. 18:1-11 (The sovereignty of

God).
5. Sign of the broken jar. – Jer. 19:1-11 (Judah must be broken).
6. Sign of the figs. – Jer. 24:1-10 (Good figs = exiles; Bad figs = Jews in Judah).
7. Sign of the joke. – Jer. 27:1-11 (Judah must submit to Babylon).
8. Sign of the field. – Jer. 32:6-15 (Judah would return to the land).
9. Sign of the scroll. – Jer. 51:59-64 (Babylon would fall).

Christ Revealed

1. The righteous branch of David. – Jer. 23:5-6; 30:8-9; 33:14-16.
   a. He will be a king like David.
   b. He will be a descendant of David.
   c. He will execute justice and righteousness.
   d. His name: The Lord our Righteousness. – Rom. 3:22; I Cor. 1:30

2. Christ is author of a better Covenant. – Jer. 31:31-34; Heb. 8:6-13
   a. It will be both inward and spiritual. – Heb. 8:10
   b. It will be both individual and universal. – Heb. 8:11
   c. It will make gracious provision for sin. – Heb. 8:12

3. Christ the "Smitten One." – Lam. 3:30; (cf. Isa. 50:6; 53:4; Matt. 26:68; Mark 14:65; Luke 22:64).

4. Jeremiah has been compared to Christ as the "most Christ-like man in the Old Testament." (cf. Matt. 16:14; 23:37-39; Luke 13:34-35). Jeremiah was a Christ-like:
   a. In his spiritual sensitivity.
   b. In his faith concerning the future of the kingdom.
   c. In his compassion and tenderness.
   d. In his life for his people.
   e. In his suffering and rejection.
   f. In his message of hope.
   g. In his courage and fidelity.

Ezekiel

Nebuchadnezzar, the king of Babylon, captured Jerusalem in 597 B.C. and among those he took were King Jehoiachin, 10,000 leading citizens and the prophet Ezekiel, II Kings 24:10-16; Ezek. 1:1-3. Ezekiel's ministry was focused mainly on the exiles in Babylon, Ezek. 3:11. Ezekiel also served as a counselor and spiritual advisor to the exiles and elders of Judah, Ezek. 8:1; 14:1; 20:1. There are two parts to the book of Ezekiel. The first part, chapters 1-24, were written as warnings before the exile and the second part, chapters 25-48, were written as consolations during the exile. Ezekiel's ministry to the exiles lasted for at least 22 years, 592-570 B.C. (cf. Ezek. 1:2 and Ezek. 29:17). Jeremiah and David's work in Judah and Babylon overlapped with Ezekiel's work.

Breakdown

A. Ezekiel's call. – Ezek. Chapters 1-3

B. Ezekiel's ministry to Judah before the exile. – Ezek. Chapters 4-24

C. Ezekiel's message to foreign nations. – Ezek. Chapters 25-32

D. Ezekiel's ministry to Judah during exile. – Ezek. Chapters 33-39

E. Ezekiel's vision of the New Spiritual Israel, "the church." – Ezek. Chapters 40-48

Pivotal Word – Son of man

"Son of man" is a title that was emphatically used by God to address Ezekiel. The term is found some 420 times in 94 verses in the book. It was used to remind Ezekiel that he was merely a mortal man in contrast to the majestic and mighty God, Ezek. 2:1.

Characters of Importance

Ezekiel – Known as the watchman prophet.

1. Ezekiel's background.
   a. His name means – "God strengthens."
   b. He was a priest, the son of Buzi. – Ezek. 1:3
   c. Ezekiel was married but his wife died suddenly in 587 B.C. – Ezek. 24:16
   d. Ezekiel lived in Babylon near the river of Chebar. – Ezek. 1:3, 3:15

2. Ezekiel's work.
   a. Ezekiel was appointed a "watchman" to warn Israel. – Ezek. 3:17
   b. Ezekiel was a spokesman for God. "The word of the Lord came to me" is found 53 times in the book.
   c. Ezekiel worked to build the morale of the Jewish exiles and taught them to believe in and hope for a future.

3. Ezekiel's character.
   a. Ezekiel was very persistent. – Ezek. 3:8-9
   b. Ezekiel had empathy. – Ezek. 3:15
   c. Ezekiel was a spiritual man.
      1. The Spirit entered him. – Ezek. 2:2; 3:24
      2. The Spirit lifted him up. – Ezek. 3:12, 14' 8:3; 11:1, 24; 43:5.
      3. The Spirit fell upon him. – Ezek. 11:5
      4. The Spirit showed him visions. – Ezek. 11:24; 37:1

Important Verses

Ezek. 3:3 – The scroll was "sweet as honey."

Ezek. 3:15 – Sitting where others sit.

Ezek. 3:17-21 – Duties of a spiritual watchman.

Ezek. 14:13-14 – Three righteous men: Noah, Daniel, and Job.

Ezek. 18:1-4 – "… the soul that sinneth, it shall die."

Ezek. 34 – False shepherds (vs. 1-10) and true shepherds (vs. 11-16).

Ezek. 33:11 – "… I have no pleasure in the death of the wicked;"

Ezek. 37:3-5 – "… can these bones live? …"

Ezek. 39:21-24 – God's explanation of His judgment on Israel.

Major Themes

A. Ezekiel's visions:
    1. Vision of the Glory of the Lord. – Ezek. 1:4-28
    2. Vision of wicked in the Temple. – Ezek. 8:1-18
    3. Vision of death in Jerusalem. – Ezek. 9:1-11
    4. Vision of Jerusalem burning. – Ezek. 10:1-22
    5. Vision of wicked princes and departed glory. – Ezek. 11:1-25
    6. Vision of the valley of dry bones. – Ezek. 37:1-14
    7. Vision of the return of the Glory of the Lord. – Ezek. 43:1-5

B. Symbolic acts.
    1. Sign of the brick – The siege of Jerusalem. – Ezek. 4:1-3
    2. Sign of laying on side – Duration of exile. – Ezek. 4:4-8
    3. Sign of bread – Scarcity of food. – Ezek. 4:9-17
    4. Sign of sharing – destruction of Jerusalem. – Ezek. 5:1-17
    5. Sign of prophet's baggage – Captivity. – Ezek. 12:1-16
    6. Sign of trembling – captivity. – Ezek. 12:17-28
    7. Sign of death of Ezekiel's wife – Sudden destruction.
       – Ezek. 24:15-27

C. Parables:
    1. The fruitless vine. – Ezek. 15:1-8
    2. The adulterous woman. – Ezek. 16:1-63
    3. The two eagles. – Ezek. 17:1-24
    4. The lion and the vine. – Ezek. 19:1-14

5. The two sisters. – Ezek. 23:1-49
6. The boiling pot. – Ezek. 24:1-14
7. The sinking ship. – Ezek. 27:1-9
8. The two sticks. – Ezek. 37:15-28

Christ Revealed

1. Glory of the Lord. – Ezek. 1:26-28; Rev. 1:12-16

2. Tender sprig. – Ezek. 17:22-24; Isa. 11:1; Jer. 23:5; Zech. 3:8.

3. The next King of Israel. – Ezek. 21:26-27

4. My servant David. – Ezek. 34:23-24; 37:24, David's greatest
    descendant, Christ, will be:
    a. The one Shepherd.
    2. The Prince among them.
    3. The King over them.

Daniel

During their exile the Jews were encouraged by the writing of Jeremiah, Dan. 9:2; Jer. 25:11-12; II Chron. 36:20-21, and the presence of two great prophets, Ezekiel and Daniel. Though Daniel was a prophet, his actual job or duty was to serve as an administrator in the King's palace. However, God used Daniel to write a prophetic book, Dan. 12:4 that bore his name. He probably penned the book toward the end of his life. Daniel's length of service in Babylon spanned nearly 70 years from 605-536 B.C., (cf. Dan. 1:1, 21; 10:1). Ezekiel reveals to us that Daniel was a righteous and wise man, Ezek. 14:14, 20; 28:3. Jesus spoke of Daniel as a prophet, Matt. 24:15; Mark 13:14. The book of Daniel is considered apocalyptic literature and is similar in nature to the book of Revelation. Something else that is interesting about Daniel is that between Dan. 2:4-7 and Dan. 7:28 the book is written in Aramaic, a language the Jews learned during their exile. This language was so much a part of their lives following their exile that the Aramaic language remained their primary language during the life of Christ, Matt. 27:46. As mentioned before Daniel is considered apocalyptic. Apocalyptic writing is characterized by numbers, allegories, figurative language, symbolisms, visions, prayers and hymns, and conflict between cosmic powers. Sometimes it is difficult to define details in such literature, however it is quite apparent that both Daniel and Revelation were inspired by God to encourage God's faithful people during periods of persecution and trial letting them know that ultimate victory would come.

Breakdown

A. Daniel and King Nebuchadnezzar. – Dan. Chapters 1-2

B. Daniel and the fiery furnace. – Dan. Chapter 3

C. Daniel and the handwriting on the wall. – Dan. Chapters 4-5

D. Daniel in the lion's den. – Dan. Chapter 6

E. Daniel and his visions. – Dan. Chapters 7-12

Pivotal Word – Vision

Some variable of the words "vision" or "dream" appear 32 times and 26 times respectively. The Babylonian kings had dreams which Daniel was able to interpret by the help of God, Dan. 1:17; 2:27-30. God chose select people and through the medium of dreams revealed His will and future events, Dan. 10:14.

Characters of Importance

Daniel – Administrator in the palace/ palace prophet.

    A. Daniel's background.
        1. Daniel's name means – "God is my judge."
        2. Daniel's Babylonian name, "Belteshazzar" – means "May Bel protect his life." – Dan. 1:7
        3. Daniel has royal heritage. – Dan. 1:3
        4. Daniel was obviously well educated and possessed a keen intelligence. – Dan. 1:4-5, 17

    B. Daniel's work.
        1. His job was to interpret visions and dreams. – Dan. 1:17
        2. Daniel was appointed chief prefect of the wise men. – Dan. 2:48
        3. Daniel was promoted to third ruler in the kingdom. – Dan. 5:16, 29
        4. Daniels service lasted through four kings: Nebuchadnezzar and Belshazzar of Babylon, Darius and Cyrus of Persia. – Dan. 1:21; 5:30-31; 6:1-3, 28; 10:1

    C. Daniels character was strong.
        1. Daniel had deep convictions. – Dan. 1:8

2. Daniel exerted a powerful influence on those in power because of his "extraordinary spirit." – Dan. 5:12, 14; 6:3
3. Daniel faithfully prayed to God. – Dan. 6:10; 9:3-19; 10:12
4. Daniel was a man of "high esteem." – Dan. 9:23; 10:11, 19

Important Verses

Dan. 1:8 – Daniel's dedication as a youth.

Dan. 2:44 – "… which shall never be destroyed:"

Dan. 3:17-18 – Our God is able to deliver!

Dan. 4:33 – Nebuchadnezzar's strange insanity.

Dan. 5:5-6, 24-29 – The handwriting on the wall.

Dan. 6:25-28 – Darius' decree of faith in God.

Dan. 12:2 – The resurrection of the righteous.

Major Themes

A. God's power and wisdom.
   1. God is a God of wisdom and power. – Dan. 2:20-23
   2. God is a God who is sovereign and reveals mysteries. – Dan. 2:28
   3. Daniel uses one title in particular for God and it is "Most High." Following are a few of the many verses: – Dan. 3:26; 4:2, 17, 24, 25, 32, 34; 5:18, 21; 7:25; 9:24

B. God's protection.
   1. In the fiery furnace. – Dan. 3:17-18, 28-29
   2. In the lion's den. – Dan. 6:18-20

C. The providence of God.
   1. Shown in Daniel's rise to fame and his position in a foreign government (compare to Joseph's favor and rise to 2nd only to Pharaoh).
   2. Shown in the prediction and fulfillment of the seventy-year captivity. – Jer. 25:11-12; Dan. 9:2
   3. Shown in the Daniel's possible involvement with Cyrus' writing of "The Decree of Cyrus" that freed the Jews in 538 B.C. (cf. II Chron. 36:22-23; Ezra 1:1-4)
   4. Shown in the prediction and fulfillment of four hundred years of world events from Daniel's day through the inter-testamental period with special focus on the rise and fall of the Greek Empire. – Dan. 8-11

D. God's eternal kingdom.
   1. The four earthly kingdoms of Daniel chapter 2 and the four beasts of Daniel 7 represent: Babylon, Medo-Persia, Greece, and Rome.
   2. The focus is this: God's eternal kingdom, the church, would be established during the days of the Roman Empire.
      a. The church would be a great mountain that would fill the whole earth. – Dan. 2:35; Isa. 2:1-4; Micah 4:1-3
      b. The church would be a kingdom that would never be destroyed. – Dan. 2:44; 7:13-14, 27; Heb. 12:28
      c. The first-century church would be persecuted by the Roman Empire, the church would stand and Rome would fall. – Dan. 7:19-27

Christ Revealed

1. Christ's Kingdom, the church. – Dan. 2:35, 44; 7:14, 27

2. A possible re-incarnate appearance of Christ. – Dan. 3:24-25

3. Son of Man. – Dan. 7:13-14; Rev. 1:7, 13; 14:14

4. Commander of the host. – Dan. 8:11

5. Prince of princes. – Dan. 8:25; Isa. 9:6

6. Messiah. 9:24-27; John 1:41; 4:25
   (See Christ Revealed in I Samuel)

Hosea

Summation

Hosea ministered for fifty years in Israel during the 8th century, 760-710 B.C. He lived during the time of Amos, Isaiah, and Micah who possible knew him. Hosea's historic record is found in II Kings 14:23-17:41. Hosea prophesied to Israel during prosperous days warning her of judgment to come because of her sins before God. Israel was often referred to as Ephraim after the largest tribe in the north. Hosea was a witness to the fall of Israel to Assyria in 722 B.C. and continued to minister for several years after the fall. The main theme of Hosea is the steadfast love of God for Israel. This theme is demonstrated vividly in Hosea's marriage to Gomer who became unfaithful, but because of Hosea's persistent love and forgiveness the marriage was reconciled. There are several New Testament passages that allude to thoughts found in Hosea: Matt. 2:15 (Hos. 11:1); Luke 23:30; Rev. 6:16 (Hos. 10:8); I Cor. 15:55 (Hos. 13:14); I Cor. 15:4 (Hos. 6:2); Rom. 9:25-26; I Pet. 2:10 (Hos. 2:23; 1:10); Matt. 9:13; 12:7; Mark 12:33 (Hos. 6:6).

Breakdown

A. Hosea's marriage and its applications to Israel.
   – Hos. Chapters 1-3

B. Hosea's preaching and its impact on Israel. – Hos. Chapters 4-14

Pivotal Word – Harlot

"Harlot" means "to commit fornication." Israel was guilty of "playing the harlot," Hos. 2:5. Israel had forsaken her true husband (God) for other lovers (the sins of the world, other gods). – Hos. 1:2; 4:12; 6:10; 3:1.

Characters of Importance

Hosea – Known as the prophet of steadfast love.

106

1. Hosea' background.
   a. Hosea's name means "salvation." (symbolism of God as a living husband)
   b. Hosea's wife was Gomer. (symbolism of Israel as an unfaithful wife) – Hosea 1:2; 2:5-7; 3:1
   c. Hosea's children. (symbolism of God's message to Israel)
      1. Jezreel – "God sows" – Hos. 1:4
      2. Lo-ruhamah – "not pitied" – Hos. 1:6
      3. Lo-ammi – "not my people" – Hos. 1:9
      4. Eventually these attitudes toward Israel would be reversed. – Hos. 2:23

2. Hosea's work.
   a. Hosea preached the word of the Lord to Israel. – Hos. 1:1
   b. Hosea pronounced the judgments of God. – Hos. 6:5
   c. Hosea interpreted God's message for the people of his day. – Hos. 12:10

3. Hosea's character.
   a. Hosea was obedient in marrying Gomer. – Hos. 1:2-3
   b. Hosea was patient and forgiving in buying Gomer back after her unfaithfulness. – Hos. 3:1-5
   c. In spite of tragedy at home and around him, Hosea remained steadfast to God and his marriage.

Important Verses

Hosea 1:2 – Key verse in Hosea.

Hosea 4:6 – "My people are destroyed for lack of knowledge…"

Hosea 6:6 – "For I desired mercy, and not sacrifice…"

Hosea 8:4 – Israel's kings were not appointed by God.

Hosea 8:7 – "For they sown the wind, and they shall reap the whirlwind…"

Hosea 10:12-13 – Sowing and reaping.

Hosea 11:1 – "… and called my son out of Egypt."

Hosea 11:9 – "… I am God and not man…"

Hosea 14:9 – "… For the ways of the Lord are right…"

Major Themes

A. The results of marital infidelity.
   1. Divorce and broken homes. – Hos. 2:1-3
   2. The children suffer. – Hos. 2:4
   3. No lasting satisfaction. – Hos. 2:7
   4. Illegitimate children. – Hos. 5:7; 2:4

B. Spiritual adultery.
   1. Israel then. – Hos. 1:2; 2:2; 4:2, 11-18; (cf. Isa. 54:5)
   2. The church today. – James 4:4; I John 2:15-17

C. Israel's transgressions.
   1. Sins against God.
      a. Israel lacked knowledge of God. (intimate acquaintance)
         – Hos. 2:20; 4:1, 6, 14; 5:4; 6:3, 6; 8:12; 13:4; (cf. John 17:3
         Phil. 3:10)
      b. Israel lacked love for and loyalty to God. (idolatry)
         – Hos. 2:13; 6:4; 11:2; 13:1
      c. Israel lacked trust and faith in God. (foreign alliances)
         – Hos. 5:13; 7:11; 8:10; 12:1
      d. Israel lacked leadership for God. (worldly priests and kings)
         – Hos. 4:9; 6:9; 7:7; 8:4; 9:7
   2. Sins against man.
      a. Corruption. – Hos. 4:2
      b. Crime. – Hos. 7:1
      c. Bad covenants. – Hos. 10:4
   3. Hosea contains many metaphors and similes for those who
      commit sin that are as follows:

a. adulterous wife. – Hos. 3:1

b. drunkard. – Hos. 4:11

c. stubborn heifer. – Hos. 4:16

d. raiders. – Hos. 6:9

e. hot oven. – Hos. 7:4-7

f. cake not turned. – Hos. 7:8

g. silly dove. – Hos. 7:11

h. deceitful bow. – Hos. 7:16

i. un-honorable vessel. – Hos. 8:8

j. wild donkey. – Hos. 8:9

k. trained heifer. – Hos. 10:11

l. disobedient youth. – Hos. 11:1

m. morning cloud. – Hos. 13:3

n. dew. – Hos. 13:3

o. chaff. – Hos. 13:3

p. smoke. – Hos. 13:3

4. As many do today, Israel tried to "rationalize" her wrongs as not being sinful. – Hos. 12:8 (cf. 14:1)

D. God's love is steadfast.

1. It is like that of a faithful husband. – Hos. 2:16, 19-20; 3:1

2. God's love is like that of a loving father. – Hos. 11:1-11

3. God's love demands justice. – Hos. 5:9; 9:7; 13:16;
God's judgment will be like:

a. an eagle. – Hos. 8:1

b. a lion. – Hos. 13:7a; 5:14

c. a leopard. – Hos. 13:7b

d. a bear. – Hos. 13:8a

e. a wild beast. – Hos. 13:8b

4. Israel once she was restored would be like:

a. the lily. – Hos. 14:5a

b. the cedars of Lebanon. – Hos. 14:5b

c. the olive tree. – Hos. 14:6

d. the wine of Lebanon. – Hos. 14:7

Christ Revealed

1. Christ is a leader. – Hos. 1:11; Jer. 30:21; Acts 5:31

2. David their king. – Hos. 3:5; Jer. 30:9; Ezek. 34:24

3. Christ the Son. – Hos. 11:1
    a. This was first applied to Israel while in Egyptian bondage.
       – Ex. 4:22-23
    b. It was later applied to Christ, by Matthews, as a fulfilled
       prophecy. – Matt. 2:14-15

4. Christ is the resurrected redeemer. – Hos. 6:2; 13:14
    a. Christ was raised on the third day. – Hos. 6:2; I Cor. 15:4
    b. Christ conquered death, sin, and Satan. – Hos. 13:14;
       I Cor. 15:55-58

Joel

Summation

Joel was a prophet in Judah and lived in the 9th century around 835 B.C. There are some difficulties with the date associated with Joel. Some of the suggested dates range from the 9th century to the 5th century. If the date for Joel places him during the pre-exilic period he would be considered one of the earliest writing prophets. It has been estimated that 27 of the 73 verses in Joel are paralleled in the other prophets. For those who chose an earlier date for Joel the explanation for the parallel is that Joel is quoted by the later works. New Testament references to Joel include: Acts 2:16-21 (Joel 2:28-32); Rom. 10:13 (Joel 2:32), and terminology similar to Revelation 6:12 (Joel 2:31), 14:17 (Joel 3:13); 19:15 (Joel 3:13); 9:3-11 (Joel 2:1-11). However, the dating of Joel aside, Joel's mission was to point out the sad condition of Judah's spiritual life as the reason why God's judgment (a locust plague) was sent. Joel's message exhorted national repentance as the essential step in returning to God.

Breakdown

A. Talk of destruction. – Joel 1:1-2:17
   1. The plague of locust. – Joel 1:1-20
   2. Call to repent. – Joel 2:1-17

B. The Lord speaks of deliverance. – Joel 2:18-3:21
   1. Israel is blessed. – Joel 2:18-32
   2. Nations judged. – Joel 3:1-16
   3. Future glory. – Joel 3:17-21

Pivotal Word – Locust

A locust plague devastated Judah and Joel's message is built on this occurrence. God used the plague of locust to bring about repentance and spiritual renewal. – Joel 1:4; 2:25.

Characters of Importance

Joel – Known as the Prophet of Pentecost.

    A. Joel's background.
       1. Joel's name means "Jehovah is God."
       2. Joel was the son of Pethuel. – Joel 1:1
       3. There are no other details known about Joel's life.

    B. Joel's work.
       1. Joel spoke the "word of the Lord." – Joel 1:1; Luke 1:70;
         Acts 3:21
       2. Joel had to minister in turbulent days. –
         II Chron. 24:17-21

    C. Joel's character.
       1. Joel was a man of high spiritual status selected by God to
         be a spiritual spokesman for his day.
       2. Joel spoke with urgency, trying to call people to turn to
         God.

Important Verses

Joel 1:15 – "For the day of the Lord is at hand…"

Joel 2:12-13 – Repentance must come from the heart.

Joel 2:21 – "… for the Lord will do great things."

Joel 2:28 – The prophecy of Pentecost.

Joel 3:14 – The valley of decision.

Major Themes

A. A plague of Locust. – Joel 1:4-20; 2:3-11
   1. The plague was real and was not uncommon in Palestine.
   2. What was unique about this plague was its devastation. –
     Joel 1:2-3

3. There are four kinds of locust mentioned. – Joel 1:4; 2:25

4. Using a natural source, the invasion of locust was sent by God as punishment for sin. – Joel 2:25; (cf. Amos 4:6-11; 7:1-3)

5. Joel used the plague of Locust as a means of illustration.

B. The Day of the Lord.

1. The "day of the Lord" was a common theme in the prophets: – Isa. 2:12; 13:6-9; Ezek. 13:5; Amos 5:18-20; Obadiah 15; Zeph. 1:7, 14; Zech. 14:1; Mal. 4:5

2. The "day of the Lord" in Joel:

   a. Is near. – Joel 1:15; 3:14

   b. Is coming. – Joel 2:1

   c. Is great and awesome. – Joel 2:11, 31

3. What the phrase, "day of the Lord" means.

   a. The "day of the Lord" was any day when God intervened in history to bring judgment upon a people or nation.

   b. To those that were unfaithful and wicked it was a day of doom, destruction and darkness. – Joel 1:15; 2:1, 11; 3:14

   c. For the faithful it was a day of deliverance, salvation and light. – Joel 2:28-32

   d. The final day of the Lord will come on the Day of Judgment. – II Pet. 3:7-12

C. Joel speaks to the importance of repentance. – Joel 2:12-17

1. The call to repentance. – Joel 2:12-13a

2. The consequences of repentance. – Joel 2:13b-14

3. The character of repentance. – Joel 2:15-17

Christ Revealed

Joel 2:28-32 points to the time of Christ.

1. New Testament application of Joel 2:28-32.

   a. Peter quoted it to explain the outpouring of the Holy Spirit on Pentecost. – Acts 2:16-21

   b. Paul quoted it in reference to salvation. – Rom. 10:13ff

2. Through the inspiration of God Peter applied and interpreted Joel 2:28-32.
   a. Peter knew how to apply prophecy. – I Pet. 1:10-12, 20
   b. Peter applied Joel 2 to the events which happened on Pentecost.
   c. Peter did not explain in detail every statement of Joel 2. (cf. Acts 2:19-20).
      1. These verses may refer to the events that transpired at Calvary (seven weeks earlier).
      2. Or, they may refer to events associated with the end of time, the second coming, and the final judgment.
      3. Peter did not give further interpretation, and it is safe for us to do the same. Speak where the Bible speaks be silent where it is silent.
      4. Peter mainly applied Joel's prophecy to the outpouring of the Holy Spirit (vs. 17-18) and the gift of salvation through Christ to the Christian or church age which began in Acts 2. (cf. Acts 2:38).

3. Joel 2:28-32 ties in with Christ in this manner.
   a. Christ's first coming ushered in the "last days." – Acts 2:16-18; I Pet. 1:20
   b. Christ's church was ushered in with preaching from and partial fulfillment of Joel 2.
   c. Christ's second coming and final judgment will completely fulfill Joel's prophecy. – Acts 2:19-20
   d. Christ's death made salvation available to all who call on His name. This means to recognize Him as our Lord and follow through with the gospel plan of salvation authored by Him being baptized for the remission of sins by His authority, "And now why tarriest thou? arise, and be baptized, and wash away thy sins, calling on the name of the Lord." (Acts 22:16). Acts 2:21; Rom. 10:13ff

Amos

Amos lived at the same time as Hosea who also preached in Israel. Amos dates his prophetic activity during the days of Uzziah in Judah and Jeroboam II in Israel, Amos 1:1; (cf. II Kings 14:23-15:7; II Chron. 26), this puts Amos around 750 B.C. making him an 8ᵗʰ century prophet. Amos's ministry took place "two years before the earthquake," a disaster that was still recalled 250 years later during the days of Zechariah, "And ye shall flee *to* the valley of the mountains; for the valley of the mountains shall reach unto Azal: yea, ye shall flee, like as ye fled from before the earthquake in the days of Uzziah king of Judah: and the LORD my God shall come, *and* all the saints with thee." (Zech. 14:5). In the New Testament Stephen quoted Amos 5:25-27 in his defense before the Sanhedrin in Acts 7:42-43. James quoted Amos 9:11-12 in Acts 15:16-18. During the time of Amos both Judah and Israel were at the height of their power and influence among world powers. It was during this time that Amos was called to deliver his message of doom to Israel. Amos however had to overcome some obstacles. Amos did not consider himself to be a prophet of God by his birth or his training, Amos 7:14-15. He was what we today would call a country boy who was called to preach in another country. Amos delivered his message to Israel at a time they did not want to hear it and his message came true about thirty years later when Assyria conquered Israel.

Breakdown

A. Amos's prophecies. – Amos Chapters 1-2
    (against other nations)

B. Amos preaches. – Amos Chapters 3-6
    (against Israel)

C. Amos's visions. – Amos Chapters 7-9
    (visions verify his call and message)

Pivotal Word – Justice

"Justice" is found only four times in Amos; it is, however, a primary theme in the book. Israel was accused of turning justice into wormwood, bitterness, sorrow, calamity, and poison, Amos 5:7; 6:12; (cf. Rev. 8:11). Justice needed to "roll down" and be "established," Amos 5:15, 24.

Characters of Importance

Amos – Known as the prophet of Justice. – Amos 5:24

A. Amos's background.
1. Amos's name means "burden-bearer."
2. Amos's hometown was the small village of Tekoa about ten miles south of Jerusalem and five miles southeast of Bethlehem.
3. Amos was a shepherd and a grower of sycamore figs. Amos 1:1; 7:14-15; (cf. I Chron. 27:28)

B. Amos's work.
1. Amos was called to be a prophet to Israel. Amos 7:14-17
2. Amos was referred to as a "seer." – Amos 7:12; I Sam. 9:9-11
3. The priest of Israel opposed Amos. – Amos 2:12; 7:10-13
4. Amos was God's obedient servant. Amos 3:7-8

C. Amos's character.
1. Amos was spiritually mature and willing to leave his profession to preach. – Amos 7:14
2. Amos was an outdoorsman type. He was rugged, energetic and hard working.
3. Amos proclaimed the truth fearlessly and courageously.

Important Verses

Amos 3:2 – Privilege and opportunity bring responsibility.

Amos 4:12 – "… prepare to meet thy God…"

Amos 5:18-20 – The day of the Lord will bring doom.

Amos 5:23 and 6:5 – These verses are not valid arguments against the issue of instrumental music in the church. (These verses show the inventor of the musical instruments as being David and the unacceptance of worship by God when sin is in our lives.)

Amos 6:1 – Spiritual lethargy and unconcern.

Amos 7:11-12 – A famine of the word of the Lord.

Major Themes

A. Israel has sinned.
   1. Social: Oppression of poor and helpless. – Amos 2:6-8; 4:1
   2. Injustice: – Amos 5:7; 6:12
   3. Moral: Sexual sins, – Amos 2:7; Materialism, – Amos 3:15; 4:1-3; Pleasure and extravagance, – Amos 5:11; 6:4-6; Dishonesty, – Amos 8:4-6
   4. Political: Violence, – Amos 3:9-10; Bribes, – Amos 5:12
   5. Religious: Insincerity, – Amos 4:4-5; Rites and Ceremonies, – Amos 5:21-27; Spiritual lethargy, – Amos 6:1

B. God portrayed in Amos.
   1. God is the God of election. – Amos 3:2
   2. Israel's sins have brought burden upon god. – Amos 2:13; (cf. Isa. 1:14)
   3. God is a God of creative power. – Amos 4:13; 9:6
   4. God is a God pf wrath and judgment. – Amos 1:2; 3:8; 6:14; 9:6
   5. God is righteous and full of justice. – Amos 5:24

C. Israel called to repentance.
    1. "...yet have ye not returned unto me..." – Amos 4:6, 8, 9, 11
    2. "... prepare to meet thy God, O Israel." – Amos 4:12
    3. "Seek Me that you may live." – Amos 5:4, 6, 14
    4. What god requires: – Amos 5:15; (cf. Micah 6:8)

D. Visions in Amos.
    1. Vision of Locust. – Amos 7:1-3
    2. Vision of Fire. – Amos 7:4-6
    3. Vision of a Plumb line. – Amos 7:7-9
    4. Vision of Summer Fruit. – Amos 8:1-14
    5. Vision of Lord Judging. – Amos 9:1-10

Christ Revealed

Amos 9:11-15 the Messianic Kingdom: Christ's church

1. Amos 9:11-15 explained.
    a. Israel would eventually be restored to the land after her captivity, Amos 9:14; Jer. 30:3. (This however would not happen until under the leadership of Zerubbabel, Ezra, and Nehemiah between the years of 536-445 B.C.)
    b. As some like to believe, this passage does not refer to the so-called millennial reign of Christ on earth.
    c. This passage is metaphorical and not literal as in the reference to an actual earthly kingdom, but is spiritual referring to the form of the church, spiritual Israel. (cf. John 18:36)
    d. The entire passage is Messianic, and it has been fulfilled under Christ.

2. Amos 9:11-15 fulfilled in the New Testament.
    a. David's dynasty is restored.
        1. David's booth (tent, tabernacle, house) fell when Zedikiah, Judah's last king, was conquered by Babylon. – Ezek. 21: 26-27; (cf. II Sam. 7:8-16)
        2. The writers of the New Testament looked to Christ as the descendant of David who fulfilled the Messianic prophecies,

and who once again established the lineage of David. – Luke 1:67-79; Acts 2:26-27; 3:18-26

b. Gentiles were included in the church. – Acts 15:14-19
  1. James, at the council of Jerusalem, quoted Amos 9:11-12 from the Greek Old Testament (Septuagint).
  2. James point was that David's tabernacle had been restored (in Christ), therefore, people from all nations (Gentiles, and not just the Jews) may be called by God's name.
  3. Salvation through Christ and His church is available for all – Now!

Obadiah

Edom was rejoicing over the calamity that had befallen Jerusalem and Obadiah focused his prophecy of doom and destruction against them for doing so. The dating of Obadiah is very difficult to do since there are no specifics about Jerusalem's enemy and her defeat. There were four invasions during the Old Testament days: by Shishak of Egypt, 926 B.C. – II Kings 14:25-26; II Chron. 12:1-12; by the Arabians and the Philistines between 848-841 B.C. – II Kings 14:13-14; II Chron. 25:17-24; and by Nebuchadnezzar of Babylon in 586 B.C. – II Kings 24-25; II Chron. 36. Many of the biblical scholars of our day think that Obadiah's message is in regards to the second invasion by the Arabians and the Philistines or perhaps in reference to the fourth invasion by Nebuchadnezzar. These dates, if correct, would make Obadiah the earliest writing prophet, after 841 B.C., or one of the latest writing prophets, after 586 B.C. Obadiah is not alluded to in the New Testament and it is the shortest book in the Old Testament.

Breakdown

A. The doom of Edom. – Obad. Vs. 1-14

B. The day of the Lord. – Obad. Vs. 15

C. Zion delivered. – Obad. Vs. 16-21

Pivotal Word – Disaster

Disaster had befallen Jerusalem, v. 13. It was a time of destruction and distress, vs. 12, 14 for God's people. But a day was coming, vs. 15 when disaster would strike the people of Edom, vs. 6-9.

Characters of Importance

Obadiah – Known as the prophet of doom.

A. Obadiah's background.
   1. Obadiah's name means, "Servant of the Lord."
   2. In the Old Testament there are over a dozen men named Obadiah, but none of them can be identified with Obadiah, the prophet.

B. Obadiah's work.
   1. The book of Obadiah is described as a vision. Vs. 1
   2. Obadiah revealed the sins of Edom and proclaimed doom. Vs. 4, 15
   3. There are other prophecies against Edom; – Ps. 137:7; Isa. 63:1-6; Jer. 49. 49:7-22; Ezek. 35:1-10

C. Obadiah's character.
   1. Obadiah was a devoted follower of God.
   2. Obadiah comforted Jerusalem as he voiced protest against her enemy.

Important Verses

Obadiah vs. 3 – Edom's sinful arrogance and pride.

Obadiah vs. 4 – "Though thou exalt *thyself* as the eagle, and though thou set thy nest among the stars, thence will I bring thee down, saith the LORD."

Obadiah vs. 15 – The day of the Lord.

Obadiah vs. 17 – Possessing your possessions.

Obadiah vs. 21 – "…and the kingdom shall be the Lord's."

Major Themes

A. The sin of pride or arrogance. Vs. 3a; (cf. Jer. 49:16)
   1. Pride is a deceitful sin of the heart.
   2. Prov. 11:2; 16:18; 18:2; 29:23

B. The sin of false security. Vs. 3b-4
    1. In arrogance Edom asked, "…who will bring me down to the ground?"
    2. God gives Edom an answer, "thence will I bring thee down, saith the Lord."
    3. All nations are vulnerable before God.

C. The sin of lacking brotherly love. Vs. 10, 12a
    1. The background for this lost love: – Gen. 25:21-26; 27:36-41; (Israel descended from Jacob – Edom descended from Esau) (cf. Rom. 9:6-13)
    2. When brotherly love is lacking: struggle, conflict, violence, servitude, and war. – Num. 20:14-21; Joel 3:19; Amos 1:11-12; Ma. 1:2-5
    3. The need for brotherly love: – Gen. 13:8; John 13:34-35; Rom. 12:10; Heb. 13:1

D. Sin of exulting over others misfortunes. Vs. 12-13
    1. Job 31:29; Prov. 17:5; 24:17; Jer. 50:29

Christ Revealed

Obadiah vs. 16-21 The Lord's kingdom: Christ's church

1. The church would be established on Mt. Zion (in Jerusalem). Vs. 17a; Isa. 2:3; Micah 4:2, it would offer escape, deliverance and salvation. Vs. 17b.

2. The church would be a spiritual, eternal kingdom comprised of men from all nations who would find salvation in Christ. Vs. 18-20; Gen. 49:10; Num. 24:17-19; Luke 1:32-33.

3. The church would be aided by "deliverers", possibly the apostles and preachers who proclaimed the gospel. Vs. 21a; Rom. 1:16.

4. The church would belong to Christ – "…and the kingdom shall be the Lord's." vs. 21b; Zech. 14:9; Eph. 1:20-23; Rev. 11:15.

Jonah

The capital city of Assyria was Nineveh. Jonah's ministry was directed to Nineveh rather than toward Israel. There have been some critiques that have alleged that the book of Jonah is not in any way historical but rather an allegory. Johan was an 8th century prophet and the strongest evidence for the historicity of Jonah is the historical background of II Kings 14:23-29, and the use Jesus made of Jonah's experience in Matt. 12:38-41. For someone to reject the historicity of Jonah in essence is to reject Christ and the scriptures. For added emphasis, Jonah was the only minor prophet mentioned by Jesus. Unlike other books the book of Jonah is more like a biographical account about the prophet himself rather than a collection of sermons or teachings. The obvious theme of this book is that God's mercy extends even to those nations other than just Israel if they will repent.

Breakdown

A. Jonah tried to run from God. – Jonah Chapter 1

B. Jonah's faith in God is demonstrated in his praying to God.
   – Jonah Chapter 2

C. Jonah obeyed God and Nineveh repents. – Jonah Chapter 3

D. Jonah is angry and God reasons with him. – Jonah Chapter 4

Pivotal Word – Compassion

Jonah lacked something special, he lacked compassion for lost souls. God's compassion, Jonah 4:2, 10, 11, spared Jonah and Nineveh. When someone feels compassion he is moved into action, Matt. 9:36-38.

Characters of Importance

Jonah – He is known as the reluctant prophet.

A. Jonah's background.
    1. Jonah's name means "Dove."
    2. Jonah's home was north of Nazareth and was called Gath-
       hepher. 1:1; II Kings 14:25.
    3. Jonah's belief: he was a Hebrew. – Jonah 1:9

B. Jonah's work.
    1. Jonah was called to preach to a city called Nineveh, the capital
       of Assyria. – Jonah 1:2; 3:2-3, Nineveh was approx. 500 miles
       N.E. of Israel.
    2. Jonah's preaching. – Jonah 3:2-5
       a. God's message: "preach unto it the preaching that I bid thee."
          – Jonah 3:2b
       b. The theme of the message was to repent or perish.
       c. The message itself was short, "Yet forty days and Nineveh
          will be overthrown." – Jonah 3:4
       d. The message was effective, "So the people of Nineveh
          believed God..."– Jonah 3:5a

C. Jonah's character.
    1. Jonah was a reluctant man. Instead of heading east, he headed
       west to Tarshish, 2,000 miles away in the south of Spain.
    2. Jonah was a repentant man. The experience of the great fish
       changed his mind, and he accepted God's commission.
    3. Jonah was a responsible man, though he tried to escape his duty,
       he did eventually fulfill it.

Important Verses

Jonah 1:3 – Jonah's attempt to run from God.

Jonah 1:17 – The Lord appointed a great fish to swallow Jonah.

Jonah 3:2 – Jonah's commission from God.

Jonah 3:5 – Nineveh's response to Jonah's preaching.

Jonah 3:10 – God changed His mind about Nineveh.

Jonah 4:2 – The compassion of God.

Major Themes

A. God's miracles in Jonah.
    1. The great storm. – Jonah 1:4
    2. The calming of the storm. – Jonah 1:15
    3. The great fish. 1:17; 2:1, 10; (cf. Matt. 12:40 "sea monster")
    4. The plant, the worm, and the wind. – Jonah 4:6-8

B. The inability to escape God's presence. – Jonah 1:3, 10; Ps. 139:7-11; Heb. 4:13

C. God cares for all people. – Jonah 4:2; I Tim. 2:3-6; II Pet. 3:9
    God's mercy is great.

D. Prejudice can cause man to become blind. – Jonah 4:1-2; Acts 10:34-35; Rom. 1:16   Man has a narrow point of view sometimes.

E. Sense of values. (things over people) – Jonah 4:10-11

Christ Revealed

    A. There are similarities between Jonah and Jesus. Matt. 12:38-41; 16:4; Luke 11:29-32
        1. Both were sent by God to sinful people.
        2. Both preached a message of repentance.
        3. Both had a unique three-day experience; Jonah in the fish, and Jesus in the grave.

    B. "Salvation is from the Lord." Jonah 2:9
        1. Salvation for: Jonah 2:9-10; Nineveh 3:9-10; and us today, II Cor. 6:1-2
        2. Christ is the: Person – Matt. 1:21; Luke 19:9-10;

Source – Acts 4:12; and Place – II Tim. 2:10 of salvation.

Micah

Micah was a prophet of Judah during the 8th century, approximately 730-700 B.C. who ministered in the days of Jotham, Ahaz, and Hezekiah, Kings of Judah, Micah 1:1. The historic account of Micah's day is found in II Kings 15:32-20:21 and II Chron. 27-32. Micah possibly knew Isaiah, Amos, and Hosea. Micah predicted the fall of both Samaria, Micah 1:5-7 and Jerusalem, Micah 3:12. One century after the time of Micah, a quote from his writing, Micah 3:12 helped to save Jeremiah's life, Jer. 26:14-24, vs. 18. There are two quotations from Micah in the New Testament, Matt. 2:5-6 (Micah 5:2) and Matt. 10:35-36 (Micah 7:6). The quotation from Micah 5:2 paved the way for Christ and the other quote, Micah 7:6, prepared the disciples for persecution.

Breakdown

A. Hear to the judgment of God. – Micah 1:1-2:13
      1. Judgment against Samaria and Jerusalem. – Micah 1:1-16
      2. Judgment because of their sins. – Micah 2:1-13

B. Hear the justice of God. – Mocha 3:1-5:15
      1. The present injustice. – Micah 3:1-12
      2. The coming kingdom of Justice. – Micah 4:1-13
      3. The coming king of Justice. – Micah 5:1-15

C. Hear the indictment of God. –Micah 6:1-7:20
      1. God's case against His people. – Micah 6:1-7:10
      2. God's future blessings for His people. – Micah 7:11-20

Pivotal Word – Hear

Micah's message was one they needed to hear, Micah 1:2; 3:1, 9; 6:1, 9; 7:7. God's proclamation was addressed to the people, 1:2, the rulers,

3:1, and the mountains, 6:1-2. To "hear" has more meaning than just to "listen;" it summons one to pay heed and obey.

Characters of Importance

Micah – He is known as the people's prophet.

    A. Micah's background:
        1. Micah's name means "who is like Jehovah." (cf. 7:18)
        2. Micah's home was about 20 miles S.W. of Jerusalem and was called Moresheth. – Micah 1:1, 14

    B. Micah's work:
        1. Micah was concerned for what are referred to as the common people of Judah such as the peasants, the poor, the down trodden, and the rural people.
        2. Micah was upset by the way the rich and nobility exploited the poor farmers.
        3. Micah pointed out sins and warned of certain punishment if the people did not repent.

    C. Micah's character:
        1. Micah was a bold preacher. – Micah 3:8
        2. Micah's view of God's holiness, righteousness, and compassion were lofty.

Important Verses

Micah 3:4 – God's hatred of sin.

Micah 4:1-3 – The church of Christ predicted.

Micah 5:2 – The birth of Christ predicted.

Micah 6:8 – God's basic requirements.

Micah 6:14-15 – The paradoxical consequences of sin.

Micah 7:2 – The scarcity of godliness.

<u>Micah 7:6</u> – The gospel divides families. (cf. Matt. 10:35-36.)

<u>Major Themes</u>

A. God hates injustice.
    1. Exploitation by the wealthy. – Micah 2:1-13; 6:11-12
    2. Oppression from rulers. – Micah 3:1-4, 9-10; 7:3
    3. Deception by false prophets. – Micah 3:5-8
    4. Corruption among the priests. – Micah 3:11; (cf. Jer. 6:13)

B. God hates ritualism. – Micah 6:6-7 God does not want:
    1. Burnt offerings. – Ps. 51:16-17; Hos. 6:6
    2. Rivers of oil.
    3. Sacrifices of the first-born child. – Lev. 18:21; 20:1-5

C. God delights in spiritual worship. – Micah 6:8
    1. To do justice. – Isa. 56:1; Jer. 22:3
    2. To love kindness. – Eph. 4:31-32
    3. To walk humbly with God. – Isa. 57:15; 66:2; James 4:6, 10
    4. These three qualities constitute the essence of true religion.
       (cf. Matt. 23:23)

D. God delights in pardon. – Micah 7:18-19
    1. God forgives sin. vs. 18
    2. God forgets forgiven sin. – Jer. 31;34; Heb. 8:12; 10:17

<u>Christ Revealed</u>

1. The Breaker. Christ is the liberator who breaks down the wall of sin. – Micah 2:13

2. The mountain of the House of the Lord. – Micah 4:1-3, 7; (cf. Isa. 2:2-4)
    The nature of Christ's kingdom, the church:
    a. Universal. – Isa. 2:1-2a
    b. Authoritative. – Isa. 2:2b-3a
    c. Peaceful. Isa. – Isa. 2:3b-4

d. Spiritual. – Micah 4:5-6

e. Eternal. – Micah 4:7

3. Ruler in Israel. – Micah 5:2; Matt. 2:5-6

a. His birthplace: Bethlehem Ephrathah. – I Sam. 16:1

b. His eternal existence: "from the days of eternity." – John 1:1-4

4. Shepherd of the flock. – Micah 5:4; John 10:10-15; I Pet. 5:4

5. Our peace. – Micah 5:5; Isa. 9:6; Luke 2:14; Eph. 2:14; Col. 1:20

Nahum

A 7th century prophet, 650-612, Nahum is an oracle against Nineveh, the capital of the Assyrian Empire, Nahum 1:1; 2:8; 3:1, 7. Nahum possibly knew Jeremiah, Habakkuk and Zephaniah as they lived during this time. Nahum's book was written prior to the fall of Nineveh to Babylon in 612 B.C. Nineveh had repented at the preaching of Jonah some 150 years earlier but sin had once again returned to Nineveh and through the voices of Nahum and Zephaniah, Zeph. 2:13-15, God announced that Nineveh would perish. The Assyrians had a reputation as being savage, ruthless and violently aggressive as warriors. God had allowed the Assyrians to be the world power for over 100 years but because of her sins God was soon to bring divine judgment against her. Nahum's message was designed to condemn sinful Nineveh and to comfort oppressed and afflicted Judah.

Breakdown

A. Nahum has faith in God. – Nahum Chapter 1
   1. God will punish the wicked.
   2. Those who trust God find Him strong and good.

B. Nineveh's fall before God. – Nahum Chapters 2-3
   1. How Nineveh would fall. – Nahum Chapter 2
   2. Why Nineveh would fall. – Nahum chapter 3

Pivotal Word – Cut off

God proclaims He would "cut off" Nineveh, Nahum 1:12, 14, 15; 2:13; 3:15. To be "cut off" means to be completely destroyed or annihilated. "The face of the LORD *is* against them that do evil, to cut off the remembrance of them from the earth." (Ps. 34:16).

Nahum – Known as the prophet of doom.

  A. Nahum's background.
     1. Nahum's name means: "Consolation, comfort, compassion."
     2. Nahum's home was Elkosh whose exact location is unknown. Some have identified it with Capernaum ("village of Nahum") in Galilee.
     3. Nahum is not mentioned anywhere else in the Bible.

  B. Nahum's work.
     1. Nahum's written message was directed to Nineveh however his spoken message was aimed at Judah.
     2. Nahum possibly had much to do with the reforms of Josiah, king of Judah at the time. (cf. II Kings 22:1-23, 30; II Chron. 34-35)

  C. Nahum's character.
     1. Nahum held strong convictions about the sovereignty of God.
     2. Nahum attempted to comfort his people by telling them of Nineveh's certain downfall.

Important Verses

Nahum 1:3 – God's patience and justice.

Nahum 1:7 – God is a stronghold and refuge.

Nahum 2:8 – Nineveh's certain doom.

Nahum 2:13 – "Behold I am against thee…"

Nahum 3:1 – "Woe to the bloody city…"

Nahum 3:7 – "…Nineveh is laid waste…"

Nahum 3:19 – Nineveh's downfall would cause rejoicing.

Major Themes

A. God's attributes.
    1. His power and majesty. – Nahum 1:3-5
    2. God's wrath and indignation. – Nahum 1:6, 8
    3. God's goodness. – Nahum 1:7; (cf. Rom. 11:22)

B. God's vengeance.
    1. God is patient but has His limits. God had once spared Nineveh
       through Jonah's preaching but now He will destroy Nineveh.
       – Nahum 1:3a
    2. Deut. 32:35-36; Ps. 94:1; Matt. 26:52; Rom. 12:19; Heb. 10:30

C. God is sovereign.
    1. Nineveh portrayed the image that no nation could conquer her.
    2. God acted and gave His divine judgment and Assyria fell.
    3. The world is ruled by God. – Nahum 1:5

Christ Revealed

Christ is portrayed as the messenger of good news. – Nahum 1:15

1. Good news to the captives. – Isa. 40:9

2. Good news to Zion. – Isa. 52:7

3. Good news to Judah. Nineveh is destroyed. – Nahum 3:7

4. Good news to all mankind. – "Jesus saves!"
    a. Jesus came preaching good news, – Isa. 61:1-2; Luke 4:18-19;
       Mark 1:14-15.
    b. Gospel preachers have good news to proclaim. – Rom. 10:15
       1. An announcement of peace. – John 14:27; Rom. 5:1
       2. An announcement of happiness. – Matt. 5:1-12
       3. An announcement of salvation. – Rom. 1:16

Habakkuk

Summation

The book of Habakkuk is different from other prophetic books since it does not contain sermons, addresses, or a warning. The book of Habakkuk is instead a dialogue that occurs between the prophet and God. This dialogue contains complaints and answers. Habakkuk is not God's messenger to the people but rather a prophet who complains to God and ultimately praises God. Habakkuk possibly knew Jeremiah, Zephaniah and Nahum. His ministry to Judah took place during the last decade of the seventh century, 612-606 B.C., this placed his ministry during the last days of King Jehoiakim, II Kings 23:34-24:7. This book was possibly written just before the invasion of Jerusalem by Nebuchadnezzar of Babylon, 605 B.C., Hab. 1:5-6; 3:16. According to Habakkuk those days were filled with distress, wickedness, and injustice, Hab. 1:2-4.

Breakdown

A. Problems of faith. – Hab. 1:1-2:20
    1. Why does God allow Judah's sins to go unpunished?
    – Hab. 1:1-4
    God's answer: Babylon will be God's instrument of judgment against Judah. – Hab. 1:5-11
    2. Why would God use the wicked Babylonians to punish Judah?
    – Hab. 1:12-3:1
    God's answer: All wicked will be punished, and the righteous will live by faith. God's judgments are for the salvation of His people. – Hab. 2:2-20

B. A prayer of faith. – Hab. 3:1-19

Pivotal Word – Violence

"Violence" is found seven times in the book of Habakkuk, 1:2, 3, 9; 2:8, 12, 17. Maliciousness, wrongdoing, evil, and iniquity created turbulent times in Judah and Babylon.

<u>Characters of Importance</u>

Habakkuk – Known as the questioning prophet.

> A. Habakkuk's background.
>> 1. Habakkuk's name means: "embracer" or to embrace"
>> 2. Habakkuk is not mentioned anywhere else in scripture.
>
> B. Habakkuk's work.
>> 1. Habakkuk thought of himself as a prophet. – Hab. 1:1, 3:1
>> 2. Habakkuk was told by God to write what he saw in a vision. – Hab. 2:2
>> 3. Habakkuk could have been a Levite singer. – Hab. 3:19
>
> C. Habakkuk's character.
>> 1. Habakkuk took his nation to heart (as his name implies) and attempted to comfort her during bad times.
>> 2. Habakkuk spoke of God's holiness. – Hab. 1:12, 2:20, 3:3
>> 3. Habakkuk's questioning of God did not lead to doubt but rather lead to a trusting faith. – Hab. 2:4

<u>Important Verses</u>

<u>Hab. 1:6</u> – God's purpose for the Chaldeans (Babylon).

<u>Hab. 2:4</u> – The key verse of Habakkuk.

<u>Hab. 2:14</u> – The predicted spread of the knowledge of God.

Hab. 2:19 – The folly of idolatry.

Hab. 2:20 – "...the Lord is in His holy temple..."

Hab. 3:2 – The call for revival.

Hab. 3:3 – Teman is not where God originated! This passage is speaking of the time when God descended upon Mt. Sinai.

Hab. 3:17-19 – A declaration of personal faith in God.

Major Themes

A. Evil is self-destructive. – Hab. 2:6-19 There are five woes against five classes of people:
   1. The greedy plunderer. – Hab. 2:6-8
   2. The shameful extortionist. – Hab. 2:9-11
   3. The violent oppressor. – Hab. 2:12-14
   4. The lascivious drinker. – Hab. 2:15-17
   5. The foolish idolater. – Hab. 2:18-19

B. It isn't wrong to question God.
   1. Job did (individual), Habakkuk did (nation) the Psalmist did, Ps. 37, 49, 73, Jeremiah did, Jer. 12:1-6
   2. All who have questioned God have discovered that God is inscrutable. – His ways are unfathomable, past finding out! Deut. 29:29; Isa. 55:8-9; Rom. 11:33-36

C. In Habakkuk is a song of praise to God. – Hab. 3:1-19
   1. God's person. – Hab. 3:1-3
   2. God's power. – Hab. 3:4-7
   3. God's purpose. – Hab. 3:8-16
   4. God's praise. – Hab. 3:17-19

D. "...but the just shall live by his faith." Hab. 2:4
   1. Rom. 1:17 – The emphasis is on "righteous."
   2. Gal. 3:11 – The emphasis is on "live."
   3. Heb. 10:38 – The emphasis is on "faith."

136

<u>Christ Revealed</u>

1. Christ is the Eternal One. – Hab. 1:12a   He will never die.

2. Christ is the Holy One. – Hab. 1:12b; 2:20; Zech. 2:13   He will never do wrong.

3. Christ is the Rock. – Hab. 1:12c; Deut. 32:4; I Cor. 10:4   He is the foundation for faith.

4. Christ is the Anointed One. – Hab. 3:13; Ps. 2:2; 20:6; 28:8; John 1:41   He is the Messiah, the Christ, sent to save His people.

Zephaniah

Zephaniah served as a prophet in the 7th century in Judah during the days of King Josiah, Zeph. 1:1, 640-609 B.C., Judah had lived through fifty-seven years of evil under the rule of Manasseh and Amon, II Kings 21:9, 20 before King Josiah came to power. Josiah was a good king who worked to bring about spiritual revival and reform in Judah, II Kings 22:23; II Chron. 34-35. Nahum and Jeremiah were alive during this time also and perhaps their preaching along with Zephaniah's influenced the reforms of that time. The book of Zephaniah was written prior to the destruction of Nineveh in 612 B.C. Zephaniah's message was to Judah and it contained both warnings and promises.

Breakdown

A. Warning and judgment for Judah and others. – Zeph. 1:1-3:8
    1. Judah. – Zeph. 1:1=2:3
    2. Other nations. – Zeph. 2:4-15
    3. Jerusalem. – Zeph. 3:1-7
    4. All nations. – Zeph. 3:8

B. Blessing and promise. – Zeph. 3:9-20
    1. For the gentiles. – Zeph. 3:9-10
    2. For Israel. – Zeph. 3:11-20

Pivotal Word – Day of the Lord

"The Day of the Lord", Zeph. 1:7, 14, is referenced in some manner 15 times in the book of Zephaniah. It is referenced as "that day", Zeph. 1:9, 10, 15; 3:11, 16, and a day of the Lord's "wrath," Zeph. 1:18, or "anger," Zeph. 2:2-3.

Characters of Importance

Zephaniah – Known as the prophet of judgment.

A. Zephaniah's background.
   1. Zephaniah's name means: "the Lord hides" or "Jehovah treasures."
   2. Zephaniah was the son of Cushi and the great-great grandson of King Hezekiah.
   3. Zephaniah was of royal blood and was probably a distant relative of King Josiah.

B. Zephaniah's work.
   1. Zephaniah preached a "last hour" warning to Judah.
   2. Zephaniah probably had easy access to the royal court of Josiah and undoubtedly influenced Josiah's spiritual reforms.

C. Zephaniah's character.
   1. Zephaniah was uncompromising in his beliefs.
   2. Zephaniah had strong convictions that he demonstrated by preaching a message of judgment.

Important Verses

Zeph. 1:2 – God's sovereign right to judge the earth.

Zeph. 1:12 – "...and the punish men that are settled on their lees..."

Zeph. 1:14 – "The great day of the LORD *is* near..."

Zeph. 2:15 – "... I *am,* and *there is* none beside me..."

Zeph. 3:1 – A woe on sinful Jerusalem.

Zeph. 3:20 – A promise of future restoration.

Major Themes

A. The Day of the Lord.
   1. The Day of the Lord announced. – Zeph. 1:7, 14
   2. The Day of the Lord described. – Zeph. 1:15-18
   3. The Day of the Lord interpreted.

a. An impending day of punishment on Judah, Babylonian captivity.

b. An ultimate day of reckoning for all, final judgment.
– I Thess. 5:2; II Pet. 3:10-12

B. Repentance is needed. There are three signs of repentance. Zeph. 2:3
1. Seek the Lord. – Zeph. 1:6; Isa. 55:6
2. Seek righteousness. – Amos 5:14-15; Matt. 6:33
3. Seek humility. – Micah 6:8

C. The sins of Jerusalem. – Zeph. 3:1-7
1. Defiled by wickedness. – Zeph. 3:1; Jer. 23:13-14
2. Disobedient to God. – Zeph. 3:3
3. Unfit civil leaders. – Zeph. 3:3
4. Unfit spiritual leaders. – Zeph. 3:4; Mal. 2:7-8

D. 5. General corruption. – Zeph. 3:7b.; Gen. 6:12

Christ Revealed

1. Chris is a zealous witness. – Zeph. 3:8
He is indignant against sinful people.

2. Christ is a just judge. – Zeph. 3:15a
He clears of guilt and condemnation.

3. Christ is a royal king. – Zeph. 3:15b
He reigns to destroy evil.

4. Christ is a victorious warrior. – Zeph. 3:17
a. He is "in your midst." – Zeph. 3:5, 15, 17
b. He is mighty to save. – Isa. 63:1
c. He is joyful over His people. Isa. – 61:5

Haggai

Summation

Haggai, Zechariah and Malachi ministered in Judah after the Jews returned from Babylonian captivity and are therefore called "post-exilic" Minor Prophets. In 539 B.C. Babylon fell to Persian and the Decree of Cyrus freed the Jewish exiled, II Chron. 36:22-23; Ezra 1:1-4. Around 50,000 Jews returned with Ezra in 536 B.C. Ezra set the first priority as the rebuilding of the temple in Jerusalem, Ezra 1:5, but opposition arose causing the work to cease, Ezra 4:24 and the temple remained unfinished for sixteen years. Ezra 5:1-2 informs us that Haggai and Zechariah were called by the Lord to encourage the people to finish the temple, this agrees with Hag. 1:1. Work began on the temple and five years later, 515 B.C., the temple was finished, Ezra 6:14-15. Haggai delivered four messages recorded in the book of Haggai covering a four month period, Sept. – Dec. in 520 B.C. These messages are directed to Zerubbabel, the governor and Joshua the high priest and the remnant of the people, Hag. 1:1, 2:2, 21.

Breakdown

Haggai can be broken down into the individual messages.

A. (Call to Construction)
   First message: God's Temple needs to be rebuilt. – Hag. 1:1-15

B. (Call to Courage)
   Second message: God is in control. – Hag. 2:1-9

C. (Call to commitment)
   Third message: God wants personal dedication. – Hag. 2:10-19

D. (Call to confidence)
   Forth message: God will finally triumph. – Hag. 2:20-23

<u>Pivotal Word</u> – Consider

   In the original Hebrew the word for "consider" refers to the inner man, the mind, the will, the heart. Therefore to "consider" means to set one's mind or heart on something and to give it serious thought. The word "consider" is found five times in Haggai.

<u>Characters of Importance</u>

Haggai – Known as the prophet of arousal.

    A. Haggai's background.
       1. Haggai's name means, "my feast," "festive or joyous one."
       2. Haggai most likely came to Jerusalem from Babylon with Zerubbabel.

    B. Haggai's work.
       1. Haggai was a prophet – a messenger of the Lord. – Hag. 1:1, 13; 2:1
       2. Haggai encouraged and supported the rebuilding of the temple. – Ezra 5:1-2; 6:14-15

    C. Haggai's character.
       1. Haggai had a very caring attitude. He was concerned about the reputation of Israel and God due to the desolation of the temple.
       2. Haggai carried a burden of concern over the unfinished house of worship.
       3. Haggai was very persistent and persuasive in his message, and he got results!

<u>Important Verses</u>

<u>Haggai 1:4</u> – The temple was desolate.

<u>Haggai 1:8</u> – Rebuild the temple.

142

Haggai 1:14 – The Lord stirred up their spirit!

Haggai 2:6 – "…and I will shake the heavens, and the earth…"

Haggai 2:9 – The glory of the temple.

<u>Major Themes</u>

A. Haggai's message is from God.
   1. "…came the word of the Lord by Haggai..." Hag. 1:1, 3; 2:1, 10, 20
   2. "Says the Lord," "declares the Lord."
   3. Twenty six times in 38 verses Haggai indicates that his message had divine origin and authority. (cf. Hag. 1:12-13)

B. Material above spiritual.
   1. Many people had expensive homes while God's house was in shambles. – Hag. 1:4, 9
   2. Foolishness of materialism: "…purse with holes..." – Hag. 1:6, Matt. 6:19-20; Luke 12:15-21

C. Put God first.
   1. Build God's house, restore His worship, dedicate your life, and blessings will follow.
   2. Neglecting God will lead to scarcity, – Hag. 1:6, 9-11; 2:5-17, allowing God to have precedence will lead to blessing, Hag. 2:18-19. (cf. Matt. 6:33)

D. God encourages.
   1. His presence: – Hag. 1:13; 2:4
   2. His power: – Hag. 2:6-7, 21-22

<u>Christ Revealed</u>

1. An unshakable kingdom. – Hag. 2:6, 21-22
   a. All nations are shaken by God.
   b. God's kingdom (the church) cannot be shaken. – Heb. 12:25-29

(Heb. 12:26 is a direct quote of Hag. 2:6)

c. The Lord's church will always stand. – Matt. 16:18

2. Greater Glory. – Hag. 2:9

    a. There are some who see this verse as a reference to the presence of Christ in "this house" during the Lord's ministry.
(cf. Matt. 21:12-17)
(Zerubbabel's temple later refurbished and enlarged under Herod the Great.)

    b. Some see this as a reference to the greater glory of the greater temple – Christ's glorious church. (cf. Eph. 5:27)

3. The Chosen One. – Hag. 2:23

    a. A signet ring is a symbol of honor, authority, and ownership.

    b. Jeconiah (Coniah) had been rejected by God as King of Judah, Jer. 22:24-30, and now God revived the Davidic promise, II Sam. 7:11-14, through Zerubbabel, a descendant of David.

    c. The full honor of the revival of the Davidic promise was not realized in Zerubbabel, but in his lineage – the eventual coming of Christ. – Matt. 1:12-16; Luke 3:27

Zechariah

Zechariah's ministry to Judah lasted about three years, 520-518 B.C. He possibly knew Haggai because their ministries overlapped and they had the same mission and that mission was to encourage the people to rebuild the temple in Jerusalem, Ezra 5:1; 6:14-15. The book of Zechariah is the longest of the Minor Prophets and is perhaps the most difficult to interpret. The difficulty in understanding Zechariah is possibly due to its apocalyptic language and focus on eschatological themes such as pertaining to the end of time, final events, and last days. There are two unanswered questions pertaining to Jesus' use of Zechariah. The first is found in Matt. 23:35 and Luke 11:51 where Jesus referred to a prophet named Zechariah who was murdered. Apparently this was not the same prophet who wrote the book of Zechariah, but probably is to be identified with the Zechariah of II Chron. 24:20-22. The second question is found in Matt. 27:9-10 where Jesus quoted Zechariah 11:12-13, but He attributed the quote to Jeremiah. It is possible that Jesus used "Jeremiah" as representative of the whole group of the prophets as He similarly did of "the Law of Moses and the Prophets and the Psalms" when He referred to the Old Testament in Luke 24:44. Regardless of the difficulties associated with Zechariah it is the general consensus of many biblical scholars that Zechariah reveals more about Christ than any other prophet except Isaiah.

Breakdown

A. During the building of the Temple. – Zech. Chapters 1-8
   1. A call to repentance. – Zech. 1:1-6
   2. Eight visions and their interpretations. – Zech. 1:7-8:23

B. After the building of the Temple. – Zech. Chapters 9-14
   1. Predictions of the Messiah. – Zech. 9:1-11:17
   2. A glorious end of Jerusalem. – Zech. 12:1-14:21

145

<u>Pivotal Word</u> – Jealous

God can only be described as "exceedingly" jealous for Jerusalem and Zion, Zech. 1:14; 8:2. God had a divine love for His city and His people. Zech. 2:8 describes Zion as the apple of His eye. God's love for His people motivated Him to display wrath toward any rivals.

<u>Characters of Importance</u>

Zechariah – Known as the prophet of encouragement.

    A. Zechariah's background.
      1. Zechariah's name means, "Jehovah has remembered."
      2. Zechariah was the son of Berechiah, and the grandson of Iddo. – Zech. 1:1
      3. Zechariah was considered a "young man." – Zech. 2:4
      4. There are 29 other people in the Bible named Zechariah.

    B. Zechariah's work.
      1. Zechariah was both a priest and a prophet. – Zech. 1:1; Neh. 12: 4, 16
      2. Zechariah encouraged the people to maintain right attitudes as they rebuilt the temple.

    C. Zechariah's character.
      1. Zechariah was a young man selected by God to motivate the people in their monumental task of rebuilding the temple. This required spiritual maturity and strong dedication.
      2 Zechariah's efforts were met with immediate response and success and gave prospects of a glorious future.

Important Verses

Zech. 1:14 – "…I am jealous for Jerusalem and for Zion with a great
    jealousy."

Zech. 2:12 – The only place in scripture where Palestine is called the
    "holy land."

Zech. 4:6 – "…not by might, nor by power, but by my spirit, saith the
    Lord of hosts."

Zech. 4:10 – "For who hath despised the day of small things?"

Zech. 6:12-13 – Christ would build the church.

Zech. 9:9 – Christ's triumphal entry predicted.

Zech. 11:12-13 – Christ's betrayal price – 30 pieces of silver.
    (cf. Matt. 27:9-10)

Major Themes

A. God has love for Jerusalem. – Zech. 1:14-17
    1. God's compassion. – Zech. 1:14-16
    2. God's comfort. – Zech. 1:17a
    3. God's choice. – Zech. 1:17b
    4. God's cleansing. – Zech. 13:1-2

B. God desires the temple finished.
    1. The Temple location. Jerusalem. – Zech. 1:16
    2. The builder. Zerubbabel. – Zech. 4:9
    3. Its completion. – Zech. 8:9; Ezra 6:14-15

C. Three means of revelation.
    1. Angels.
      a. They are often addressed as "my Lord." – Zech. 1:9;
        4:4-5, 13; 6:4
      b. Also called "the angel of the Lord." – Zech. 1:12; 3:1, 6; 12:8
      c. Twenty references are made to angels in Zechariah.

2. Visions. There are 8 visions recorded: - Zech. 1:7-6:8
    a. A vision of horses and riders. – Zech. 1:7-17
    b. A vision of four horns and four workmen. – Zech. 1:18-21
    c. A vision of the surveyor. – Zech. 2:1-13
    d. A vision of Joshua and the High Priest. – Zech. 3:1-10
    e. A vision of the Golden Lampstand. – Zech. 4:1-14
    f. A vision of the flying scroll. – Zech. 5:1-4
    g. A vision of the woman in the Ephah. – Zech. 5:5-11
    h. A vision of the four chariots. – Zech. 6:1-8
3. Prophecies.
    a. They came from the Lord, "…came the word of the Lord unto Zechariah…" – Zech. 1:1, 7; 4:8; 6:9; 7:1, 4, 8; 8:1, 18; 9:1; 11:11; 12:1
    b. The spirit sent the prophecies. – Zech. 7:12; II Sam. 23:2; II Pet. 1:20-21

D. The requirements of God.
1. Zechariah – 7:8:12
    a. Handout true justice.
    b. Kindness and compassion.
    c. No oppression of widows or orphans.
    d. No oppression of strangers or the poor.
    e. Do not devise evil in your hearts against one another.
    f. A sad response: – Zech. 7:11-12
2. Zechariah – 8:14-17
    a. Speak truth to one another.
    b. Judge with truth.
    c. Let none of you devise evil in your heart against another.
    d. Do not love false oaths.

E. Looking to the future.
1. "In that day" is found repeatedly in Zechariah Chapters 12-14.
2. "In that day" is probably used in reference either to the days of Christ, or to final events that are treated in an apocalyptic way.

Christ Revealed

1. My servant the Branch. – Zech. 3:8

2. Branch: – Zech. 6:12-13
   a. Christ would build the temple (the church). – Matt. 16:18; I Cor. 3:16-17; Eph. 2:19-22
   b. Christ would combine the offices of King and Priest in one person, not in an earthly way, but in a heavenly or spiritual way. – Heb. 7:13-17; 8:4-5

3. A triumphant and humble king. – Zech. 9:9; Matt. 21:4-5; John 12:12-15

4. Christ described four ways. – Zech. 10:4
   a. Cornerstone – Ps. 118:22; Luke 20:17; Eph. 2:20; I Pet. 2:6
   b. A tent peg – to uphold and support.
   c. Bow of battle – to withstand the enemy.
   d. Ruler – to suppress the wicked.
   e. The pierced one. – Zech. 12:10; John 19:37; Rev. 1:7
   f. Fountain for cleansing sin and impurity. – Zech. 13:1; John 1:29; Eph. 1:7; Rev. 1:5
   g. Smitten or stricken shepherd. – Zech. 13:7; Matt. 26:31; Mark 14:27
   h. King over all the earth. – Zech. 14:9; I Tim. 6:15; Rev. 17:14; 19:16

Malachi

Malachi being the last of the prophets, ministered to Judah during the last half of the fifth century B.C., 450-400. Malachi probably knew Nehemiah as he was around in the year 445 B.C. During Malachi's time the Jews had been back in Judah for nearly 100 years and the Temple and the walls of Jerusalem had been rebuilt. At this time in history there was security and prosperity in the land but there was an obvious lack of spirituality in worship and daily life. Malachi reminded the people of God's love and attempted to call them back to faithfulness while lifting their spirits with the hope of the coming Messiah. Following Malachi the world experienced what has been called the silence of scripture or 400 years of silence between the testaments. For that period of time the world seemed to be in darkness for God remained silent but a Great Light was soon to shine on the world in the form of Christ, the coming Messiah. With Malachi the Old Testament ends the same way it begins, with the anticipation of Christ's coming, Gen. 3:15; Mal. 3:1; 4:2.

Breakdown

A. A message of love. – Mal. 1:1-5
   1. God declares His love. – Mal. 1:1-2
   2. God demonstrates His love. – Mal. 1:3-5

B. Rebuke. – Mal. 1:6-2:17; 3:7-18
   1. The sins of the priests. – Mal. 1:6-2:9
   2. The sins of the people. – Mal. 2:10-17; 3:7-18

C. Hope. – Mal. 3:1-6; 4:1-6
   1. A messenger to be sent. John the Baptist. – Mal. 3:1-6
   2. Christ will come. – Mal. 4:1-6

<u>Pivotal Word</u> – Yet you say

Malachi uses what is known as the dialectic method in his book. The major part of his writing is composed of assertions or charges, questions or objections raised by the charges, and a final rebuttal of each. Each of these occurrences are associated with the key phrases "yet your say", Mal. 2:14, 17; 3:13, "but you say", Mal. 1:2, 6; 3:7-8, "in that you say", Mal. 1:7, 12, and "you also say", Mal. 1:13.

<u>Characters of Importance</u>

Malachi – Known as the Prophet of Hope.

        A. Malachi's background.
           1. Malachi's name means: "my messenger" or "messenger of Jehovah."
           2. Malachi is not given mention anywhere else in the Bible.

        B. Malachi's work.
           1. Malachi was to Nehemiah what Haggai and Zechariah had been to Zerubbabel – a spiritual reformer.
           2. God in His wisdom selected Malachi to be the last of the writing prophets, this makes him significant.

        C. Malachi's character.
           1. Malachi was a sensitive man and this sensitivity made him aware of the seriousness of sin.
           2. Malachi was also aware of God's love for man, and man's need to love God back by being dedicated in worship and consecrated living.

<u>Important Verses</u>

<u>Mal. 1:2</u> – "I have loved you, saith the Lord…"

<u>Mal. 2:11</u> – The danger of marrying an unbeliever.

151

Mal. 2:16 – "...the God of Israel, saith that he hateth putting away..."

Mal. 3:1 – John the Baptist to come before Christ.

Mal. 3:6 – "For I *am* the LORD, I change not..."

Mal. 3:8-10 – "Will a man rob God? ..."

Mal. 4:5 – John the Baptist is called Elijah.

Major Themes

A. Malachi rebukes Israel for her sins.
    1. Laxity and unfaithfulness among the priests. – Mal. 1:6-14; 2:1-9; Neh. 13:4-9
    2. Spiritually mixed marriages. – Ma. 2:10-12; Ezra 9-10; Neh. 13:23-28
    3. Divorce. – Mal. 2:13-16; Deut. 24:1; Matt. 5:31; 19:6-8
    4. Love for evil. – Mal. 2:17
    5. Improper giving. – Mal. 3:7-12; Neh. 13:10-13
    6. Arrogance and pride. – Mal. 3:13-15

B. Malachi has a message for the church today.
    1. Form, ritual, ceremony, and tradition is not the totality of religion, it is more. – Mal. 1:10
    2. Marriage must be spiritual and permanent. – Mal. 2:10-16
    3. God's moral standards must be upheld. – Mal. 3:5
    4. Giving must be done generously and freely in support of God's work. – Mal. 3:10

C. A remedy for then and now.
    1. Always remember God's word. – Mal. 4:4
    2. Always repent of your sins. – Mal. 2:8-9
    3. Cling to God and return to God. – Mal. 3:7; Zech. 1:3

<u>Christ Revealed</u>

1. Messenger of the covenant. – Mal. 3:1
   a. Malachi use of "messenger" (ambassador, angel):
      1. The name Malachi means "messenger." – Mal. 1:1
      2. Levi the high priest. – Mal. 2:7
      3. John the Baptist. – Mal. 3:1a
      4. Christ. – Mal. 3:1b

The New Testament

The New Testament is unique in and of itself. It is the source for all authority in the final dispensation of time known as the Christian Age. According to its own declaration it is the last will and testament of Christ and therefore is the Law of Christ for all who live today. Its teachings will judge men and angels at the last day. It is the exclusive and final work of God through Christ, as confirmed to us by them that walked with Him and heard Him. What the New Testament looses or binds on earth will be bound or loosed eternally. All the wisdom of men on earth in the past or in the future is insufficient and insignificant in contrast to the wisdom of God revealed in the pages of the New Testament. No opinion or counter command of man can change or nullify any part of it. Within the pages of the New Testament the eternal will of God is revealed to mankind including His eternal covenant.

Though man has tried through the years to produce his own version of the Bible he has not succeeded. His feeble attempts have only strengthened the authenticity, authority and authorship of the Bible. Without question, without doubt, without evidence to the contrary the New Testament is indeed the Law from God that man must abide by today.

New Testament Themes

Matthew	Jesus, Lord of the Jews
Mark	Jesus, Lord of the Romans
Luke	Jesus, Lord of the Greeks
John	Jesus, Lord of all
Acts	Jesus at work through the Church.
Romans	Jesus in God's plan for salvation.
I Corinthians	Jesus, the life of the Church
II Corinthians	Evidences of real loyalty to Jesus.
Galatians	Jesus, the fulfillment of the Law.
Ephesians	Jesus, the head of the Church.
Philippians	The joy of living for Jesus.
Colossians	The divinity of Jesus.
I Thessalonians	The second coming of Jesus.
II Thessalonians	A second look at the second coming of Jesus.
I Timothy	Notes on serving Jesus.
II Timothy	A dying man's confidence in Jesus.
Titus	More notes on serving Jesus.
Philemon	The difference Jesus makes.

Hebrews	The superiority of Jesus and His covenant.
James	The teachings of Jesus applied to life.
I Peter	Jesus, the church's example in suffering.
II Peter	Identifying the enemies of Jesus.
I John	Jesus, the Son of God, and proof of God's love.
II John	Dealing with the enemies of Jesus.
III John	Hospitality among the followers of Jesus.
Jude	A warning against the enemies of Jesus.
Revelation	The final victory of Jesus and his followers.

Key Dates of the New Testament

Jesus' birth (Matt. 2:1; Luke 2:1-2)	6-4 B.C.
Death of Herod the Great (Matt. 2:19)	4 B.C.
John the Baptist's ministry begins (Luke 3:1-2)	26 A.D.
Jesus' Ministry begins (Luke 3:1-2)	26-27 A.D.
Jesus' death (John 19:14)	30 A.D.
Church established in Jerusalem on Pentecost (Acts 2)	30 A.D.
Stephen's death (Acts 7)	32 A.D.
Saul's conversion (Acts 9)	34 A.D.
James' death (Acts 12:1-2)	44 A.D.
Death of Herod Agrippa I (Acts 12:21-23)	44 A.D.
Famine in Palestine (Acts 13:1-14:28)	46 A.D.
First Missionary Journey (Acts 13:1-14:28)	47-49 A.D.
Expulsion of Jews from Rome (Acts 18:2)	49 A.D.
Jerusalem Council (Acts 15)	51 A.D.
Gallio, proconsul of Achaia (Acts 18:12)	51-53 A.D.
Second Missionary Journey (Acts 15:36-18:22)	51-53 A.D.
Third Missionary Journey (Acts 18:23-21:26)	53-57 A.D.
Nero becomes Roman Emperor (54-68A.D.)	54 A.D.
Paul's journey to Rome (Acts 27-28)	60 A.D.
Great fire of Rome (July)	64 A.D.
Jewish revolt in Palestine	66 A.D.
Paul's death (II Tim. 4:6-8)	67- 68 A.D.
Peter's death (II Pet. 1:13-15)	67- 68 A.D.
Vespasian becomes Roman Emperor (69-79 A.D.)	69 A.D.
Destruction of Jerusalem and the Temple	70 A.D.
The fall of Masada, the last Jewish stronghold	73 A.D.
Titus becomes Roman Emperor (79-81 A.D.)	79 A.D.
Domitian becomes Roman Emperor (81-96 A.D.)	81 A.D.
John writes Revelation on Island of Patmos (Rev. 1:9)	95 A.D.
John's death	96-98 A.D.

Some of these dates are approximate and are to help put some order to the events of the New Testament times.

Matthew

Summation

Matthew was written with the intended target being Jews. His intent was to present Jesus as the Messiah and King. To help support his efforts Matthew traces the genealogy of Jesus back to Abraham, the Father of Israel. Because the Jews were given the Law at Mt. Sinai the book of Matthew contains over 60 references to the Old Testament and 43 of them are to prove that Jesus fulfilled all prophecy. Following are examples: Matt. 1:22-23 and Isa. 7:14; Matt. 2:5 and Mic. 5:2; and Matt. 2:15 and Hos. 11:1. Matthew was what was known as a publican or tax collector by profession, Matt. 9:9. He was called to be an apostle, Matt. 9:9-13; 10:3 and is also known as Levi, Mark 2:14. The book of Matthew was written prior to the destruction of Jerusalem, Matt. 24:1-2ff; the temple was destroyed in 70 A.D. by Roman Emperor Titus. Though the probability exists that the book was written between 60-65 A.D., there are some who believe it was the first Gospel to be written around 50 A.D.

Breakdown

Jesus is the King.

A. Jesus the King's introduction. – Matt. Chapters 1-4

B. Jesus the King's preaching. – Matt. Chapters 5-7

C. Jesus the King's Miracles. – Matt. Chapters 8-10

D. Jesus the King's program. – Matt. Chapters 11-14

E. Jesus the King's destiny. – Matt. Chapters 15-18

F. Jesus the King's problems. – Matt. Chapters 19-25

G. Jesus the King's death. – Matt. Chapters 26-27

H. Jesus the King's triumph. – Matt. Chapter 28

Pivotal Word – Kingdom

"Kingdom of heaven" is found 116 times in 32 verses. It is unique to Matthew. The term "kingdom of God" is also found in Matthew, Matt. 12:28; 19:24; 21:31, 43. Kingdom is used to reference the church, a domain in which Christ rules and reigns as King supreme.

Important Verses

Matt. 1:21-23 – The virgin birth of Jesus.

Matt. 3:13-17 – The baptism of Jesus.

Matt. 4:1-11 – The temptation of Jesus.

Matt. 5:1-12 – The beatitudes.

Matt. 6:9-13 – The Lord's Prayer.

Matt. 9:36-38 – The Lord's concern for the lost.

Matt. 11:28-30 – The universal invitation.

Matt. 17:1-5 – The transfiguration of Jesus.

Matt. 22:36-40 – The two great commandments.

Matt. 25:31-46 – The final judgment scene.

Matt. 28:18-20 – The Great Commission.

Major Themes

A. Jesus' (our King) preaching and teaching.
    1. The Sermon on the Mount. – Matt. 5:1-7:29
    2. The commissioning of the Twelve. – Matt. 10:1-42
    3. The Parables. – Matt. 13:1-53
       a. The Sower. – Matt. 13:1-23

b. The wheat and Tares. – Matt. 13:24-30
　　　c. The Mustard Seed. – Matt. 13:31-32
　　　d. the Leaven. – Matt. 13:33
　　　e. The Wheat and Tares explained. – Matt. 13:34-43
　　　f. the Hidden Treasures. – Matt. 13:44
　　　g. the Pearl of Great Prices. – Matt. 13:45-46
　　　h. The Dragnet. – Matt. 13:47-50
　　　i. The Householder. – Matt. 13:51-53
　4. The principles of greatness and forgiveness. – Matt. 18:1-35
　5. The rebuking of the Pharisees. – Matt. 23:1-39
　6. The final discourse to the Disciples on Mount Olivet.
　　　– Matt. 24:1-25:46

Please note: Five of the statements end with the words, "…when Jesus had ended these sayings …"– Matt. 7:28; 11:1; 13:53; 191; 26:1.

B.　Jesus (our King) shows His power by miracles. Jesus had power over:
　1. Defilement. – Matt. 8:1-4
　2. Distance. – Matt. 8:5-13
　3. Disease. – Matt. 8:14-17
　4. Disciples. – Matt. 8:18-22
　5. Deep. – Matt. 8:23-27
　6. Demons. – Matt. 8:28-34
　7. Death. – Matt. 9:18-26
　8. Darkness. – Matt. 9:27-31
　9. Dumbness. – Matt. 9:32-34
　10. Disease. – Matt. 9:35

C.　Jesus (our King) exhibits righteousness.
　1. "Righteous," righteousness," occur more often in Matthew than in the other three gospels combined.
　2. A person who is righteous is a person who lives right because he is in a right relationship with God.

160

3. Jesus condemned "self-righteousness" using the Pharisees as an example. – Matt. 5:20; 23:25-28.
4. The righteousness that man needs is the one he acquires from God, according to Jesus man needs to seek the "righteousness of God." – Matt. 6:33; (cf. Rom. 1:17; 4:6-8; 9:30-31; 10:1-4; Phil. 3:9).

D. The church, the King's Kingdom.
   1. Matthew is the only gospel in which the word "church" appears.
      a. Matt. 16:18 – the universal church.
      b. Matt. 18:17 – the local congregation.
   2. Jesus predicted the church.
   3. The foundation of the church is that Jesus is the Son of God.
   4. The church was not founded by or built upon Peter.
   5. The church began on the Day of Pentecost, Acts 2, when Peter used the authority Christ gave him (the keys to the kingdom) to preach the gospel. – Acts 2:36-47.

Christ Revealed

1. Titles associated with Christ the Jews would understand.
   a. Son of David. – Matt. 1:1, 20; 9:27; 12:23; 15:22; 20:30-31; 21:9, 15
   b. son of Abraham. – Matt. 1:1; Gal. 3:16
   c. King of the Jews. – Matt. 2:2; 27:11, 29, 37
   d. King. – Matt. 21:5; 25:34, 40
   e. King of Israel. – Matt. 27:42
   f. Ruler. – Matt. 2:6

2. Title associating Christ with God.
   a. Jesus (Jehovah is salvation). – Matt. 1:21, 25 (total of 150 times)
   b. Immanuel (God with us). – Matt. 1:23
   c. My Son or Son. – Matt. 2:15; 3:17; 11:27; 17:5; 28:19
   d. Son of God. – Matt. 8:29; 14:3, 6, 37; 16:16; 26:63; 27:40, 43, 54

e. Christ. – (Messiah, anointed One) – Matt. 16:16; 22:42
(total of 17 times)

3. Titles connecting Christ with man and His mission on earth.
a. Son of Man. – Matt. 8:20; 9:6; 10:23; 11:19; 12:8, 32, 40;
13:37, 41; 16:13, 27, 28; 17:9, 12, 22; 18:11; 19:28; 20:18, 28;
24:27, 30, 36, 37, 39, 44; 25:31; 26:2, 24, 45; 26:64 (total of 30
times).
b. Rabbi or Teacher. – Matt. 23:7-8
c. Leader. – Matt. 23:10

Mark

Summation

The Gospel of Mark was written to a Roman audience to present Jesus as a mighty worker and servant. According to tradition and testimony of the early church, Mark wrote his gospel to give account of Peter's preaching. Mark himself was probably converted by Peter, I Pet. 5:13, and his gospel corresponds to Peter's address at Caesarea, Acts 10:34-43. Mark does not record any genealogy, the virgin birth or the childhood years of Jesus. Very little reference is made to Jewish law in the Gospel of Mark however, Mark does address Jewish terms and explains them, Mark 3:17; 5:41; 7:11; 12:42; 14:12; 15:22, 42. Mark, known also as John Mark, was the son of Mary, a woman whose home was used by the church in Jerusalem, Acts 12:12. Mark was also Barnabas's cousin, Col. 4:10, and he was with Paul and Barnabas on the first missionary journey, Acts 12:25, however he turned back at Perga in Pamphylia, Acts 13:5, 13. When plans were made for the second missionary journey it appears that John Mark was a point of contention between Paul and Barnabas, Acts 15:36-40. John Mark is also thought to be the man who fled from Jesus on the night of His betrayal, Mark 14:51-52. John Mark wrote his gospel at a time no later than 70 A.D. and probably as early as A.D. 50. Evidently just prior to his death Paul sent for Mark to join him, II Tim. 4:11.

Breakdown

Jesus the servant.

A. Jesus' preparation. – Mark 1:1-13
   1. The ministry of John the Baptist. – Mark 1:1-8
   2. The baptism of Jesus. – Mark 1:9-11
   3. Jesus' temptation. – Mark 1:12-13

B. Jesus' preaching. – Mark 1:14-10:52
    1. Galilee. – Mark 1:14-9:50
    2. Judea and Perea. – Mark 10:1-52

C. Jesus' passion. – Mark 11:1-16:20
    1. Jesus' triumphal entry. – Mark 11:1-19
    2. Jesus' final teaching. – Mark 11:20-13:37
    3. Jesus' betrayal. – Mark 14:1-52
    4. Jesus' trials and death. – Mark 14:53-15:47
    5. Jesus' resurrection and ascension. – Mark 16:1-20

Pivotal Word - Immediately

Mark focused on the continual activity of our Lord. Some 40 times the word "immediately" is found. Some translations render the word "straightway, at once, as soon, etc.

Important Verses

Mark 1:14-15 – Jesus came preaching.

Mark 2:17 – "… I came not to call the righteous, but sinners…"

Mark 4:11 – "… but unto them that are without, all these things are done in parables."

Mark 5:19-20 – "… how great things the Lord hath done for thee…"

Mark 7:6-7 – Vain worship (lips but not hearts).

Mark 9:41 – A cup of water in Christ's name.

Mark 10:27 – "… but not with God: for with God all things are possible."

Mark 10:45 – The key verse of the book.

Mark 12:17 – "… Render to Caesar the things that are Caesar's, and to God the things that are God's."

Mark 15:34 – "… My God, my God, why hast thou forsaken Me?"

Mark 16:15-16 – The Great Commission.

Major Themes

A. An attitude of service from the servant. – Mark 10:45
   1. Mark shows Jesus as a might wonder worker going from one deed to the next. – Mark 1:10ff
      a. Mark stresses the deeds and works of Jesus more than His words. – Acts 10:38
      b. Mark presents 18 miracles in rapid succession.
   2. Those Jesus was always busy, he never gave the appearance of being in a hurry.
   3. Mark shows that Jesus took time for people such as the sick, children, disciples and even his enemies.

B. Jesus' tender touch.
   1. Those who received the touch of the Master's hand:
      a. Lepers. – Mark 1:41
      b. Afflicted. – Mark 3:10
      c. Woman. – Mark 5:25-34
      d. Sick. – Mark 6:53-56
      e. Deaf. – Mark 7:31-37
      f. Blind. – Mark 8:22
      g. Children. – Mark 10:13

C. Jesus' emotions.
   1. Jesus wondered. – Mark 6:6
   2. Jesus felt compassion. – Mark 6:34
   3. Jesus became indignant. – Mark 10:14
   4. Jesus was deeply grieved. – Mark 14:34

D. Jesus' shameful death. – Mark 8:31; 10:32-34; Matt. 16:21; Luke 9:22
   1. Jesus suffered.

2. Jesus was rejected.

3. Jesus was delivered up.

4. Jesus was condemned.

5. Jesus was mocked.

6. Jesus was spit upon.

7. Jesus was scourged.

8. Jesus was killed.

9. Jesus was raised from the dead.

Christ Revealed

1. Son of God. – Mark 1:1; 3:11; 15:39

2. My beloved Son. – Mark 1:11; 9:7

3. Jesus of Nazareth. – Mark 1:24; 10:47; 14:67; 16:6

4. Hoy One of God. – Mark 1:24

5. Son of Man. – Mark 2:10; 10:45 (total of 14 times)

6. Physician. – Mark 2:17

7. Lord of Sabbath. – Mark 2:28

8. Teacher or Rabbi. – Mark 4:38; 9:5 (total of 14 times)

9. Son of the Most High God. – Mark 5:7

10. Prophet. – Mark 6:3-4

11. Christ or Messiah. – Mark 8:29; 12:35-37; 13:21-23; 15:32

12. Son of David. – Mark 10:47-48; 12:35

13. Rabboni or My Master. – Mark 10:51

14. King of the Jews or Israel. – Mark 15:2, 9, 12, 18, 26, 32

Luke

Summation

   Luke is the only New Testament author that was not a Jew. He was a Gentile physician, Col. 4:14. Luke penned his gospel for the Gentles in order to present to them Jesus as the Son of Man and the Divine Savior and in order to do this Luke traced Jesus' lineage back to Adam, the father of all. During Paul's second missionary journey Luke was with him, Acts 16:10-17, and on the third journey, Acts 20:5; 21:18, as well as the journey to Rome, Acts 27:1; 28:16. By using the "we" pronoun in the previous verses the inclusion of Luke is understood indicating his presence as well as his authorship. During both of Paul's imprisonments Luke was with him, Phil. 24: II Tim. 4:11, and some believe Luke was Paul's personal physician, Col. 4:14. Luke, being an excellent historian, gives precise dates for his narratives, Luke 1:5; 2:1-2; 3:1-2. Luke penned both Luke and Acts to someone named Theophilus (friend of God) in an effort to give an accurate account of the beginning of Christ's ministry and the continuation of it through the actions of the apostles, Luke 1:1-4; Acts 1:1-5. In Luke's effort to give accurate information he provides more information on the birth, childhood, and growth of Jesus than the other gospels. It is believed that the book of Luke was written before the book of Acts probably around 58-60 A.D. Matthew, Mark and Luke have many similar passages, some word for word. They together are called the "Synoptic Gospels" meaning (to see together) because they take a common view of Jesus. Some skeptics and critics say the authors either copied, collaborated, or used common sources. The differences of the writers, however, exemplifies their independence and their similarities associate them with a common inspiration of the Holy Spirit.

Breakdown

The Son of Man – Jesus Christ as He is:

A. Identified with men. – Luke 1:1-4:13

B. Ministering to men. – Luke 4:14- 9:50

C. Rejected by men. – Luke 9:51-19:27

D. Condemned for men. – Luke 19:28-23:56

E. Vindicated before men. – Luke 24:1-53

<u>Pivotal Word</u> – Sinner

In some form (sins, sinners, sinned) "sinner" appears some 31 times in Luke. We are told that Jesus came to call sinners to repentance, Luke 5:32. In Luke 15:1 sinners came to listen to Jesus. Jesus was called a friend of sinners, Luke 7:34, and He ate with sinners and received them, Luke 15:2; 19:7.

<u>Important Verses</u>

<u>Luke 1:1-4</u> – Luke's method and purpose.

<u>Luke 1:30-33</u> – Gabriel's announcement to Mary.

<u>Luke 2:40, 52</u> – Jesus' early growth.

<u>Luke 4:16-21</u> – Jesus' first recorded sermon.

<u>Luke 6:12-16</u> – Choosing the twelve disciples.

<u>Luke 6:31</u> – The Golden Rule.

<u>Luke 9:58</u> – "… the Son of Man hath nowhere to lay His head."

<u>Luke 10:25-37</u> – Parable of the Good Samaritan.

<u>Luke 14:25-35</u> – The cost of discipleship.

<u>Luke 16:19-31</u> – The rich man and Lazarus.

<u>Luke 22:54-62</u> – Peter's denial of Christ.

168

<u>Luke 24:44-48</u> – The Great Commission.

<u>Major Themes</u>

A. Hymns
   1. Mary's song. – Luke 1:46-55
   2. Zacharias' song. – Luke 1:67-79
   3. Angel's song. – Luke 2:13-14
   4. Simeon's song. – Luke 2:29-32
   A characteristic found in each of these songs, they each praise God for sending Jesus as our Savior.

B. Salvation from sin.
   1. Christ loved the lost. – Luke 19:10
      a. Salvation for all people. – Luke 2:10-11
      b. Salvation for a sinful woman. – Luke 7:36-50
      c. Salvation for Zaccheus. – Luke 19:1-10
      d. Salvation for a penitent thief. – Luke 23:39-43
      e. Salvation for social outcasts: publicans, sinners, Samaritans, lepers, etc.
   2. There are two parables that emphasize salvation from sin:
      a. The lost sheep, coin, and sons. – Luke 15:1-32
      b. Publican and Pharisee. – Luke 18:9-14
   3. There is a universal need for salvation.
      a. Good news for all people. – Luke 2:10-11
      b. "And all flesh shall see the salvation of God." – Luke 3:6
      c. All nations are to hear the gospel. – Luke 24:47

C. Prayer in Luke.
   1. The prayer life of Christ:
      a. After His baptism. – Luke 3:21
      b. After a day of miracles. – Luke 5:15-16
      c. Before selecting the twelve. – Luke 6:12
      d. Before predicting His death. – Luke 9:18-22
      e. At the transfiguration. – Luke 9:29
      f. On the return of the seventy. – Luke 10:17-22

169

g. Before teaching His disciples to pray. – Luke 11:1

h. In Gethsemane. – Luke 22:39-46

i. On the cross. – Luke 23:34, 46

D. Concerns with money.
1. The two debtors. – Luke 7:41-42
2. The rich farmer. – Luke 12:13-21
3. The tower builder. – Luke 14:28-30
4. The lost coin. – Luke 15:8-10
5. The unjust steward. – Luke 16:1-9
6. The rich man and Lazarus. – Luke 16:19-31
7. The ten minas (pounds). – Luke 19:11-27

E. The Holy Spirit
1. The main characters are empowered by the Spirit.
   a. John the Baptist. – Luke 1:15
   b. Mary. – Luke 1:35
   c. Elizabeth. – Luke 1:41
   d. Zacharias. – Luke 1:67
   e. Simeon. – Luke 2:25-26
2. Jesus Christ:
   a. Conceived by the Spirit. – Luke 1:35
   b. Attested by the Spirit. – Luke 3:22
   c. Led by the Spirit. – Luke 4:1
   d. Anointed by the Spirit. – Luke 4:14, 18
   e. Rejoiced in the spirit. – Luke 10:21
3. The Twelve were told to wait in Jerusalem for "power from on high." – Luke 24:49; Acts 1:4-5, 8; 2:1-4

Christ Revealed

1. Son of the Most High. – Luke 1:32, 35, 76; 828

2. Son of God. – Luke 1:35; 4:3, 9, 41; 22:70

3. Sunrise. – Luke 1:78; (cf. Mal. 4:2)

4. Savior. – Luke 1:47; 2:11

5. Child. – Luke 2:17, 34, 40

6. Jesus. – Luke 2:21 (86 times)

7. Teacher. – Luke 3:12; 7:40; 22:11 (14 times)

8. Christ. (12 times) – Luke 3:15; Christ the Lord, 2:11; Lord's Christ, 2:26; Christ of God, 9:20; 23:25

9. Son. – Luke 10:22; Beloved son, 3:22; My Son, My Chosen One, 9:35

10. Prophet. – Luke 4:24; 7:16

11. Jesus of Nazareth. – Luke 4:34; 18:37; 24:19

12. Master. – Luke 5:5; 8:24 (8 times)

13. Son of Man. – Luke 5:24; 19:10; 24:7 (24 times)

14. Lord of Sabbath. – Luke 6:5

15. Lord. – Luke 2:11; 3:34; 5:12; 6:46 (46 times)

16. Expected One. – Luke 7:19-20

17. Son of David. – Luke 18:38-39; 20:41

18. King. – Luke 19:38; (cf. Ps. 118:26)

19. King of the Jews. – Luke 23:3, 38

20. Living One. – Luke 24:5

John

Summation

The gospel of John was authored by John, whom Jesus called "Son of thunder," Mark 3:17, though he only identifies himself by referring to himself as the "disciple whom Jesus loved," John 13:23; 19:26; 20:2; 21:7, 20. John clearly states that the purpose of his gospel was to produce initial faith in Christ, John 20:30-31. It was written as a gospel for a universal audience not just the Jew or the Greek. John was a member of what we can call the "inner circle" and kept company with Peter and James, Matt. 17:1. John occupied a place next to Jesus at the last supper, John 13:25, and he courageously stood near the cross of Calvary, John 19:26. John is also known to have provided bold leadership in the Jerusalem church, Acts 4:13; Gal. 2:9. There is a tradition that tells us that John spent his last days in Ephesus caring for Mary, John 19:26-27, and he later died in Ephesus following his exile on the island of Patmos, Rev. 1:9. John wrote the Gospel of John, the letters of First, Second, and Third John, and the Book of Revelation, sometime between 85 and 100 A.D. The Gospel of John has some unusual characteristics compared to the other Gospels: John has noticeable deletions and its unique vocabulary. John omits Christ's genealogy, birth, youth, baptism, temptation, transfiguration, and ascension, and he does not list the twelve apostles. John also makes no mention of the church and very little reference to baptism and repentance. John also does not record any of the Sermon on the Mount, and parables, or any of the prophecies of the destruction of Jerusalem and the end of the world. Listed here are some of the important words used by John and their frequency of use: Father (124), know (94), believe (93), world (78), I am (75), life (47) witness (39), love (30), truth (27), and abide (17).

Breakdown

A. Presenting the Son of God. – John 1:1-18

172

B. Public ministry of the Son of God. – John 1:19-12:50

C. Private ministry of the Son of God. – John 13:1-17:26

D. Passion of the Son of God. – John 18:1-20:31

E. Personal appeal of the Son of God. – John 21:1-25

Pivotal Word – Believe

It could easily be said that John is the Gospel of Belief. A form of the word believe is used numerously: believe (55 times), believed (24 times), and believes (14 times). John poses a question, "do you believe?" – John 1:50; 9:35; 11:26; 16:31. As John records, some did believe, John 2:11, 22, 23; 4:39, 42, 50; 10:42, and some did not believe on Him, John 4:48; 8:48; 10:25-26; 12:37.

Important Verses

John 1:1-4 – "In the beginning was the Word ..."

John 1:10-13 – The rejection and reception of Jesus.

John 1:14 – The incarnation.

John 3:1-5 – The new birth.

John 3:14-16 – "For God so loved the world ..."

John 4:24 – Worship in spirit and truth.

John 6:63 – "... the words that I speak unto you, they are spirit..."

John 8:24 – The necessity of believing in Jesus.

John 10:10 – The abundant life.

John 11:35 – "Jesus wept."

John 12:48 – The standard of judgment.

173

John 14:1-6 – Comfort for troubled souls.

John 17:20-23 – Jesus' prayer for unity.

John 20:30-31 – The key verses in John.

John 21:25 – The Gospels do not furnish a detailed account of
        Christ's life.

Major Themes

  A. Seven signs showing Christ's power and authority.
  1. Water to wine. – John 2:1-11 (Power over quality)
  2. Nobleman's son. – John 4:46-54 (Power over distance)
  3. Lame man. – John 5:1-18 (Power over time)
  4. Feeding five thousand. – John 6:1-14 (Power over
        quantity)
  5. Walking on water. – John 6:16-21 (Power over natural
        law)
  6. Healing the blind man. – John 9:1-12 (Power over
        disease)
  7. Raising Lazarus. – John 11:1-46 (Power over death)
  Each of these signs had a purpose: – John 20:30-31
    a. Signs – attesting miracles, manifestation of God's
        power and Christ's glory. – John 2:11; 4:48
        (cf. 7:31; 10:41)
    b. Believe – the reaction signs are designed to
        produce. – John 2:11; 4:50, 53; 6:14;
        11:45
    c. Life – The result which belief in Christ brings.
        – John 3:36; 5:21; 10:10

  B. Christ seven times states "I am."
  1. The Bread of Life. – John 6:35, 48
  2. The Light of the word. – John 8:12; 9:5
  3. The Door. – John 10:7
  4. The Good Shepherd. – John 10:11, 14

174

5. The Resurrection and the Life. – John 11:25
6. The Way, the Truth, and the Life. – John 14:6
7. The True Vine. – John 15:1
Please note the use of "I Am" in John 8:56-58. This denotes Christ's eternal existence.

C. Seven witnesses of Christ:
   1. John the Baptist. – John 5:31-35
   2. The works of Jesus. – John 5:36
   3. The Father. – John 5:37-38
   4. The scriptures. – John 5:39-47
   5. Jesus Himself. – John 8:13-14
   6. The Holy Spirit. – John 15:26
   7. The apostles. – John 15:27; 19:35; 21:24

D. The characteristics of Jesus: Jesus was God and man.
   1. Jesus as God. (cf. John 5:17-18)
      a. "The Word was God." – John 1:1
      b. "Before Abraham was born, I Am." – John 2:25
      c. "I and the Father are one." – John 10:30, 33
      d. "… he who hath seen me hath seen the Father…"
         John 14:9
      e. "My Lord and my God." – John 20:28
   2. Jesus as a man.
      a. "And the Word became flesh and dwelt among us. "
         John 1:14
      b. He was social. – John 2:1-11
      c. "… for He knew what was in man." – John 2:25
      d. He was weary and thirsty. – John 4:6-7; 19:28
      e. He was sympathetic. – John 11:35
      f. He was troubled. – John 12:27
      g. He was loving. – John 13:1
      h. He died and was buried. – John 19:30, 40-42

Christ Revealed

1. Word. – John 1:1, 12 (4 times)

2. God. – John 1:1

3. Only begotten (unique, only one of His kind). – John 1:14, 18; 3:16, 18

4. Jesus Christ. – John 1:17; 17:3 (only twice)

5. Christ. – John 1:20, 25; 3:28; 7:31, 41-42; 9:22; 20:31 (17 times)

6. Prophet. – John 1:21, 25; 4:19; 6:14; 7:40; 9:17; (cf. Deut. 18:15-18)

7. Lord. – John 1:23; 6:23; 13:13-14; 21:7

8. Lamb of God. – John 1:29, 36 (only twice)

9. Son of God. – John 1:34, 49; 3:14; 10:36; 19:7

10. Rabbi or Teacher. – John 1:38, 49; 3:2, 26; 4:31; 6:25; 8:4; 11:8, 28; 13:13-14

11. Messiah. – John 1:41; 4:25 (only 2 occurrences in the New Testament)

12. Him of whom Moses and the Prophets wrote. – John 1:45

13. King of Israel. – John 1:49; 12:13, 15

14. Son of Man. – John 1:51

15. Jesus. – John 2:1 (239 times)

16. Son. – John 3:35

17. Savior of the world. – John 4:42 (only once)

18. Shepherd. – John 10:16

19. He who comes into the world. – John 11:27; (cf. 6:14)

20. Jesus the Nazarene. – John 18:5, 7; 19:19

21. Man. – John 18:29-30, 40; 19:5, 12

22. King of the Jews. – John 18:34; 19:3, 14, 15, 19, 21

23. My Lord and my God. – John 20:28

Acts

Summation

According to internal and external evidence Luke is the author of the book of Acts, too. Some consider the book of Acts to be a second volume to Luke's writings. In the book of Acts the reader is given a history of the beginnings, growth and development of the church during the first century A.D. The book tells of the spread of Christianity among the Gentiles and of the many struggles and persecutions the early church suffered. The time span of Acts is a period of about 30 years and was written approximately 30 years after the church was established approximately 61-62 A.D. Peter and Paul are the two main figures the book of Acts follows, Peter chapters 1-12 and Paul chapters 13-28. Acts provides the background for ten of Paul's letters: Romans, I & II Corinthians, Galatians, Ephesians, Philippians, Colossians, I & II Thessalonians, and Philemon. A precise outline of the book of Acts is provided by Luke in Acts 1:8.

Breakdown

      A. Witnesses in Jerusalem. – Acts 1:1-8:3
         1. Days of waiting, preparing and praying. – Acts 1:1-26
         2. The Church of Christ is established. – Acts 2:1-47
         3. Healing, preaching and persecutions. – Acts 3:1-8:3

      B. Witnesses in Judea and Samaria. – Acts 8:4-12:25
         1. Christians scattered. – Acts 8:4-40
         2. Paul converted. – Acts 9:1-43
         3. Gentiles converted. – Acts 10:1-11:30
         4. Christians persecuted. – Acts 12:1-25

      C. Witnesses to the all the earth. – Acts 13:1-28:31
         1. First missionary journey. – Acts 13:1-14:28
         2. Jerusalem council. – Acts 15:1-35
         3. Second missionary journey. – Acts 15:36-18:22

4. Third missionary journey. – Acts 18:23-21:26

5. Journey to Rome. – Acts 21:27-28:31

Pivotal Word – Witness

A form of the word "witness" occurs 21 times in the book of Acts. This word is closely related to the word "testify" that appears ten times. Both of these words are derived from the root word for martyr, and they mean "to affirm solemnly and boldly on the basis of what one knows, sees, hears, and believes." – Acts 1:8, 5:32; 10:39-43.

Important Verses

Acts 1:8 – Power of the Holy Spirit and propagation of the gospel.

Acts 1:11 – The ascension and promised return of Christ.

Acts 2:1-4 – The coming of the Holy Spirit on the apostles.

Acts 2:36-38 – A great affirmation, a great question, a great answer.

Acts 4:13 – The secret of boldness and confidence.

Acts 4:18-20 – "… we cannot but speak the things which we have seen and heard."

Acts 6:3-4 – The priority of praying and preaching.

Acts 8:4 – "Therefore they that were scattered abroad went everywhere preaching the word."

Acts 11:26 – "… And the disciples were called Christians first in Antioch."

Acts 17:30-31 – Christ, the righteous judge.

Acts 20:7 – "And upon the first day of the week, when the disciples came together to break bread…"

Acts 20:28 – Elders are to shepherd the church of God.

Acts 20:35 – "… It is more blessed to give than to receive."

Acts 22:16 – "… and now why tarriest thou? Arise, and be baptized, and wash away thy sins, calling on the name of the Lord."

Acts 26:28 – "… Almost thou persuades me to be a Christian."

Major Themes

A. Working of the Holy Spirit.
   1. Promise of the Holy Spirit. Acts – 1:4-5, 8; (cf. Luke 24:49)
   2. Baptism of the Holy Spirit.
      a. On the Apostles. – Acts 2:1-4, 14-18; 33
      b. On the Gentiles. – Acts 10:44-48; 11:15-16; 15:8
      c. On believers.
         1. At baptism, the Spirit of adoption. – Acts 2:38; 5:32; Rom. 8:15
         2. By laying on of the Apostle's hands. – Acts 8:14-19; 19:1-7
   3. Those filled with the Holy Spirit.
      a. Apostles. – Acts 2:4
      b. Peter. – Acts 4:8
      c. All present. – Acts 4:31
      d. The seven. – Acts 6:3
      e. Stephen. – Acts 6:5, 10; 7:55
      f. Saul. – Acts 9:17
      g. Barnabas. – Acts 11:24
      h. Paul. – Acts 13:9
      i. Disciples. – Acts 13:52
   4. Power of the Holy Spirit.
      a. The written Word. – Acts 1:16; 4:25; 28:25
      b. Holy Spirit lied to, Acts 5:3, tested Acts 5:9, and resisted Acts 7:51
      c. Spoke to people. – Acts 8:29, 10:19; 11:12; 13:2; 20:23; 21:11
      d. Holy Spirit directed disciples. – Acts 8:39; 15:28; 16:6-7; 19:21; 21:4

      e. Brought comfort to the churches. – Acts 9:31

      f. Empowered Christ. – Acts 10:38

      g. Prompted prophecy. – Acts 11:28

      h. Selected and sent out missionaries. – Acts 13:2-4

      i. Made men overseers in the church. – Acts 20:28

B. The Church.

    1. Established. – Acts 2:1-41

    2. Devotion of the church. – Acts 2:42-47

    3. Unity of the church. – Acts 4:32

    4. The organization of the church. – Acts 6:1-7; 11:30; 14:23;
       15:2, 4, 6, 22; 16:4; 20:17; 21:18

    5. Worship. – Acts 20:7

    6. Growth. – Acts 2:41, 47; 4:4; 5:14; 6;1, 7; 9:31, 35; 11:21; 16:5;
       21:20

    7. The church is referenced as "the way." – Acts 9:2; 19:9, 23;
       22:4; 24:14, 22

C. Preaching

    1. Peter on Pentecost. – Acts 2:14-40

    2. Stephen before the Sanhedrin. – Acts 7:1-53

    3. Peter at Cornelius' home. – Acts 10:34-43

    4. Paul preaching to the Greek philosophers on Mar's Hill in
       Athens. – Acts 17:22-31

D. Evangelism

    1. The answer some many ask is given in Acts, "What must I do to
       be saved?" – Acts 2:37; 16:30; 22:10

    2. Conversions listed in Acts.

      a. Jews on Pentecost. – Acts 2:14-41

      b. Samaritans. –Acts 8:5-13

      c. Ethiopian Eunuch. – Acts 8:26-40

      d. Saul. – Acts chapter 9, 22, 26

      e. Cornelius and his household. Acts chapter 10

      f. Lydia and her household. – Acts 16:12-15

     g. Philippian jailor and his household. – Acts 16:19-34

     h. Corinthians. – Acts 18:1-8

Christ Revealed

A. Jesus. – Acts 1:1; 8:35; 9:5 (70 times)

B. Jesus Christ the Nazarene. – Acts 2:22; 3:6; 4:10; 6:14; 10:38; 22:8; 26:9; (cf. 24:5)

C. Holy One. – Acts 2:27; 13:35

D. Lord. – Acts 2:25, 34, 36; 4:26; 9:5; 10:36; 18:8; 22:10

E. Christ. – Acts 2:36; 3:18, 20; 4:26; 5:42; 8:5; 9:22; 17:3; 18:5, 28; 26:23

F. Jesus Christ. – Acts 2:38; 8:12; 9:34; 10:36, 48; 16:18

G. Servant Jesus. – Acts 3:13, 26; 4:27, 30

H. Holy and Righteous One. – Acts 3:14

I. Prince of Life – Acts 3:15

J. Prophet. – Acts 3:22-23; 7:37

K. Stone. – Acts 4:11

L. Lord Jesus. – Acts 4:33; 7:59; 9:17; 11:20; 15:11; 16:31; 19:13; 20:24

M. Prince and Savior. – Acts 5:31

N. Righteous One. – Acts 7:52; 22:14

O. Son of God. – Acts 9:20

P. One who has been appointed by God as Judge of the living and the dead. – Acts 10:42

Q. Lord Jesus Christ. – Acts 11:17; 15:26; 28:31

R. Savior. – Acts 13:23

S. My Son. – Acts 13:33; (cf. Ps. 2:7)

T. Man. – Acts 17:31

Romans

Summation

The Roman letter was written to the church in Rome, Rom. 1:1, 7, 15, by the Apostle Paul. Paul very much wanted to visit the church in Rome, and share the gospel with the people of Rome, Rom. 1:11-16, but he also desired to go on beyond Rome to share the gospel, Rom. 15:24. The scheme of redemption from its beginning to its end is revealed by Paul in the book of Romans and he declares boldly that the gospel is the "… power of God unto salvation…" (Rom. 1:16). While declaring the gospel in his letter Paul also lays out precisely the doctrines of the Christian faith: condemnation, justification, sanctification, glorification, and consecration. Paul wrote the letter from Corinth around 58 A.D., and it was delivered to the church in Rome by a godly woman named Phoebe, Rom. 16:1, 23.

Breakdown

A. Condemnation. – Rom. 1:1-3:20

B. Justification. – Rom. 3:21-5:21

C. Sanctification. – Rom. 6:1-8:13

D. Glorification. – Rom. 8:14-39

E. Problem of the Jews. – rom. 9:1-11:36

F. Consecration. – Rom. 12:1-16:27

Pivotal Word – Righteousness

Righteousness is a pivotal word in Romans, used 35 times, it is also the major theme. Righteousness is an attribute of God, Rom. 3:25, and is given by God to man on the basis of faith in Christ, Rom. 3:22, 26; 4:3-5; 10:4; (cf. Phil. 3:9). Righteousness is not gained by keeping the law, Rom. 3:21, nor is it gained by one's self-made righteousness, Rom. 10:3. A righteous person is one who is right with God and who lives right as a result. Righteousness carries with it the idea of justified, (19 times), innocent, cleared of guilt. The question of Romans is, "How can a righteous God save unrighteous man and maintain His holiness and justice?" The answer is: through Christ, Rom. 3:21-26.

<u>Important Verses</u>

<u>Rom. 1:16-17</u> – The theme of Romans.

<u>Rom. 2:16</u> – The standard of judgment.

<u>Rom. 3:23-24</u> – "… all have sinned … justified freely…"

<u>Rom. 4:7-8</u> – The blessedness of forgiveness. (cf. Ps. 32:1-2)

<u>Rom. 5:18</u> – Justification resulted from Christ's death.

<u>Rom. 6:3-4</u> – Baptism is a burial.

<u>Rom. 7:24-25</u> – Christ sets man free!

<u>Rom. 8:28</u> – The providence of God.

<u>Rom. 9:32</u> – The Jews stumbled over Christ.

<u>Rom. 10:9-10</u> – Confession from the believing heart.

<u>Rom. 11:22</u> – The kindness and the severity of God.

<u>Rom. 12:1-2</u> – "… present your bodies a living sacrifice…"

<u>Rom. 13:7</u> – "Render therefore to all their dues…"

<u>Rom. 14:7-8</u> – Whether we live or die, we are the Lord's.

<u>Rom. 15:1</u> – The strong and weak brother.

<u>Rom. 16:25-27</u> – The obedience of faith.

<u>Major Themes</u>

Righteousness of God

A. Righteousness of God is revealed. – Rom. 1:16-17
   1. Revealed in the gospel. – Rom. 1:16
   2. The response from man. The just live by faith. – Rom. 1:17;
      Hab. 2:4; Gal. 3:11; Heb. 10:38; (cf. Rom. 16:26)

B. God's righteousness is needed. – Rom. 3:10, 23
   1. Jews and Greeks are under sin. – Rom. 3:9
   2. All are under sin and in need of a savior. – Rom. 3:19, 23

C. God demonstrates His righteousness. – Rom. 3:21-26
   1. Shown at Calvary when Christ was displayed publicly as a
      propitiation through faith in His blood. – Rom. 3:25; I John 2:2;
      4:10; Heb. 2:17
   2. God the Just offered Christ the Justifier that man might become
      the justified.

D. God's righteousness reckoned. Rom. 4:3, 9, 22; (cf. Gen. 15:6)
   1. Abraham was "reckoned" righteous – imputed, imparted,
      bestowed, to charge to one's account.
   2. Abraham's righteousness was:
      a. Not by works. – Rom. 4:1-8
      b. Not by circumcision. – Rom. 4:9-12
      c. Not by the Law. – Rom. 4:13-15
      d. By faith. – Rom. 4:16-22
   3. This was written "for our sake." – Rom. 4:23-25

E. God's righteousness given. – Rom. 5:12-21
   1. Sin and death reigned under Adam. – Rom. 5:12-14
   2. Grace and life reign under Christ. – Rom. 5:15-21

F. God's righteousness appropriated. – Rom. 6:3-4, 13, 16-18
   1. Appropriated at baptism. – Rom. 6:3-4

2. Instruments of righteousness. – Rom. 6:13

3. Slaves of righteousness. – Rom. 6:16-18

G. God's righteousness confirmed.
   1. Justified in Christ. – Rom. 5:1, 9
   2. United with Christ. – Rom. 6:5
   3. Married to Christ. - Rom. 7:4, 24-25
   4. Saved in Christ. – Rom. 8:1, 37-39

H. God's righteousness is practiced.
   1. In the church. – Rom. 12:1-21
   2. In the world. – Rom. 13:1-14
   3. In conscience. – Rom. 14:1-23
   4. In brotherly relationships. – Rom. 5:1-16:27

Christ Revealed

1. Christ Jesus. – Rom. 1:1; 2:16; 6:3, 11; 8:1, 2, 11, 34; 15:16, 17; 16:3

2. His Son. – Rom. 1:3, 4, 9; 5:10; 8:3, 29, 32

3. Seed of David. - Rom. 1:3; (cf. II Sam. 7:12-16)

4. Jesus Christ. – Rom. 1:6; 16:25, 27

5. Lord Jesus Christ. – Rom. 1:7; 5:1, 11; 13:14; 14:14; 15:30; 16:18, 20, 24

6. Justifier. – Rom. 3:25-26

7. Jesus our Lord. – Rom. 4:24; 5:21

8. Christ. – Rom. 5:6, 8; 6:4; 8:9, 17, 35; 9:1, 3, 5; 10:4, 6, 7, 17; 12:5; 14:9, 18; 15:3, 7, 8, 18, 19, 20, 29; 16:5, 7, 9, 10, 16

9. Second Adam. – Rom. 5:14; (cf. I Cor. 15:45)

10. Man, Jesus Christ. – Rom. 5:15

11. The One, Jesus Christ. – Rom. 5:17, 19

12. Christ Jesus our Lord. – Rom. 6:23; 7:25; 8:39

13. Husband. – Rom. 7:4

14. The Stumbling stone. – Rom. 9:32-33; (cf. Isa. 28:16)

15. Lord. – Rom. 10:9, 12, 13; 14:4, 6, 8, 9; 16:2, 8, 11, 12, 13, 22

16. The Deliverer. – Rom. 11:26; (cf. Isa. 59:20-21)

17. The Root of Jesse. – Rom. 15:12; (cf. Isa. 11:10)

I Corinthians

Summation

    Corinth was a Roman colony and the capital of Achaia not to mention a leading commercial city of the Mediterranean world. The Temple of Aphrodite (Venus) was located on the Acro-Corinth and it boasted of having 1,000 temple prostitutes. Needless to say immorality was widespread in Corinth, so much so that the term "Corinthian" was often used to describe the vilest kind of behavior. Paul established the Corinthian church amidst this vile worldly climate on his second missionary journey, Acts 18:1-17. Some consider the possibility that Paul wrote as many as four letters to the Corinthians, look at I Cor. 5:9ff for the possibility of a lost letter and II Cor. 12:14; 13:1-2 for a possible third letter. There are two possibilities for the purpose of writing I Corinthians. The first is centered on some information that Paul received from a family in Corinth, I Cor. 1:11 and the second is centered on some questions the Corinthian church sent to Paul probably at the hands of Stephanas, Fortunatus and Achaicus, I Cor. 16:15-18; (cf. "now concerning" in I Cor. 7:1, 25; 8:1; 12:1; 16:1, 12). The possible date for I Corinthians is 54-55 A.D. from the city of Ephesus, I Cor. 16:8, and the letter was most likely delivered by Timothy, I Cor. 4:17; 16:10.

Breakdown

A. Problems in the Corinthian church Paul became aware of.
    1. Divisions. – I Cor. 1:1-4:21
    2. Sexual immorality. – I Cor. 5:1-13
    3. Litigation. – I Cor. 6:1-11
    4. Defilement. – I Cor. 6:12-20

B. Problems the Corinthian church wrote to Paul about.
    1. Marriage, celibacy, divorce, and remarriage. – I Cor. 7:1-16:24
    2. Conscience. – I Cor. 8:1-10:33
    3. Subjection and the Lord's Supper. – I Cor. 11:1-34

4. Spiritual gifts. – I Cor. 12:1-14:40

5. Resurrection. – I Cor. 15:1-58

6. Collection. – I Cor. 16:1-24

Pivotal Word – Body

The word "body" appears some 43 times in I Corinthians. Paul uses the word in two distinct ways: First Paul uses it to refer to the human body which was never to be used for immorality, I Cor. 6:13-18, but instead for the glory of God because it is the temple or sanctuary of the Holy Spirit, I Cor. 6:19-20. Secondly Paul uses the word "body" to refer to the church 16 times, (cf. 12:12-27), which is the spiritual body of Christ made up of many "members."

Important Verses

I Cor. 1:18 – "... preaching of the cross... power of God."

I Cor. 2:2 – "For I determined not to know any thing among you, save Jesus Christ, and Him crucified."

I Cor. 3:16-17 – "Know ye not that ye are the temple of God ..."

I Cor. 4:2 – "Moreover it is required in stewards, that a man be found faithful."

I Cor. 5:6 – "... Know ye not that a little leaven leaveneth the whole lump?"

I Cor. 6:19-20 – "... Know ye not that your body is the temple of the Holy Ghost which is in you..."

I Cor. 7:7 – "... But every man hath his proper gift of God, one after this manner, and another after that."

I Cor. 8:12 – "But when ye sin so against the brethren, and wound their weak conscience, ye sin against Christ."

I Cor. 9:9 – "… thou shalt not muzzle the mouth of the ox that treadeth out the corn…"

I Cor. 10:13 – "There hath no temptation taken you but such as is common to man…"

I Cor. 11:23-26 – The institution of the Lord's Supper.

I Cor. 12:12-13 – The church is one body made up of many members.

I Cor. 13:13 – "And now abideth faith, hope, charity, these three; but the greatest of these is charity."

I Cor. 14:33 – "For God is not the author of confusion, but of peace, as in all churches of the saints."

I Cor. 15:57-58 – Victory in Christ motivates faithful living.

I Cor. 16:1-2 – The collection for the saints.

Major Themes

A. Corinth a worldly place, a worldly church. (signs of immorality)
    1. No spiritual appetite. – I Cor. 2:12-16
    2. Divisions, quarrels, strife, jealousy, party spirit. – I Cor. 1:10-13; 3:3-4; 11:18-19; 12:25
    3. Immaturity. – I Cor. 3:1-2
    4. Immorality. – I Cor. 5:1-13; 6:9-11; 13-18
    5. Law suits among the brethren. – I Cor. 6:1-8
    6. Pride, arrogance, conceit. – I Cor. 4:6, 18-21; 8:1; 13:4
    7. Marital problems. – I Cor. 7:1-40
    8. Lack of Love. – I Cor. 13:1-13
    9. Confusion and disorder in worship over spiritual gifts. – I Cor. 14:12-26
    10. Denial of the resurrection. – I Cor. 15:12

B. The Spiritual church. (signs of spirituality)
    1. An appreciation, appraisal, and understanding of spiritual things.

       – I Cor. 2:12-16

  2. Unity and maturity. – I Cor. 1:10; 3:2

  3. Understanding that the body, I Cor. 3:16-17, and I Cor. 6:19-20, is the temple of the Holy Spirit.

  4. Discipline for the wicked in the church. – I Cor. 5:6-7, 12-13

  5. Devotion to the Lord is essential no matter what the marital status is, (married, single, widowed, separated, and divorced). – I Cor. 7:7, 17, 32, 35

  6. As a Christian, freedom and liberty is used for the benefit of all. – I Cor. 10:23-24

  7. Observing the Lord's Supper correctly. – I Cor. 11:17-29

  8. Realizing the Lordship of Christ. – I Cor. 8:6; 12:3

  9. Proper function and involvement in the body. – I Cor. 12:12-27

  10. Supremacy of love. – I Cor. 13:1-13

  11. Edification instead of confusion in the assembly. – I Cor. 14:4, 5, 12, 17, 26

  12. Firm convictions about the gospel. – I Cor. 15:1-4 (received, stand, saved, hold fast)

  13. Strong belief in the resurrection. – I Cor. 15:20-22

  14. Steadfast service and faithfulness. – I Cor. 15:58; 16:13-14

C. Comparison of Corinth to the church of today.

  1. Like today Corinth was plagued with many problems sinful nature such as: moral, ethical, social, doctrinal.

  2. With every problem a solution was found to be a spiritual one.

  3. I Corinthians was addressed to the whole church though there were problems of diversity of beliefs, different levels of maturity and other things plaguing the congregation, I Cor. 1:2.

  4. As today the church of Corinth existed for sinners who needed grace and forgiveness of God.
"And such were some of you…"– I Cor. 6:11

    a. You were washed (baptized). – Acts 18:8; 22:16

    b. You were sanctified (set apart). – I Cor. 1:2, 30

    c. You were justified (cleared of guilt). – Rom. 3:24

  5. The goal of every church is to overcome carnality and worldliness with spirituality and maturity.

Christ Revealed

1. Jesus Christ. – I Cor. 1:1, 2:1

2. Christ Jesus. – I Cor. 1:2, 4; 4:15; 16:24

3. Lord Jesus Christ. – I Cor. 1:2, 3, 7, 8, 10; 6:11; 15:57

4. Christ. – I Cor. 1:6, 12, 13, 17, 23; 2:16; 3:1, 23; 4:1, 10, 15, 17; 6:15; 8:11, 12; 9:12, 21; 10:16; 11:1, 3; 12:12; 15:3, 12-20, 22 23 (total of 59 times)

5. His Son. – I Cor. 1L9; 15:28

6. Jesus Christ our Lord. – I Cor. 1:9

7. Christ the power of God and the wisdom of God. – I Cor.1:24

8. Fourfold description of Christ: – I Cor. 1:30
   a. Wisdom from God. – I Cor. 1:24
   b. Righteousness. – II Cor. 5:21; Phil. 3:9
   c. Sanctification. – I Cor. 1:2; 6:11; I Thess. 5:23
   d. Redemption. – Rom. 3:24; Eph. 1:7, 14; Col. 1:14

9. Lord (Kurios – Lord, master). – I Cor. 1:31; 3:5; 4:4, 5, 19; 6:13, 14, 17; 7:10, 12, 17, 22, 25, 32, 34, 35, 39; 8:6; 9:1, 5, 14; 10:9, 21, 22, 26; 11:11, 20, 23, 26, 27; 12:3, 5; 14:21, 37; 15:58; 16:10, 19, 22 (total of 61 times)

10. Foundation. – I Cor. 3:11

11. Lord Jesus. – I Cor. 5:4, 5; 10:23; 16:23

12. Christ our Passover. – I Cor. 5:7; Mark 14:12; I Pet. 1:19

13. Christ the rock. – I Cor. 10:4; (cf. Ex. 17:6; Num. 20:11; Ps. 78:15)

14. Christ's body, the church. – I Cor. 12:12, 27

15. Christ the first fruits (first to be resurrected). – I Cor. 15:23

16. Christ the one who reigns over all. – I Cor. 15:24-28

17. Christ Jesus our Lord. – I Cor. 15:31

18. The last Adam. – I Cor. 15:45

II Corinthians

Summation

Paul writes II Corinthians in a very personal and defensive manner and yet he lovingly bears his soul as he defends his ministry, vindicates his character and validates his authority as an apostle. After the Corinthian church had received I Corinthians and a possible second sorrowful letter, II Cor. 2:4, 9; 7:8, 12, from Paul, some of the brethren, maybe a majority, had repented of their sins, II Cor. 2:5-11; 7:8-12, while others still needed to repent, II Cor. 12:19-21. There had been some who voiced serious criticisms and accusations against Paul, II Cor. 10:10-11 prompting the writing of II Corinthians. Paul wrote the letter some time about 54-55 A.D. while in Macedonia, possibly Philippi, II Cor. 2:13; 7:5-7; 8:1; 9:2-4. Titus possibly delivered the letter to Corinth, II Cor. 7:6, 13-15; 8:6, 16-17; 12:18.

Breakdown

A. Paul defends his ministry. – II Cor. 1:1-7:16
    1. His comfort. – II Cor. 1:1-24
    2. His triumph. – II Cor. 2:1-17
    3. His confidence. – II Cor. 3:1-18
    4. His commitment. – II Cor. 4:1-18
    5. His motivation. – II Cor. 5:1-21
    6. His appeal. – II Cor. 6:1-18
    7. His joy. – II Cor. 7:1-16

B. The collection for the Saints. – II Cor. 8:1-9:15
    1. Example of liberality, the Macedonians. – II Cor. 8:1-6
    2. Motives for liberality. – II Cor. 8:7-16
    3. Liberality in ministry. – II Cor. 8:16-9:5
    4. Encouragement for liberality. – II Cor. 9:6-15

C. His apostleship vindicated. – II Cor. 10:1-13:14
    1. His authority. – II Cor. 101-18

195

2. His credentials. – II Cor. 11:1-33
3. His strength. – II Cor. 12:1-21
4. His plans and final exhortations. – II Cor. 13:1-14

Pivotal Word – Boast

There is some form of the word "boast" found 24 times in II Corinthians. To boast means to "exult, glory or to take pride in." Paul is not guilty of being boastful about himself, his achievements, or his accomplishments, II Cor. 12:5, as some had wrongly accused him of being, II Cor. 10:8, 15. Paul had however boasted about the Corinthians, II Cor. 7:4, 14; 8:24; 9:2-3, about his sufferings (in jest or foolishness, II Cor. 11:16-18, about his weaknesses, II Cor. 11:30; 12:9, and about his confidence in the Lord, II Cor. 10:17; (cf. I Cor. 1:31).

Important Verses

II Cor. 1:21-22 – "Who hath also sealed us, and given the earnest of the Spirit in our hearts."

II Cor. 2:14 – "Now thanks be unto God, which always causeth us to triumph in Christ…"

II Cor. 3:17 – "Now the Lord is that Spirit: and where the Spirit of the Lord is, there is liberty."

II Cor. 4:16-18 – The temporal and the eternal.

II Cor. 5:21 – The gospel in one verse!

II Cor. 6:14 – "Be ye not unequally yoked together with unbelievers: …"

II Cor. 7:9-10 – Godly sorrow leads to repentance.

II Cor. 8:9 – The example of Jesus in giving.

II Cor. 9:6-8 – Principles of giving.

II Cor. 10:17 – "But he that glorieth, let him glory in the Lord."

II Cor. 11:28 – "Beside those things that are without, that which cometh upon me daily, the care of all the churches."

II Cor. 12:9 – "… My grace is sufficient for thee: for my strength is make perfect in weakness."

II Cor. 13:5 – "Examine yourselves, whether ye be in the faith; prove your own selves…"

Major Themes

A. Accusations against Paul as an Apostle.
   1. Selling the word of God. – II Cor. 2:17; (cf. 4:2; 11:7-9; 12:13)
   2. Paul possessed no credentials. – II Cor. 3:1
   3. Embezzlement of funds entrusted to him. – II Cor. 8:20-23
   4. Paul was cowardly, II Cor. 10:1, fleshly, II Cor. 10:2, boastful, II Cor. 10:8, 15, and deceitful, II Cor. 12:16.
   5. Paul was weighty and strong in his letters, but unimpressive and weak in his personal presence and contemptible in his speech. II Cor. 10:10-11
   6. Paul was not a true apostle, therefore unqualified and unauthoritative in his teaching. – II Cor. 11:5; 12:11-12; 13:3
   7. Paul's accusers were:
      a. False apostles. – II Cor. 11:13
      b. Haughty and domineering personalities. – II Cor. 11:20
      c. Judaizing teachers. – II Cor. 11:23

B. The hardships Paul suffered as an Apostle.
   1. What he suffered:
      a. Despair. – II Cor. 1:8-10
      b. Difficulties. – II Cor. 4:8-10; 12:10
      c. Distresses. – II Cor. 6:3-10
      d. Dangers. – II Cor. 11:22-28
   2. The reason for his suffering.
      a. He did not want the ministry discredited. – II Cor. 6:3

b. He loved the church. – II Cor. 11:11; 12:15

c. He was a true apostle. – II Cor. 12:12; (cf. I Cor. 9:1-2)

d. For Christ's sake. – II Cor. 4:5; 12:10

C. Paul took comfort in Christ.

1. Comfort (19 times) – "a calling to one's side, encouragement."

2. Through Christ one can find abundant comfort. – II Cor. 1:3-7

3. Comfort is derived from fellowship in Christ. – II Cor. 7:5-7

4. Those who are comforted comfort the comfortless. – II Cor. 1:4

D. Principles of giving.

Note: II Cor. 8 and 9 contain the most concise and comprehensive teaching on giving found anywhere in the New Testament.

1. Giving liberally reaps a harvest. – II Cor. 9:6

2. Liberality comes from the heart. – II Cor. 9:7

3. Giving liberally is rewarded of God. – II Cor. 9:7-11

a. God loves the cheerful giver. – II Cor. 9:7

b. God compensates the liberal giver. – II Cor. 9:8-9

c. God supplies the liberal giver. – II Cor. 9:10

d. God enriches the liberal giver. – II Cor. 9:11

4. Giving liberally has many fringe benefits. – II Cor. 9:12-14

5. Giving liberally is motivated and transcended by God's indescribable gift. – II Cor. 9:15; (cf. II Cor. 8:9)

E. A fivefold final exhortation by Paul. – II Cor. 13:11

1. Rejoice (farewell, we wish you all joy). – Phil. 4:4

2. Be made complete (perfect, mature, in order). – II Cor. 13:9

3. Be comforted (take courage). – II Cor.1:3-7

4. Be like-minded (of one mind, agree together). – II Cor. 1:10

5. Live in peace (keep peace among you). – Rom. 12:18; Eph. 4:3

F. A threefold benediction by Paul. – II Cor. 13:14

This benediction affirms the existence of three distinct, yet equal, personalities in the Godhead, (cf. Matt. 28:19).

1. The grace of the Lord Jesus Christ. – II Cor. 8:9; Rom. 16:20

2. The love of God. – Rom. 5:5; 8:39; Jude 21

3. The fellowship of the Holy Spirit. – Phil. 2:1

<u>Christ Revealed</u>

1. Christ Jesus. – II Cor. 1:1, 19; 4:5

2. Lord Jesus Christ. – II Cor. 1:2, 3; 8:9; 13:14

3. Christ. – II Cor. 1:5, 21; 2:10, 12, 14, 15, 17; 3:3, 4, 14; 4:4, 6; 5:10, 14, 16-20; 6:15; 8:23; 10:1, 5, 7, 14; 11:2, 3, 10, 13, 23; 12:2, 9-10, 19; 13:3 (44 total times)

4. Lord Jesus. – II Cor. 1:14; 4:14; 11:31

5. Son of God. – II Cor. 1:19

6. Lord. – II Cor. 2:12; 3:17; 4:5; 5:6, 8, 11; 8, 19, 21; 10:8, 17, 18; 11:17; 12:8; 13:10 (30 total times)

7. The Lord is the Spirit. – II Cor. 3:17-18

8. Jesus. – II Cor. 4:5, 10, 11, 14; 11:4

9. Indescribable Gift. – II Cor. 9:15; (cf. Rom. 5:15-17)

10. Jesus Christ. – II Cor. 13:4-5

Galatians

The book of Galatians was most likely written to the churches of Antioch, Lystra, Derbe, and Iconium that are located in southern Galatia. A historical account of Paul's association with the churches of southern Galatia is found in Acts chapters 13, 14 and 16:1-7. Assuming that this letter was written prior to the Jerusalem council mentioned in Acts chapter 15, it would make it Paul's earliest letter possibly written around 49 to 50 A.D. A strong argument for the early date of the writing of this letter stems from the fact that Paul does not mention the decision of the Jerusalem council. The council's decision would have had strong bearing on the issue of the so called Judaizers in Galatia. Judaizers were working to discredit Paul's authority and message and they were perverting the gospel by insisting on continued observance of portions of the Law of Moses. In Paul's letter to the Galatians he insists that there is only one way to salvation and that is through justification by faith in Christ, Gal. 2:16. Paul proclaims Christians are set free, the gospel brings liberation, Gal. 5:1.

Breakdown

A. The Gospel authenticated: The question of authority. (personal)
   Gal. 1:1-2:21
   1. The origin of the gospel. – Gal. 1:1-24
   2. The gospel confirmed. – Gal. 2:1-21

B. The gospel defended: the question of salvation (doctrinal).
   Gal. 3:1-4:31
   1. The faith of the gospel. – Gal. 3:1-29
   2. The superiority of the gospel. – Gal. 4:1-31

C. The gospel applied: The question of holiness (practical).
   Gal. 5:1-6:18

1. The freedom of the gospel. – Gal. 5:1-26
2. The application of the gospel. – Gal. 6:1-18

Pivotal Word – Gospel

The gospel spoken of in Galatians (total of 11 times), Gal. 1:6, 7, 8, 9, 11; 2:2, 5, 7, 14; 3:8; 4:13, is the gospel preached by Paul. Paul preached the gospel of Christ, Gal. 1:7, the only gospel, Gal. 1:8, revealed by Jesus Christ, Gal. 1:11-12, endorsed by other apostles, Gal. 2:2, 7-10 and even preached "beforehand to Abraham," Gal. 3:8. The gospel is essentially the "good news" of what Christ has done for man. Christ gave Himself for our sins, Gal. 1:4; Christ loved us and gave Himself for us, Gal. 2:20; Christ became a curse for us, Gal. 3:13; and Christ came at the right time and for the right reason, redemption, Gal. 4:4-5.

Important Verses

Gal. 1:8 – There is only one gospel.

Gal. 2:16 – "… by the faith of Jesus Christ..."

Gal. 3:26-28 – "… For as many of you as have been baptized into Christ have put on Christ…"

Gal. 4:6-7 – "And because ye are sons, God hath sent forth the Spirit of his Son into your hearts, crying, Abba, father…"

Gal. 5:1 – "Stand fast therefore in the liberty wherewith Christ hath made us free…"

Gal. 6:1 – The ministry of restoration.

Major Themes

A. Evidence of false teachers.
    1. Disturb the brethren. – Gal. 1:7; 5:7, 10, 12
    2. Distort the gospel. – Gal. 1:7

3. Deny liberty in Christ. – Gal. 2:4; 4:9; 5:1
4. Deceive the brethren. – Gal. 3:1

B. Justification by faith. – Gal. 2:16; 3:24
   1. Faith unites us with God's people of the past. – Gal. 3:7, 29
   2. Faith unites us with God's people of the present. – Gal. 3:26, 28
   3. Faith unites us with Christ through baptism. – Gal. 3:27
   4. Faith in Christ is the identifying mark of the family of God.
      – Gal. 6:10
   5. Faith has always been the principle by which God's people have
      lived. – Gal. 3:11; (cf. Hab. 2:4; Rom. 1:17; Heb. 10:38)

C. Freedom in Christ. – Gal. 5:1, 13; (cf. I Pet. 2:16)
   1. Christian freedom is not:
      a. Freedom to indulge in the flesh. – Gal. 5:13
      b. Freedom to exploit people. – Gal. 5:14
      c. Freedom from all restraint, control, or love. – Gal. 5:15
   2. Freedom in Christ is:
      a. Freedom from the principle of works of merit. – Gal. 2:16;
         3:10-12
      b. Freedom from the curse of the Law. – Gal. 3:21, 24
      c. Freedom from the spiritual impotency of the Law.
         – Gal. 3:21, 24
      d. Freedom from slavery and bondage under the Law.
         – Gal. 4:9; 5:1

D. Holiness and the Holy Spirit.
   1. Reception of the spirit. – Gal. 3:2-5; Acts 2:38; Rom. 8:9-11
   2. The promise of the Spirit. – Gal. 3:14; (cf. Eph. 1:13)
   3. Spirit of His Son into our hearts. – Gal. 4:5-7; Rom. 5:5
   4. Through the Spirit we wait. – Gal. 5:5
   5. Walking in the Spirit. – Gal. 5:16
   6. To be led by the Spirit. – Gal. 5:18
   7. The fruit of the Spirit. – Gal. 5:22-23
   8. Living by the Spirit. – Gal. 5:25
   9. Sow to the Spirit. – Gal. 6:8

E. The Cross and the Christian.
1. The Christian is crucified with Christ. – Gal. 2:20
2. The cross becomes a present reality through preaching.
   – Gal. 3:1; (cf. I Cor. 2:2)
3. The cross is not a stumbling-block to believers. – Gal. 5:11;
   I Cor. 1:28
4. The passions and desires of the flesh are crucified. – Gal. 5:24
5. The Christian is willing to be persecuted for the cross of Christ.
   – Gal. 6:12
6. The Christian boasts only in the cross of Christ. – Gal. 6:14

Christ Revealed

1. Jesus Christ. – Gal. 1:1, 12; 3:1, 22

2. Lord Jesus Christ. – Gal. 1:3; 6:14, 18

3. Sacrifice for sins. – Gal. 1:4; 2:20

4. Christ. – Gal. 1:6, 7, 10, 22; 2:16, 17, 20, 21; 3:13, 24, 29; 4:19;
   5:1, 2, 4; 6:2, 12

5. His Son. – Gal. 1:16; 4:4, 6

6. Lord. – Gal. 1:19; 5:10

7. Christ Jesus. – Gal. 2:4, 16; 3:14, 26, 28; 4:14; 5:6, 24

8. Son of God. – Gal. 2:20

9. Redeemer. – Gal. 3:13; 4:5

10. Seed. – Gal. 3:16

11. Jesus. – Gal. 6:17

Ephesians

Summation

In the first century world Ephesus was considered a major commercial city. Ephesus was the home of the legendary Temple of Diana. Paul briefly visited Ephesus on his second missionary journey leaving Priscilla and Aquila there, Acts 18:18-19. On his third missionary journey Paul returned to Ephesus and conducted a profitable ministry for three years, Acts 18:24-19:41; 20:31. When Paul met with the elders from the Ephesian church in Miletus, Acts 20:17-38, he expressed his love for the Ephesian church. Within a short span of a few decades the Ephesian church had left her "first love", Eph. 6:24; (cf. Rev. 2:1-7). Paul wrote a series of letters known as the "Prison Letters" and Ephesians is part of them, Ephesians, Philippians, Colossians and Philemon. These letters were written during Paul's first Roman imprisonment sometime around 60-61 A.D., Eph. 3:1; 4:1; 6:20; Acts 28:30. Paul wrote the Ephesian letter to emphasize the spiritual blessings and riches available to the Christian because of God's eternal purpose through Christ and His church, Eph. 1:3; 3:11. Tychicus delivered the letter possibly for the purpose of being circulated among other churches in Asia Minor, Eph. 6:21-22; Col. 4:7-9, 16.

Breakdown

A. The church is called. – Eph. 1:1-3:21
   1. Members are called by the gospel. – Eph.1:1-23
   2. They are called from death to life. – Eph. 2:1-22
   3. They are called to the riches of Christ. – Eph. 3:1-21

B. How the church should conduct itself. – Eph.4:1-6:9
   1. In unity. – Eph. 4:1-16
   2. In purity. – Eph. 4:17-32
   3. In love. – Eph. 5:1-6
   4. In light. – Eph. 5:7-21

5. In family. – Eph. 5:22-6:4

6. As a slave to the master. – Eph. 6:5-9

C. The church dealing with conflict.

   1. The adversary of the Christian. – Eph. 6:10-24

   2. The armor of the Christian. – Eph. 6:10-12

   3. The alertness of the Christian. – Eph. 6:18-20

Pivotal Word – In Christ

The prepositional phrase "in Christ", "In Christ Jesus", "in the Lord", or "in Him" is found some twenty-two times in Ephesians, Eph. 1:1, 3, 4, 7, 10, 13, 20; 2:6, 7, 10, 13; 3:6, 11, 12, 21; 4:21, 32; 5:8; 6:1, 10, 21. "In Christ" describes the Christian's position, privileges, possibilities, and power! The opposite of being "in Christ" is being "separate from Christ" and thus lost, Eph. 2:12-13.

Important Verses

Eph. 1:3 – All spiritual blessings are in Christ.

Eph. 2:8-10 – The gift of Salvation by grace through faith not by works for it is the gift of God, we are created to walk in good works.

Eph. 3:20-21 – The ability of our great and powerful God.

Eph. 4:11-13 – The building up of the body of Christ.

Eph. 5:25 – "Husbands, love your wives, even as Christ also loved the church, and gave himself for it;"

Eph. 6:1-4 – Children, parents, and fathers.

Eph. 6:10 – Be strong in the Lord.

Eph. 6:11-18 – The armor of God.

Eph. 6:18 – Pray for all saints.

Major Themes

A. Spiritual blessings in Christ. – Eph. 1:3
   1. Our election. – Eph. 1:4; 2:10
   2. Our adoption. – Eph. 1:5
   3. Our redemption. – Eph. 1:7, 14
   4. Our salvation. – Eph. 1:13; 2:8-9

B. Heavenly places.
   1. Where spiritual blessings are. – Eph. 1:3
   2. Where Christ is right now. – Eph. 1:20
   3. Where the Christian is seated with Christ. – Eph. 2:6
   4. Where the manifold wisdom of God is to be made known.
      – Eph. 3:10
   5. Where spiritual forces of wickedness are to be struggled with.
      – Eph. 6:12

C. The body of Christ.
   1. The head of the body. – Eph. 1:22-23; 4:5; 5:23
   2. The kinship of the body. – Eph. 2:19; Gal. 6:10
   3. The discipleship of the body. – Eph. 4:12; Luke 14:25-33
   4. The fellowship of the body. – Eph. 4:16; Rom. 12:4-8
   5. The savior of the body. Eph. 5:23; Acts 4:12
   6. The membership of the body. – Eph. 5:30; I Cor. 12:27

D. The unity of the Spirit. – Eph. 4:1-6
   God's pattern for unity:
   1. One body. – Eph. 4:4; 2:16; I Cor. 12:12
   2. One Spirit. – Eph. 4:4; 2:18; I Cor. 12:13
   3. One hope. – Eph. 4:4; 1:18; Rom. 8:24
   4. One Lord. – Eph. 4:5; 1:19-23; I Cor. 8:6
   5. One faith. – Eph. 4:5; Jude 3
   6. One baptism. – Eph. 4:5; Matt. 28:18-20
   7. One God. – Eph. 4:6; I Cor. 8:6

E. Our daily walk.
   1. Walk in good works. – Eph. 2:10

2. Walk worthily. – Eph. 4:1
3. Walk no longer as the Gentiles walk. – Eph. 4:17
4. Walk in love. – Eph. 5:2
5. Walk as children of light. – Eph. 5:8
6. Walk carefully. – Eph. 5:15

F. The Armor of God. – Eph. 6:10-17
    The armor of God is representative of Christ. To put on Christ is to
    put on the armor of God. – Rom. 6:3-4; Gal. 3:27
    1. Girdle of truth. – John 14:6
    2. Breastplate of righteousness. – II Cor. 5:21
    3. Shoes of the gospel of peace. – Eph. 2:14
    4. Shield of faith. – Gal. 2:20
    5. Helmet of salvation. – Luke 2:30
    6. Sword of the Spirit. – John 1:1, 14

Christ Revealed

1. Christ Jesus. – Eph. 1:1; 2:6, 7, 10, 13, 20; 3:1, 6, 21

2. Lord Jesus Christ. – Eph. 1:2, 3, 17; 5:20; 6:23, 24

3. Christ. – Eph. 1:3, 10, 12, 20; 2:5, 12, 13; 3:4, 8, 17, 19; 4:7, 12,
    13, 15, 20, 32; 5:2, 5, 14, 21, 23, 24, 25, 29, 32; 6:5, 6

4. Jesus Christ. – Eph. 1:5

5. Redeemer. – Eph. 1:7

6. Lord Jesus. – Eph. 1:15

7. Head of the church. – Eph. 1:22-23; 4:15; 5:23

8. Our Peace and Reconciler. – Eph. 2:14-16

9. Cornerstone. – Eph. 2:20; Ps. 118:22; Isa. 28:16; I Pet. 2:6

10. Lord. – Eph. 2:21; 4:1, 5, 17; 5:8, 17, 19, 22; 6:1, 4, 7, 8, 10, 21

11. Christ Jesus our Lord. – Eph. 3:11

12. Son of God. – Eph. 4:13

13. Jesus. – Eph. 4:21

14. Savior. – Eph. 5:23

15. Master. – Eph. 6:9

Philippians

Summation

   Philippi was a Roman colony in Macedonia. The city was founded in 368 B.C. by King Philip, the father of Alexander the Great. Paul visited Philippi on his second missionary journey and established the church there. Lydia and her household, a young slave girl, and the jailor and his household were some of the first converts, Acts 16:9-40; 20:1-2, 6. Around ten years later Paul wrote the Philippian church to thank them for their continued support, Phil. 4:10, 14-18. The scriptures reveal Paul is thankful, Phil. 1:3, hopeful, Phil. 1:6, loving, Phil. 4:1, and joyful, Phil. 4:4. This is Paul's most personal letter to a local church. Paul wrote the letter while a prisoner in Rome, Phil. 1:7, 13, 17; 4:22 and sent it to Philippi by the hand of Epaphorditus, Phil. 2:25-30; 4:18.

Breakdown

A. The Christian's purpose. – Phil. 1:1-30
    1. Peace from God. – Phil. 1:1-2
    2. Participation in the gospel. – Phil. 1:3-11
    3. Progress of the gospel. – Phil. 1:12-20
    4. Purpose of life. – Phil. 1:21-30

B. A pattern for the Christian to follow. – Phil. 2:1-30
    1. The mindset of believers. – Phil. 2:1-4
    2. The mind of Christ. – Phil. 2:5-11
    3. The attitude of believers. – Phil. 2:12-18
    4. The attitude of a servant. – Phil. 2:19-30

C. The Christian's goal. – Phil. 3:1-21
    1. To gain Christ. – Phil. 3:1-8
    2. To be found in Christ. – Phil. 3:9
    3. To know Christ. – Phil. 3:10-16
    4. To see Christ. – Phil. 3:17-21

D. The Christian's advantage. – Phil. 4:1-23
    1. Peace of God – Phil. 4:1-9
    2. Power of Christ. – Phil. 4:10-13
    3. Needs fulfilled. – Phil. 4:14-23

Pivotal Word – Joy or to Rejoice

The word "joy" is used 7 times and the word "rejoice" is used 9 times and describe the tone of the Philippian letter. True joy for Paul was not was not derived from the circumstance that one found themselves in, but in a personal relationship with Christ. "Rejoice in the Lord alway; and again I say, Rejoice." (Phil. 4:4).

Important Verses

Phil. 1:1 – The Philippian church was fully organized: saints, overseers, deacons.

Phil. 1:21 – "For to me to live is Christ, and to die is gain."

Phil. 2:5-11 – Christ is our example in attitude, disposition, and temperament.

Phil. 3:14 – "I press toward the mark for the prize of the high calling of God in Christ Jesus."

Phil. 3:20 – "For our conversation is in heaven; from whence also we look for the Saviour, the Lord Jesus Christ."

Phil. 4:6-8 – Prayer, peace, and proper thinking.

Phil. 4:13 – "I can do all things through Christ which strengtheneth me."

Major Themes

A. The gospel.
    1. Participation in the gospel. – Phil. 1:5
    2. Defense and confirmation of the gospel. – Phil. 1:7

3. Progress of the gospel. – Phil. 1:12
4. Defense of the gospel. – Phil. 1:16
5. Worthy of the gospel. – Phil. 1:27
6. Faith of the gospel. – Phil. 1:27
7. Furtherance of the gospel. – Phil. 2:22
8. Struggle in the gospel. – Phil. 4:3
9. Preaching of the gospel. – Phil. 4:15

B. Our joy in Christ.
1. Joy of prayer. – Phil. 1:4
2. Joy that Christ is preached. – Phil. 1:18
3. Joy in the faith. – Phil. 1:25
4. Joy of seeing Christian unity. – Phil. 2:2
5. Joy of suffering for Christ. – Phil. 2:17-18
6. Joy of seeing a loved one. – Phil. 2:28
7. Joy of Christian hospitality. – Phil. 2:29
8. Joy of being in the Lord. – Phil. 3:1; 4:4
9. Joy of bringing souls to Christ. – Phil. 4:1
10. Joy of helping fellow Christians. – Phil. 4:10

C. The mind of Christ in attitude. – Phil. 2:5-11
1. Denying self – "emptied Himself." – Phil. 2:6-7
2. Self-discipline – "bond-servant." – Phil. 2:7
3. Humility – "humbled Himself." – Phil. 2:8
4. Submission – "obedient." – Phil. 2:8
5. Self-sacrifice – "death on a cross." – Phil. 2:8
6. Abasing ourselves – God highly exalted Him. – Phil. 2:9-11

D. The mind of Christ in knowledge. – Phil. 3:7-11
1. That we might gain Christ. – Phil. 3:7-8
2. That we may be found in Christ. – Phil. 3:9
3. That we may know Christ. – Phil. 3:10-11

E. Our power in Christ. – Phil. 4:1-13
1. We can love. – Phil. 4:1
2. We can live in harmony. – Phil. 4:2

3. We can help. – Phil. 4:3

4. We can rejoice. – Phil. 4:4

5. We can be patient. – Phil. 4:5

6. We can pray. – Phil. 4:6-7

7. We can think. – Phil. 4:8-9

8. We can be content. – Phil. 4:10-12

9. We can do all things through Christ. – Phil. 4:13

Christ Revealed

1. Christ Jesus. – Phil. 1:1, 6, 8, 26; 2:5, 21; 3:3, 12, 14; 4:7, 19, 21

2. Lord Jesus Christ. – Phil. 1:2; 3:20; 4:23

3. Christ. – Phil. 1:10, 13, 15, 17, 18, 20, 23, 27, 29; 2:1, 16, 30; 3:7, 8, 9, 18

4. Jesus Christ. – Phil. 1:11; 2:11

5. Lord. – Phil. 1:14; 2:11, 24, 29; 3:1; 4:1, 2, 4, 5, 10

6. Spirit of Jesus Christ. – Phil 1:19

7. Jesus. – Phil. 2:10

8. Lord Jesus. – Phil. 2:19

9. Christ Jesus my Lord. – Phil 3:8

10. Savior. – Phil. 3:20

Colossians and Philemon

Colossae was a city in Asia Minor and was located some 100 miles east of Ephesus and near Laodicea and Hierapolis, Col. 2:1; 4:13-16. Both Colossians and Philemon are letters grouped with Ephesians and Philippians and recognized as the Prison Letters which Paul wrote around 60-61 A.D. while he was in his first Roman imprisonment, Col. 4:3, 18; Philemon 9, 10, 13, 23. Similar to Romans, Rom. 1:13, Colossians was written to a church Paul had not personally visited, Col. 2:1, even though he hoped to do so, Philemon 22. While Paul was at Ephesus the gospel may have spread to Colossae, Acts 19:10, and Epaphras was someone who was very involved in the establishment of the Colossian congregation, Col. 1:7-8; 4:12-13; Philemon 23. Colossians and Philemon have a great deal in common and are closely associated. They were both written at the same time by Paul, Col. 4:18; Philemon 19, they were both delivered by Tychicus and Onesimus, Col. 4:7-9. Both Philemon and Onesimus lived in Colossae, Col. 4:7-9, and it is a possibility that the church in Colossae met in Philemon's home, Philemon 2. The letter of Colossians focuses primarily on the problem of heresy, a problem that was threatening the all-sufficiency of Christ. Philemon pertains to a personal problem, the request that a slave owner, Philemon, receive back and forgive his runaway slave, Onesimus, who had become a Christian.

Breakdown

Colossians:

A. The preeminence of Christ. – Col. 1:1-29
   1. Christ is first in the church. – Col. 1:1-8
   2. Christ is first in daily life. – Col. 1:9-14
   3. Christ is first in all creation. – Col. 1:15-23
   4. Christ is first in preaching. – Col. 1:24-29

B. Christ is preeminent in doctrine. – Col. 2:1-3:4
    1. Preeminent over Greek Philosophy. – Col. 2:1-10
    2. Preeminent over Jewish Legalism. – Col. 2:11-17
    3. Preeminent over false asceticism. – Col. 2:18-19
    4. Preeminent over earthly materialism. – Col. 3:4

C. Christ is preeminent in ethics. – Col. 3:5-4:18
    1. Ethics of daily life. – Col. 3:5-17
    2. Ethics of family life. – Col. 3:18-4:1
    3. Ethics of prayer life. – Col. 4:2-6
    4. Ethics in church life. – Col. 4:7-18

Philemon:

A. Paul's prayer for Philemon. – Philemon 1-7

B. Paul's petition for Onesimus. – Philemon 8-20

C. Paul's plans for the future. – Philemon 21-25

Pivotal Word – in Colossians and Philemon

Colossians: Christ

Christ is the central theme of the book of Colossians and it stresses living a Christ-centered life. "Christ" is referred to 24 times. Colossians tells us that Christ is full of Deity, Col. 1:19; 2:9, and the Christians is to be full of Christ, Col. 1:28; 2:10. Christ is to occupy a position in our life that places Him first in everything, Col. 1:18, especially in the life of the Christian, Col. 3:3-4, 11.

Philemon: Brother

The affectionate term "brother" is used by Paul 5 times in this short book, Philemon 1, 7, 16, and 20. Paul not only refers to Philemon as his brother but to Onesimus too, Philemon 1, 16. The brotherhood in Christ presented an entirely new association between a master and his slave. In Christ, brothers and sisters can come from all walks of life and be equal.

Important Verses

Col. 1:13-14 – Two Kingdom's contrasted.

Col. 1:18 – The key verse of the book.

Col. 1:27-28 – The goal of Christian living.

Col. 2:9 – "For in him dwelleth all the fullness of the Godhead bodily."

Col. 2:12 – One of two New Testament verses which describe baptism as a burial. (cf. Rom. 6:4)

Col. 2:14 – "Blotting out the handwriting of ordinances that was against us, which was contrary to us, and took it out of the way nailing it to his cross."

Col. 3:16 – "Let the word of Christ dwell in you richly in all wisdom; teaching and admonishing one another in psalms and hymns and spiritual songs, singing with grace in your hearts to the Lord."

Col. 3:23-24 – "And whatsoever ye do, do it heartily, as to the Lord, and not unto men; …"

Col. 4:6 – Gracious and godly speech.

Col. 4:16 – The lost letter to Laodicea?

Philemon 7 – Philemon's refreshing love.

Philemon 11 – Onesimus – from useless to useful.

Philemon 16 – Onesimus – from slave to brother.

Major Themes – Colossians and Philemon

A. Christ is supreme.
1. Christ is supreme over creation. – Col. 1:15-17
2. Christ is supreme over the church. – Col. 1:18a; 2:19

3. Christ is supreme over everything. – Co. 1:18b
4. Christ is supreme over all rule and authority. – Col. 2:10;
   Matt. 28:18
5. Christ is supreme over human relationships. – Col. 3:18-4:1
   a. Husband-wife; parent-child; master-slave
   b. Note the emphasis on Lordship in these verses. "Lord"
      appears six times.

B. Christ is all-sufficient.
   1. Christ in us and hope of glory. – Col. 1:27
   2. We are complete in Christ. – Col. 1:28
   3. We walk in Him. – Col. 2:6
   4. We are rooted and built up in Him. – Col. 2:7
   5. We are full in Christ. – Col. 2:10
   6. We are buried with Him in baptism. – Col. 2:12
   7. We are raised up with Him. – Col. 3:1
   8. We died with Christ. – Col. 2:20
   9. We will appear with Him in glory. – Col. 3:4
   10. We are hidden with Christ. – Col. 3:3
   11. He is our life. – Col. 3:4
   12. Christ is all, and in all. – Col. 3:11

C. Morality of Christ. – Col. 3:5-14; (cf. Gal. 5:19-23; Eph. 4:22-24)
   1. We must put to death the members of our earthly body.
      – Col. 3:5-7
   2. Put off our old self. – Col. 3:8-9
   3. Put on the new self. – Col. 3:12-14

D. Brotherhood in Christ.
   1. The common denominator is faith in Christ. – Col. 1:4;
      Philemon 5
   2. The common experience is forgiveness of sins. – Col. 1:14; 2:14
   3. A common equality in the family of God. – Col. 3:11; 3:22-4:1;
      Philemon 16
   4. A common work in the fellowship of the gospel.
      a. Fellow bond-servant. – Col. 1:7; 4:7

b. Fellow prisoner. – Col. 4:10; Philemon 23
c. Fellow workers. – Col. 4:11; Philemon 1, 24
d. Fellow soldier. – Philemon 2

Christ Revealed

1. Jesus Christ. – Col. 1:1, 4:12

2. Christ. – Col. 1:2, 7, 24, 27, 28; 2:2, 5, 8, 11, 17, 20; 3:1, 3, 4, 11, 15, 16; 4:3

3. Lord Jesus Christ. – Col. 1:3

4. Christ Jesus. – Col. 1:4

5. Lord. – Col. 1:10; 3:13, 18, 20, 22, 23, 24; 4:7, 17

6. His beloved Son (Son of His love). – Col. 1:13

7. Redeemer. – Col. 1:14

8. The Pre-eminent One. – Col. 1:15-23
a. Image of the invisible God. – Col. 1:15a; John 1:18; Heb. 1:3
b. First born of all creation. – Col. 1:15b; Rom. 8:29
c. Creator. – Col. 1:16-17; John 1:3
d. Head of the body, the church. – Col. 1:18a; 2:19; Eph. 1:22
e. The Beginning. – Col. 1:18b; Rev. 3:14
f. First born from the dead. – Col. 1:18c; Acts 26:23; I Cor. 15:20
g. First place or Preeminence. – Col. 1:18d
h. Fullness of deity. – Col. 1:19; 2:9
i. Reconciler. – Col. 1:20-22; II Cor. 5:18-19; Eph. 2:16

9. Christ Jesus the Lord. – Col. 2:6

10. Head over all rule and authority. – Col. 2:10

11. Head of the body. – Col. 2:19

12. Christ, who is our life. – Col. 3:4; Gal. 2:20

13. The One. – Col. 3:10

14. Christ is all, and in all. – Col. 3:11; Eph. 1:23

15. Lord Jesus. – Col. 3:17

16. Lord Christ. – Col. 3:24

17. Master. – Col. 4:1

Philemon:

1. Christ Jesus. – Philemon 1, 9, 23

2. Lord Jesus Christ. – Philemon 3, 25

3. Lord Jesus. – Philemon 5

4. Christ. – Philemon 6, 8, 20

5. Lord. – Philemon 16, 20

I and II Thessalonians

Summation

Thessalonica was located 100 miles southwest of Philippi in an area called Macedonia (northern Greece). During his second missionary journey, Acts 17:1-14, Paul, Silas, and Timothy took the gospel to Thessalonica. Their attempt was violently opposed by the leading Jews of the city, Acts 17:5, 13. A short amount of time after Paul left he wrote I Thessalonians to encourage the new church to be faithful and to wait, I Thess. 1:10, and watch, I Thess. 5:2, for the Lord to return. A brief few months later Paul wrote II Thessalonians to clarify any misunderstandings or misrepresentations concerning the Lord's second coming, II Thess. 2:1-2. There were some members of the Thessalonian church who had stopped working in anticipation of the Lord's immediate return. Paul encouraged those members to work and not grow weary of doing good until the Lord did return, II Thess. 3:10-14. Both of the Thessalonian letters were written from Corinth in 51 A.D. Both of the letters are considered authentic, II Thess. 3:17 and authoritative, I Thess. 4:8; II Thess. 3:14, and they were to be read aloud to the church, I Thess. 5:27.

Breakdown

A. I Thessalonians
   1. Paul's association with the Thessalonian church.
      – I Thess. 1:1-3:13
   2. Paul's exhortation to marital fidelity. – I Thess. 4:1-12
   3. Paul's communication about the dead and Christ's second coming. – I Thess. 4:13-5:11
   4. Paul's applications to Christian living. – I Thess. 5:12-28

B. II Thessalonians
   1. Christ's second coming anticipated. – II Thess. 1:1-12

2. Christ's second coming described. – II Thess. 2:1-17

3. Christ's second coming and proper conduct. – Thess. 3:1-18

Pivotal Word – Coming of the Lord

The coming of the Lord is mentioned some 6 times in both books, I Thess. 2:19; 3:13; 4:15; 4=5:23; II Thess. 2:1, 8. The word "coming" (parousia) means "presence or appearance." When Christ comes or returns He will descend from heaven, I Thess. 4:16; 1:10, or be revealed from heaven, II Thess. 1:7. His return is also referred to as that "day", I Thess. 5:4; II Thess. 1:10, and the "day of the Lord", I Thess. 5:2; II Thess. 2:2. When Christ returns He will bring wrath, judgment, and vengeance on the ungodly and disobedient, I Thess. 1:10; II Thess. 1:7-9, and He will bring deliverance and salvation for the godly, I Thess. 1:10; 5:9.

Important Verses – I and II Thessalonians

I Thess. 1:8 – "… your faith to God-ward is spread abroad…"

I Thess. 2:13 – The reception of God's message.

I Thess. 3:11-13 – Paul's prayer for the Thessalonian church.

I Thess. 4:13-18 – Words of hope and comfort.

I Thess. 5:9-10 – Christians are destined for salvation and not wrath.

I Thess. 5:12-13 – Appreciation, esteem, and love for spiritual leaders.

I Thess. 5:23 – The whole man – spirit, soul, and body.

II Thess. 1:7-9 – Retribution for the ungodly and disobedient.

II Thess. 2:3 – Apostasy, man of lawlessness, son of destruction.

II Thess. 2:13-15 – God calls people to salvation through the gospel.

II Thess. 3:6 – Discipline for the undisciplined.

II Thess. 3:10 – "… that if any would not work, neither should he eat."

Major Themes – I and II Thessalonians

A. The measure of a church. – I Thess. 1:3; 5:8; II Thess. 1:3
   1. Work of faith. – I Thess. 3:7, 10; II Thess. 1:11
   2. Labor of love. – I Thess. 3:6, 12
   3. Steadfastness of hope. – I Thess. 4:13; II Thess. 2:16

B. How the preacher and congregation relate.
   1. What we preached, the Gospel:
      a. In word and in power. – I Thess. 1:5
      b. Boldly amidst opposition. – I Thess. 2:2
      c. Not as pleasing men but God. – I Thess. 2:4
      d. In labor and hardship. – I Thess. 2:8-9
      e. As the word of God. – I Thess. 2:13
      f. The necessity of obeying the gospel – II Thess. 1:8
      g. The privilege of being called by the gospel.
        – II Thess. 2:13-14
   2. The preacher as an example.
      a. Godly example. – I Thess. 1:6; II Thess. 3:7, 9
      b. Caring mother. – I Thess. 2:7
      c. Beloved brother. – I Thess. 2:8-9
      d. Loving father. – I Thess. 2:10-12
   3. The church for the preacher is: I Thess. 2:19-20; (cf. Phil. 4:1)
      a. Hope.
      b. Joy.
      c. Crown.
      d. Glory and joy.
      e. Price. – II Thess. 1:4; (cf. II Cor. 1:14)

C. Relationships in the church.
   1. Love one another. – I Thess. 3:12
   2. Love one another. – I Thess. 4:9
   3. Comfort one another. – I Thess. 4:18
   4. Encourage one another. – I Thess. 5:11a

5. Build up one another. – I Thess. 5:11b
6. Live in peace with one another. – I Thess. 5:13
7. Seek after that which is good for one another. – I Thess. 5:15
8. Love toward one another. – II Thess. 1:3

D. Christ's second coming.
1. Coming of the Lord (comfort). – I Thess. 4:13-18
2. Day of the Lord (be ready). – I Thess. 5:1-11, 23
3. Retribution of the Lord (obey). – II Thess. 1:6-10
4. Coming of the Lord (stand firm). – II Thess. 2:1-12

E. Exhortations.
1. Responsibilities to spouse. – I Thess. 4:1-8
2. Responsibilities to leaders. – I Thess. 5:12-13a
3. Responsibilities to one another. – I Thess. 5:13b-15
4. Responsibilities to self. – I Thess. 4:11-12; 5:16-22
5. Responsibilities to the undisciplined. – II Thess. 3:6-15

Christ Revealed

I Thessalonians

1. Lord Jesus Christ. – I Thess. 1:1, 3; 5:9, 23, 28

2. Lord. – I Thess. 1:6, 8; 3:8, 12; 4:6, 15, 16, 17; 5:2, 12, 27

3. His Son. – I Thess. 1:10

4. Jesus. – I Thess. 1:10; 4:14

5. Christ. – I Thess. 2:6; 3:2; 4:16

6. Christ Jesus. – I Thess. 2:14; 5:18

7. Lord Jesus. – I Thess. 2:15, 19; 3:13; 4:1, 2

8. Jesus our Lord. – I Thess. 3:11

II Thessalonians

1. Lord Jesus Christ. – II Thess. 1:1, 2, 12; 2:1, 14, 16; 3:6, 12, 18

2. Lord Jesus. – II Thess. 1:7, 8, 12

3. Lord. – II Thess. 1:9; 2:2, 8, 13; 3:1, 3, 4, 5, 16

4. Christ. – II Thess. 3:5

I and II Timothy and Titus

Summation

I and II Timothy and Titus are often called the Pastoral Letters because they deal with the work of preaching and church organization. Paul in these letters affectionately refers to Timothy and Titus as "son" "beloved son" revealing the possibility that he may have converted them to Christ, I Tim. 1:2, 18; II Tim. 1:2; 2:1; Tit. 1:4. What is known of Timothy is that he was relatively young, I Tim. 4:12; II Tim. 2:22, he was sickly or in poor health, I Tim. 5:23, and he was shy or timid, II Tim. 1:6-7. Of the two young preachers, Titus seems to be the stronger personality. Paul's Pastoral Letters are dated around 64-68 A.D. He wrote I Timothy from Macedonia, I Tim. 1:3, in 64 or 65 A.D. Titus was written from Nicopolis, Tit. 3:12, about the same time. Paul's last letter, II Timothy, was written from Rome during his second imprisonment, II Tim. 1:8, 16-17; 2:9; 4:14, 16, just prior to his death at the hands of the Roman Emperor Nero in 67 or 68 A.D. At the time the letters were received Timothy was ministering to the church in Ephesus, I Tim. 1:3, and Titus was ministering on the island of Crete, Tit. 1:5.

Breakdown

I Timothy

A. Timothy's commission. – I Tim. 1:1-20
    1. False doctrines. – I Tim. 1:1-11
    2. Paul is faithful. – I Tim. 1:12-17
    3. Fight the good fight. – I Tim. 1:18-20

B. The conduct of the church. I Tim. 2. 1-3:16
    1. Prayer in the church. – I Tim. 2:1-8
    2. Women in the church. – Tim. 2:9-15
    3. Elders in the church. – Tim. 3:1-7
    4. Deacons in the church. – I Tim. 3:8-13
    5. Conduct and confession. – I Tim. 3:14-16

224

C. Timothy's charge. – I Tim. 4:1-6:21
   1. Sound doctrine – duty to truth. – I Tim. 4:1-16
   2. Special groups – duty to church. – I Tim. 5:1-20
      a. Older and younger. – I Tim. 5:1-2
      b. Widows. – I Tim. 5:3-16
      c. Elders. – I Tim. 5:17-20

D. Solemn charge - duty to self. – I Tim. 5:21-6:21
   1. Personal matters. – I Tim. 5:21-25
   2. Godliness and gain. – I Tim. 6:1-10
   3. The man of God. – I Tim. 6:11-21
      (flee, pursue, fight, keep, guard)

II Timothy

A. Thankfulness for Timothy. – II Tim. 1:1-18
   (Guard the Gospel – II Tim. 1:1-18)
   1. His family. – II Tim. 1:1-5
   2. His faith. – II Tim. 1:6-18

B. Exhortations to Timothy. – II Tim. 2:1-26
   (Suffer for the gospel. – II Tim. 2:3)
   1. As a child. – II Tim. 2: 1-2
   2. As a soldier. – II Tim. 2:3-4
   3. As an athlete. – II Tim. 2:5
   4. As a farmer. II Tim. 2:6-13
   5. As a workman. – II Tim. 2:14-19
   6. As a vessel. – II Tim. 2:20-23
   7. As a servant. – II Tim. 2:24-26

C. Warnings
   (Continue in the gospel. – II Tim. 3:14)
   1. The last days. – II Tim. 3:1-13
   2. The inspired scriptures. – II Tim. 3:14-17

D. Timothy's final charge. – II Tim. 4:1-22
   (Preach the gospel. – II Tim. 4:2)

1. Timothy's responsibilities. – II Tim. 4:1-5
2. Reward for faithfulness. – II Tim. 4:6-8
3. Final requests. – II Tim. 4:9-22

Titus

A. Administer sound doctrine. – Tit. 1:1-16
    (An orderly church.)
    1. The source of sound doctrine. – Tit. 1:1-4
    2. Elders appointed. – Tit. 1:5-9
    3. Exposing false teachers. – Tit. 1:10-16

B. Preach sound doctrine. – Tit. 2:1-15
    (The health of the church.)
    1. The application of sound doctrine. – Tit. 2:1-10
    2. The definition of sound doctrine. – Tit. 2:11-15

C. The counsel of sound doctrine. – Tit. 3:1-15
    (A working church.)
    1. Citizenship/ - Tit. 3:1-3
    2. Salvation. – Tit. 3:4-7
    3. Good deeds. – Tit. 3:8-15

Pivotal Word – Instruction

"Instruction" means to transmit a message, to order, to command. "Instruction" is used in I Tim. 1:5; 2:11; II Tim. 4:2, "instruct" is used in I Tim. 1:3; 6:17, and "instruction" is used in Tit. 2:12, these are key words in the Pastoral Letters. Timothy and Titus were instructed in truth and doctrine for the purpose of instructing others, II Tim. 2:2. In order to instruct the church Paul told these two young preachers to: prescribe, I Tim. 4:11; 5:7, teach, I Tim. 1:3; 2:12; 3:2; 4:11; 6:2 II Tim. 2:2, 24, exhort, II Tim. 4:2; Tit. 1:9 2:15, and preach, I Tim. 6:2; II Tim. 4:2. The biblical method for instruction in the church includes three things found in I Tim. 4:13: (1) Public reading of the scripture, (2) preached explanation of the scripture, and (3) personal application of the scripture.

<u>Important Verses</u>

<u>I Tim. 1:15</u> – "… that Christ Jesus came into the world to save sinners; of whom I am chief."

<u>I Tim. 2:12</u> – "But I suffer not a woman to teach, nor to usurp authority over the man, but to be in silence."

<u>I Tim. 3:15</u> – The key verse in I Timothy.

<u>I Tim. 4:1</u> – The source of false doctrines.

<u>I Tim. 4:12</u> – "Let no man despise thy youth…"

<u>I Tim. 5:8</u> – The responsibility to provide for one's family.

<u>I Tim. 6:7</u> – "For we brought nothing into this world, and it is certain we can carry nothing out."

<u>II Tim. 1:12</u> – "… for I know whom I have believed…"

<u>II Tim. 2:15</u> – Diligent study is required in handling accurately the word of truth.

<u>II Tim. 3:16-17</u> – "All scripture is given by inspiration of God…"

<u>II Tim. 4:6-8</u> – Paul's confidence at the end of life.

<u>Tit. 1:5</u> – "… set in order the things that are wanting, and ordain elders in every city …"

<u>Tit. 2:11-14</u> – A concise statement of the Christian faith.

<u>Tit. 3:5</u> – The basis of salvation.

<u>Major Themes</u>

A. The necessity of sound doctrine.
   1. Sound doctrine defined: Sound doctrine is healthy or wholesome in contrast to false doctrine which is unhealthy and diseased.

2. Sound doctrine introduced: "This is a faithful saying…"
   I Tim. 1:15; 3:1; 4:9; II Tim. 2:11; Tit. 3:8
3. Sound doctrine classified:
   a. Sound mind. – II Tim. 1:7
   b. Sound words. – I Tim. 6:3-5; II Tim. 1:13
   c. Sound doctrine. – I Tim. 1:10; 4:6; II Tim. 4:3; Tit. 1:9; 2:1
   d. Sound faith. – Tit. 1:13
   e. Sound speech. – Tit. 2:8
4. Sound doctrine contrasted:
   a. Myths and endless genealogies. – I Tim. 1:4
   b. Worldly fables. – I Tim. 4:7
   c. Worldly and empty chatter. – I Tim. 6:20
   d. Wrangling about words. – II Tim. 2:14
   e. Worldly and empty chatter. – II Tim. 2:16
   f. Foolish and ignorant speculations. – II Tim. 2:23
   g. Myths. – II Tim. 4:4
   h. Jewish myths and commandments of men. – Tit. 1:14
   i. Foolish controversies, genealogies, strife, and disputes about
      the Law. – Tit. 3:9

B. Qualifications for church leaders.
   1. Elders (also known as overseer, bishop, pastor, presbyter, each
      of these titles describes a part of their duty), I Tim. 3:1-7; 5:17-
      20; Tit. 1:5-9; (cf. Acts 11:30; 14:23; 15:2, 4, 6, 22ff; 16:4;
      20:17; 21:18; Heb. 13:17; James 5:14; I Pet. 5:1-4)
   2. Deacons (servant). I Tim. 3:8-13; (cf. Acts 6:1-6; Phil. 1:1)
   3. The qualifications for both elders and deacons can be noted in
      four categories: personal life, family life, social life, and
      spiritual life.

C. The duties of the preacher.
   1. To preach. – I Tim. 4:13; II Tim. 4:1-5
   2. To teach. – I Tim. 6:2; II Tim. 2:2
   3. To study. – I Tim. 4:6; II Tim. 2:15; 4:13
   4. To serve. – II Tim. 2:20-26

5. To lead. – I Tim. 4:12; II time. 3:1-13; Tit. 1:5-9

6. To save souls. – I Tim. 4:16

D. Good works.

1. Having a reputation for good works. – I Tim. 5:10

2. Rich in good works. – I Tim. 6:18

3. Prepared for every good work. – II Tim. 2:21

4. Unbelieving worthless for any good deed. – Tit. 1:16

5. An example of good deeds. – Tit. 2:7

6. Zealous for good deeds. – Tit. 2:14

7. Ready for every good deed. – Tit. 3:1

8. Careful to engage in good deeds. – Tit. 3:14

9. Learn to engage in good deeds. – Tit. 3:14

10. Note: The Christian is not saved by good deeds, but is steadfast in them. – Tit. 3:5; (cf. Eph. 2:8-10; James 2:26)

Christ Revealed

I Timothy

1. Christ Jesus. – I Tim. 1:1, 14, 15; 2:5; 3:13; 4:6; 5:21; 613

2. Christ Jesus who is our hope. – I Tim. 1:1

3. Christ Jesus our Lord. – I Tim. 1:2, 12

4. Lord. – I Tim. 1:14

5. Jesus Christ. – I Tim. 1:16

6. King. – I Tim. 1:17

7. Mediator. – I Tim. 2:5

8. Ransom – Redeemer. – I Tim. 2:6

9. A six point description of Christ. – I Tim. 3:16
   a. He who was revealed in the flesh. (Incarnation) – John 1:14
   b. Was vindicated in the Spirit. (Vindication) – Matt. 3:13-17

c. Beheld by angels. (Annunciation) – Luke 2:13; 24:4; I Pet. 1:12

d. Proclaimed among the nations. (Proclamation) – Rom. 16:26; Col. 1:23

e. Believed on in the world. (Reception) – John 1:12

f. Taken up in glory. (Ascension) – Mark 16:19; Acts 1:9-11

10. Christ. – I Tim. 5:11

11. Lord Jesus Christ. – I Tim. 6:3, 14

12. A triptych description of Christ. – I Tim. 6:15-16
    a. Sovereign. – I Tim. 1:17
    b. King of kings. – Rev. 17:14; 19:16
    c. Lord of lords.

II Timothy

1. Christ Jesus. – II Tim. 1:1, 9, 13; 2:1, 3, 10; 3:12, 15; 4:1

2. Christ Jesus our Lord. – II Tim. 1:2

3. Lord. – II Tim. 1:8, 16, 18; 2:7, 19, 22, 24; 3:11; 4:8, 14, 17, 18, 22

4. Savior Christ Jesus. – II Tim. 1:10

5. Jesus Christ. – II Tim. 2:8

6. Master. – II Tim. 2:21

7. Judge of the living and the dead. – II Tim. 4:1; Acts 1042

8. The Righteous Judge. – II Tim. 4:8; Acts 17:31

Titus

1. Jesus Christ. – Tit. 1:1

2. Christ Jesus our Savior. – Tit. 1:4

3. Our great God and Savior, Christ Jesus. – Tit. 2:13; (cf. 1:3; 2:10; 3:4; I Tim. 1:1; 2:3; 4:10)

4. Redeemer. – Tit. 2:14

5. Jesus Christ our Savior. – Tit. 3:6

Hebrews

Summation

The exact authorship of Hebrews is not known. The book of Hebrews has been referred to as the "riddle of the New Testament" because of the uncertainty of its authorship. Various authors have been suggested in times past such as, Barnabas, Silas, Luke, Aquila and Priscilla, and Clement, however the earliest tradition ascribes the authorship to Paul, Heb. 13:23-24. The character with which Hebrews is written exhibits the qualifications of Apollos, Acts 18:24-28. No one really knows for certain except God who the author of Hebrews is. The audience that the book of Hebrews was written to appears to be Jewish Christians who had suffered persecution, Heb. 10:32-36, but not to the point of death, Heb. 12:4. Hebrews tells us itself it is a, "word of exhortation," Heb. 13:22. The Jewish Christians that the book is written to possibly lived in Rome, Heb. 13:24, or maybe in Jerusalem, and they needed to be exhorted to faithfulness in their Christian life because there were signs of drifting, Heb. 2:1 and neglect, Heb. 2:3; 10:25, and even evidence of irrevocable apostasy, Heb. 6:1-6; 10:26-31. The Greek Old Testament, LXX or Septuagint, was relied upon by the author who quoted from it 29 times and clearly alluded to it some 53 times. The book of Hebrews draws heavily upon the Old Testament by contrasting the old and the new covenants. The book of Leviticus would make a good companion to the book of Hebrews. The book of Hebrews brilliantly contrasts Christianity and Judaism by showing the permanence of Christ, His preeminence, His uniqueness, and absoluteness, Heb. 3:1; 8:1-2, 6. Hebrews shows Christ and Christianity are not just better but that the Old covenant had flaws, Heb. 8:6-7. Hebrews was written some time before the destruction of Jerusalem probably between 65 and 70 A.D. The destruction of Jerusalem marked the final overthrow of the Jewish system, temple worship.

Breakdown

A. The superiority of Christ. – Heb. 1:1-4:16
   1. He is superior to the prophets. – Heb. 1:1-4
   2. He is superior to angels. – Heb. 1:5-2:18
   3. He is superior to Moses. – Heb. 3:1-19
   4. He is superior to Joshua. – Heb. 4:1-16

B. The superiority of the priesthood of Christ. – Heb. 5:1-10:39
   1. He is superior to Aaron. – Heb. 5:1-4
   2. He is superior to Melchizedek. – Heb. 5:5-7:17
   3. He is superior to all earthly High Priest. – Heb. 7:18-8:5
   4. He is superior in His covenant. – Heb. 8:6-13
   5. He is superior in His sacrifice. – Heb. 9:1-10:39

C. The superiority of Christ's power. – Heb. 11:1-13:25
   1. Superior faith – people of faith. – Heb. 11:1-40
   2. Superior hope – perfecter of faith. – Heb. 12:1-29
   3. Superior love – practice of faith. – Heb. 13:1-25

Pivotal Word – Blood

Hebrews is considered a priestly book contrasting the old and new covenants and the priesthood of Christ with earthly priest, therefore "blood" (mentioned 22 times) is a focal theme. Under the old covenant the blood of bulls and goats was inadequate to take away sins, Heb. 10:1-4, but not so with the blood of Christ, Heb. 9:12-14. "And almost all things are by the law purged with blood; and without shedding of blood is no remission." (Heb. 9:22; (cf. Lev. 17:11). The blood of Jesus is the ultimate and final sacrifice for sins, Heb. 10:10-12, 26. The New Testament or covenant is signed and sealed with the blood of Jesus, Heb. 9:20; 10:29; 13:20; Ex. 24:8; Matt. 26:28. Other significant words in Hebrews include: priest (31 times), covenant (17 times), heaven or heavenly (16 times), eternal or forever (16 times), sacrifice (15 times), perfect (14 times), better (13 times).

233

Important Verses

Heb. 1:1-2 – "God, who at sundry times and in divers manners spake in time past unto the fathers by the prophets, hath in these last days spoken unto us by his son, whom he hath appointed heir of all things, by who also he made the worlds;"

Heb. 1:14 – "Are they not all ministering spirits, sent forth to minister for them who shall be heirs of salvation?"

Heb. 2:3 – "How shall we escape, if we neglect so great salvation; ..."

Heb. 2:9 – Jesus tasted (experienced) death for everyone.

Heb. 3:12-13 – The deceitfulness of sin.

Heb. 4:12 – The power of the word of God.

Heb. 4:14-16 – Jesus is our perfect High Priest.

Heb. 5:7-9 – The necessity of obeying Jesus.

Heb. 5:11-14 – "... for the time ye ought to be teachers ..."

Heb. 6:4-6 – The possibility of apostasy.

Heb. 7:25 – Jesus always lives to make intercession for Christians.

Heb. 8:8-12 – The new covenant of Christ. (cf. Jer. 31:31-34)

Heb. 9:26-28 – Jesus is our sin bearer.

Heb. 10:1-4 – Old Testament sacrifices did not remove sin.

Heb. 10:25 – "Not forsaking the assembling of ourselves together, as the manner of some is..."

Heb. 10:38 – "Now the just shall live by faith: ..." (cf. Hab. 2:4; Rom. 1:17; Gal. 3:11)

Heb. 11:1 – "Now faith is the substance of things hoped for, the evidence of things not seen."

Heb. 11:6 – "But without faith it is impossible to please him: for he that cometh to God must believe that he is, and that he is a rewarder of them that diligently seek him."

Heb. 12:1-2 – Run the race with your eyes on Jesus.

Heb. 13:8 – "Jesus Christ the same yesterday, and today, and forever."

Heb. 13:17 – "Obey them that have the rule over you, and submit yourselves: for they watch for your souls, as they that must give account, that they may do it with joy, and not with grief: for that is unprofitable for you.

Major Themes

A. Better things.
   1. Better than the angels. – Heb. 1:4
   2. Better things. – Heb. 6:9
   3. Better hope. – Heb. 7:19
   4. Better covenant. – Heb. 7:22; 8:6
   5. Better promises. – Heb. 8:6
   6. Better sacrifices. – Heb. 11:4
   7. Better possession. – Heb. 10:34
   8. Better sacrifice. – Heb. 11:4
   9. Better country. – Heb. 11:16
   10. Better resurrection. – Heb. 11:35
   11. Better provision. – Heb.; 11:40
   12. Better message. – Heb. 12:24

B. Eternal things.
   1. Eternal salvation. – Heb. 5:9
   2. Eternal judgment. – Heb. 6:2
   3. Eternal redemption. – Heb. 9:12
   4. Eternal spirit. – Heb. 9:14

5. Eternal inheritance. – Heb. 9:15

6. Eternal covenant. – Heb. 13:20

C. Salvation.

   1. Inherit salvation. – Heb. 1:14

   2. "How shall we escape, if we neglect…salvation …" – Heb. 2:3

   3. Jesus is the author of salvation. – Heb. 2:10

   4. Jesus is the source of eternal salvation. – Heb. 5:9

   5. Things that accompany salvation. – Heb. 6:9

   6. Christ shall appear a second time for salvation. – Heb. 9:28

   7. Noah prepared an ark for the salvation of his household.
     – Heb. 11:7

D. Approaching God.

   1. Draw near with confidence. – Heb. 4:16

   2. Draw near through a better hope. – Heb. 7:19

   3. Draw near through Christ. – Heb. 7:25

   4. Old Testament sacrifices did not make perfect those who drew
     near. – Heb. 10:1

   5. Draw near with a sincere heart in full assurance of faith.
     – Heb. 10:22

E. What Christians have in Christ.

   1. We have a High Priest. – Heb. 4:14; 8:1; 10:21

   2. We have an altar or sacrifice. – Heb. 13:10-13

   3. We have a sure and steadfast hope. – Heb. 6:19

   4. We have a lasting, abiding, permanent city. – Heb. 13:14; 11:10,
     13-16; 12:22; Rev. 21:2

F. Warnings.

   1. Warning against Neglect. – Heb. 2:1-4

   2. Warning against unbelief. – Heb. 3:7-19

   3. Warning against disobedience. – Heb. 4:11-13

   4. Warning against immaturity. – Heb. 5:11-6:12

   5. Warning against apostasy. – Heb. 10:19-31

   6. Warning against refusal. – Heb. 12:25-29

G. Exhortations.
1. Let us fear. – Heb. 4:1
2. Let us be diligent. – Heb. 4:11
3. Let us hold fast our confession. – Heb. 4:14
4. Let us therefore draw near. – Heb. 4:16
5. Let us press on to maturity. – Heb. 6:1
6. Let us draw near. – Heb. 10:22
7. Let us hold fast the confession of our hope. – Heb. 10:23
8. Let us consider. – Heb. 10:24
9. Let us also lay aside every encumbrance. – Heb. 12:1
10. Let us run with endurance. – Heb. 12:1
11. Let us show gratitude. – Heb. 12:28
12. Let us go out to Him. – Heb. 13:13
13. Let us continually offer up a sacrifice of praise. – Heb. 13:15

H. Finality.
1. Final revelation through Jesus. – Heb. 1:1-4; 2:1-4; Jude 1:3
2. Final sacrifice by Jesus. – Heb. 1:3; 2:9; 7:27; 9:12, 26, 28;
    10:10-12, 14, 26
3. Final rest in Jesus. – Heb. 4:9-11; Rev. 14:13

Christ Revealed

1. Concise description of Christ. – Heb. 1:1-4
    a. Christ's authority: He is the spokesman for God. Matt. 28:18;
       John 12:48-50
    b. Christ's inheritance: He is heir of all things. – Rom. 8:17
    c. Christ's ability: He created the world. – John 1:3; Col. 1:16
    d. Christ's essence: He is the radiance of God's glory. – II Cor. 4:4
    e. Christ's nature: He is the exact representation of God's nature.
       – John 1:18; 14:9
    f. Christ's power: He upholds all things by the word of His power.
       - Col. 1:17
    g. Christ's gift: He made purification of sins. – Heb. 9:14; Tit. 2:14
    h. Christ's position: He sat down at the right hand of the Majesty
       on high. – Heb. 8:1; 10:12; 12:2; Mark 16:19; I Pet. 3:22

i. Christ's name: He has a more excellent name than angels.
   – Eph. 1:21; Phil. 2:9-11

2. My Son. – Heb. 1:5; 5:5

3. Son. – Heb. 1:2, 5, 8; 3:6; 5:8; 7:28

4. First-born. – Heb. 1:6

5. Lord. – Heb. 2:3; 7:14; 12:14; 13:6

6. Son of man. – Heb. 2:6-8; quote from Ps. 8:4-6

7. Jesus. – Heb. 2:9; 6:20; 7:22; 10:19; 12:2, 24; 13:12

8. Author (leader, captain, pioneer). – Heb. 2:10; 12:2

9. High Priest. – Heb. 2:17; 3:1; 4:144-16; 5:5, 10; 6:20; 8:1; 9:11;
    10:21
    Characteristics of Christ our High Priest:
    a. with an oath. – Heb. 7:18-22
    b. Permanent. – Heb. 7:23-24
    c. Eternal. – Heb. 7:25
    d. Holy. – Heb. 7:26
    e. Innocent. – Heb. 7:26
    f. Undefiled. – Heb. Heb. 7:26
    g. Separated from sinners. – Heb. 7:26
    h. Exalted above the heavens. – Heb. 7:26
    i. Final sacrifice. – Heb. 7:27
    j. Perfect. – Heb. 7:28

10. Apostle. – Heb. 3:1 This is the only reference in the Bible to
                Christ as an Apostle (one sent with authority).

11. Christ. – Heb. 3:6, 14; 5:5; 6:1; 9:11, 14, 24, 28; 11:26

12. Jesus the Son of God. – Heb. 4:14; 6:6;7:3; 10:29

13. A priest forever according to the order of Melchizedek. – Heb. 5:6; 6:20; 7:17; quote from Ps. 110:4

14. Source of eternal salvation. – Heb. 5:9

15. Forerunner. – Heb. 6:20

16. Descendent of Judah. – Heb. 7:14; (cf. Gen. 49:9-10; Num. 24:17; Micah 5:2; Matt. 2:6; Rev. 5:5)

17. Guarantee (surety). – Heb. 7:22

18. Intercessor. – Heb. 7:25

19. Mediator. – Heb. 8:6; 9:15; 12:24

20. Perfect and final sacrifice for sins. – Heb. 9:12-14, 23-28; 10:10-12, 14, 26

21. Jesus Christ. – Heb. 10:10; 13:8, 21

22. Him who is unseen. – Heb. 11:27

23. A fivefold description of Christ. – Heb. 12:2-3
    a. Author and captain of faith. – Heb. 2:10
    b. Perfecter or finisher of faith.
    c. Crucified savior. – Heb. 2:9
    d. Humiliated savior. – Heb. 13:12-13; Acts 8:32-33; I Cor. 1:18, 23
    e. Exalted savior. – Heb. 1:3; 8:1; 10:12

24. Great Shepherd. – Heb. 13:20; John 10:11; I Pet. 2:25; 5:4

25. Jesus our Lord. – Heb. 13:20

James

Summation

James is one of the group of letters known as the General or Universal Letters that were not restricted to one specific congregation but were written for believers everywhere. This group of letters consists of James, I and II Peter, I, II, and II John, and Jude. The manner in which James is addressed "...the twelve tribes which are scattered abroad...," (James 1:1), indicates that the book of James was intended for Jewish Christians scattered throughout the world, James 2:1, 7; 5:7 (cf. Acts 8:1-4). There are four men named James in the New Testament: (1) James the son of Zebedee who was beheaded by Herod Agrippa I in 44 B.C., Matt. 4:21; Acts 12:1-2; (2) James the son of Alphaeus, Matt. 10:3; (3) the James of Luke 6:16; and (4) James the Lord's half-brother, Matt. 13:55. It is generally agreed that the author of the book of James is James the half-brother of Jesus and the brother of Jude, (cf. Jude 1). According to John 7:5 James was an unbeliever during the ministry of Jesus but after the resurrection appearance, I Cor. 15:7, we are shown how he emerged as a staunch leader in the Jerusalem church, Acts 12:17; 15:13-29; 21:18; Gal. 2:9. The book of James focuses on Christian conduct and has been called "the Proverbs of the New Testament." James speaks of duty more than he does doctrine and is concerned about the balance between right behavior and right belief, James 1:22, 27; 4:17. In the content of James, he makes reference to 22 Old Testament books. The time of the writing of James is 45-50 A.D., this makes it one of the earliest New Testament books.

Breakdown

A. Genuine faith. – James 1:1-27
    1. Faith and trials, (outward). – James 1:1-12
    2. Faith and temptations, (inward). – James 1:13-18
    3. Faith and true religion, (upward). – James 1:19-27

B. Nature of genuine faith. – James 2:1-26
    1. Faith does not show partiality. – James 2:1-13
    2. Faith shows, itself in good works. – James 2:14-26

C. Evidence of genuine faith. – James 3:1-4:17
    1. Faith controls the tongue. – James 3:1-12
    2. Faith seeks wisdom from above. – James 3:13-18
    3. Faith avoids worldliness. – James 4:1-4
    4. Faith remembers God. – James 4:5-17

D. Applying genuine faith. – James 5:1-20
    1. Concerning riches. – James 5:1-6
    2. Concerning the coming of the Lord. – James 5:7-11
    3. Concerning oaths. – James 5:12
    4. Concerning prayer. – James 5:13-18
    5. Concerning an erring brother. – James 5:19-20

Pivotal Word – Perfect

"Perfect" (teleios) a word that means, having reached its end, accomplished, complete, or mature, appears six times, James 1:4, 17, 25; 2:22; 3:2. James talks about endurance having its "perfect result," James 1:4 so the Christian can be "perfect." James speaks about every "perfect gift," James 1:17, and being "perfected," James 2:22, the "perfect law," James 1:25 and the "perfect man," James 3:2.

Important Verses

James 1:12 – "Blessed is the man that endureth temptation for when he is tried, he shall receive the crown of life, which the Lord hath promised to them that love him."

James 1:22 – "But be ye doers of the word, and not hearers only, deceiving your own selves."

James 1:27 – "Pure religion and undefiled before God and the Father is this, to visit the fatherless and widows in their affliction, and to keep himself unspotted form the world."

James 2:10 – "For whosoever shall keep the whole law, and yet offend in one point, he is guilty of all."

James 2:14-26 – Faith and works.

James 3:1-12 – The power of the tongue.

James 4:2-3 – Why some prayers are not answered.

James 4:14-15 – Life is like a vapor that vanishes away.

James 4 17 – Sin by omission.

James 5:11 – The only New Testament reference to Job.

James 5:16 –"… The effectual fervent prayer of a righteous man availeth much."

James 5:19-20 – Duty to the erring brother.

Major Themes

A. The nature of sin. – James 1:13-16
   1. It is ungodly. – James 1:13
   2. It is progressive. – James 1:14-15
   3. It is deadly. – James 1:15
   4. It is deceptive. – James 1:16

B. The nature of the word of God.
   1. It is involved in bringing about salvation. – James 1:18, 21
   2. It is to be received, obeyed, and acted upon. – James 1:19-22
   3. It is a mirror for reflecting man's defects. – James 1:23-24
   4. It is an ethical guide for Christian living. – James 1:25; 2:8
   5. It is to be the standard of judgment. – James 2:12

C. The nature of true religion. – James 1:26-27
   1. Religion that is worthless. – James 1:26
   2. Religion that is pure and undefiled. – James 1:27

D. THE NATURE OF SAVING FAITH.
   1. Faith and endurance. – James 1:2-4
   2. Faith and prayer. – James 1:5-8; 5:15
   3. Faith and partiality. – James 2:1-13
   4. Faith and works. – James 2:14-26
      a. There is no contradiction between Paul and James. The both use Abraham to illustrate justification, Rom. 4:3; Gal. 3:6; James 2:23; Gen. 15:6.
      b. Paul explains than an unsaved man cannot be justified by works of merit. James on the other hand explains that a saved man will prove his faith by works or acts of obedience.
      c. Paul portrays Abraham as being justified by faith when he believed God concerning Isaac's birth, Rom. 4:16-25, and James explains that Abraham was justified by works when he obeyed God in offering up Isaac, James 2:21-24.

E. The nature of the tongue. – James 3:1-12
   1. Power of direction: bits and rudder. – James 3:1-4
   2. Power of destruction: fire and deadly poison. – James 3:5-8
   3. Power of delight: fountain and tree. – James 3:9-12

F. The nature of wisdom.
   1. Wisdom is needed by man. – James 1:5; (cf. I Kings 3:9-12)
   2. Wisdom is provided by God. – James 1:5; Prov. 2:6
   3. Wisdom that is not from above. – James 3:13-16
   4. Wisdom that is from above. – James 3:17-18

G. The nature of prayer.
   1. Ask in faith, (expectation). – James 1:5-8
   2. Ask with the right motives, (motivation). – James 4:2-3
   3. Ask earnestly and fervently, (determination). – James 5:14-18

Christ Revealed

1. Lord Jesus Christ. – James 1:1; 2:1

2. Lord. – James 1:7, 12; 3:9; 4:10, 15; 5:7, 8, 10, 11, 14, 15

3. Lawgiver. – James 4:12; (cf. Isa. 33:22)

4. Judge. – James 4:12; 5:9; (cf. I Cor. 4:5; I Pet. 4:5)

5. The One who is able to save and to destroy. – James 4:12; cf. Matt. 10:28

6. Lord of Sabaoth (hosts). – James 5:4; (cf. Rom. 9:29; Isa. 1:9) the Lord of Hosts was a familiar Old Testament title describing the Lord almighty as the omnipotent sovereign.

I and II Peter

Summation

The apostle Peter is obviously the author as he identifies himself as such, I Pet. 1:1; II Pet. 1:1. Along with identifying himself as the author Peter clearly states that his intended audience are the Christians scattered throughout Asia Minor, I Pet. 1:1; II Pet. 3:1. While Peter wrote these two letters he revealed some interesting things about himself. He reveals that he was an apostle, I Pet. 1:1, and elder, I Pet. 5:1, a witness of the transfiguration of Christ, II Pet. 1:16-18, and a witness of the sufferings (death) of Christ, I Pet. 5:1. Peter penned these letters from Babylon (a title used to symbolize Rome, I Pet. 5:13), and he knew his death was imminent, II Pet. 1:14-15. There is a tradition that says that Peter was crucified upside down at Rome about 65-67 A.D. Silvanus or Silas served as Peter's amanuensis (secretary) in writing these letters, I Per. 5:12; Acts 15:22. The books are dated in Peter's last years between 64 and 67 A.D. The letter of I Peter was written to encourage Christians to stand firm in the grace of God, I Pet. 5:12, during suffering and persecution, I Pet. 4:12-13. The letter of II Peter was written to remind Christians to remember God's word, II Pet. 1:12-15; 3:1-2 and to "grow in the grace and knowledge of our Lord and Savior Jesus Christ," (II Pet. 3:18).

Breakdown

I Peter

A. Suffering and salvation. – I Pet. 1:1-25
    1. Salvation and hope. – I Pet. 1:1-5
    2. Salvation and faith. – I Pet. 1:6-12
    3. Salvation and the blood of Christ. – I Pet. 1:13-21
    4. Salvation and the word of the Lord. – I Pet. 1:22-25

B. Suffering and Christ. – I Pet. 2:1-25
    1. The kindness of the Lord: salvation. – I Pet. 2:1-3

2. The people of the Lord: Spiritual House. – I Pet. 2:4-12
3. The submission of the Lord: Sacrifice. – I Pet. 2:13-3:12
   a. Submit to government. – I Pet. 2:13-17
   b. Submit to masters. – I Pet. 2:18-19
   c. Submit to suffering. – I Pet. 2:20-25
   d. Submit to spouse. – I Pet. 3:1-12

C. Suffering and glory. – I Pet. 3:13-4:19
   1. Suffer for righteousness (blessed). – I Pet. 3:13-22
   2. Suffer as Christ suffered (rejoice). – I Pet. 4:1-11
   3. Suffer as a Christian (glorify). – I Pet. 4:12-19

D. Suffering and grace. – I Pet. 5:1-14
   1. Grace for Elders. – I Pet. 5:1-4
   2. Grace for the humble. – I Pet. 5:5-7
   3. Grace for the brethren. – I Pet. 5:8-14

II Peter

A. Knowledge and the Christian life. – II Pet. 1:1-21
   1. Divine power: For life and godliness. – II Pet. 1:1-4
   2. Divine personality: Supply Christian graces. – II Pet. 1:5-11
   3. Divine provision: Remember God's word. – II Pet. 1:12-21

B. Knowledge and false teachers. – II Pet. 2:1-22
   1. Description of false teachers. – II Pet. 2:1-3
   2. Destruction of false teachers. – II Pet. 2:4-12
   3. Deception of false teachers. – II Pet. 2:13-19
   4. Danger of false teachers. – II Pet. 2:20-22

C. Knowledge and the Second Coming. – II Pet. 3:1-18
   1. The question of His coming. – II Pet. 3:1-7
   2. The description of His coming. – II Pet. 3:8-13
   3. The anticipation of His coming. – II Pet. 3:14-18

Pivotal Word

I Peter – Suffering

The word "suffering" in some form appears 17 times in I Peter. Suffering Christians, I Pet. 1:6-7; 2:19-20; 3:14, 17; 4:1, 12-13, 15-16, 19; 5:9-10, are told they should find some consolation in knowing that Christ also suffered, I Pet. 1:11; 2:21, 23; 3:18; 4:1, 13; 5:1. Peter diligently worked to put suffering in its proper perspective by talking about hope, I Pet. 1:13, joy, I Pet. 4:13, and glory, I Pet. 1:7; 4:16 all the while Christians are in the midst of various trials and persecutions.

II Peter – Knowledge

Knowledge or some form of the word is used 12 times, II Pet. 1:2, 3, 5, 6, 8, 16, 20; 2:20, 21; 3:3, 17, 18. Peter teaches that true knowledge of the Lord and His word will protect against false teaching and promote holy conduct and godly living.

Important Verses

I Pet. 1:18-19 – Redeemed by the blood of the Lamb.

I Pet. 2:9 – A description of God's people.

I Pet. 2:21-24 – Christ suffered for sin.

I Pet. 3:15 – "… be ready always to give an answer to every man that asketh you a reason of the hope that is in you…"

I Pet. 3:21 – "… baptism doth also now save us…"

I Pet. 4:16 – "Yet if any man suffer as a Christian, let him not be ashamed; but let him glorify God on this behalf."

I Pet. 5:1-4 – Elders are spiritual shepherds.

I Pet. 5:7 – "Casting all your care upon him; for he careth for you."

II Pet. 1:3 – "… hath given unto us all things that pertain unto life and godliness…"

II Pet. 1:5-10 – The virtues or graces of the Christian life.

II Pet. 1:11 – "For so an entrance shall be ministered unto you
abundantly into the everlasting kingdom of our Lord
and Saviour Jesus Christ."

II Pet. 1:20-21 – "Knowing this first, that no prophecy of the scripture
is of any private interpretation... but holy men of
God spake as they were moved by the Holy Ghost."

II Pet. 2:20-22 – The possibility of apostasy.

II Pet. 3:9 – "... but is longsuffering to us-ward, not willing that any
should perish, but that all should come to repentance."

II Pet. 3:10 – "...the heavens shall pass away with a great noise, and
the elements shall melt with fervent heat..."

II Pet. 3:13 – "Nevertheless we, according to his promise, look for new
heavens and a new earth, wherein dwelleth
righteousness."

II Pet. 3:15-16 – Peter said Paul wrote some things hard to understand.

Major Themes

A. Precious things.
    1. Precious faith. – I Pet. 1:7
    2. Precious blood. – I Pet. 1:19
    3. Precious Corner Stone. – I Pet. 2:4, 6
    4. Precious value. – I Pet. 2:7
    5. Precious promises. – II Pet. 1:4

B. Important ingredients of the Christian life.
    1. Hope. – I Pet. 1:3, 13, 21; 3:5, 15
    2. Salvation. – I Pet. 1:5, 9, 10; 2:2; II Pet. 3:15
    3. Glory. – I Pet. 1:7; 4:11, 13, 14, 16; 5:1, 4
    4. Calling. – I Pet. 1:15; 2:19, 21; 3:9; 5:10; II Pet. 1:3, 10
    5. Submission. – I Pet. 2:13-3:12
    6. Suffering. – I Pet. 1:6-7; 3:17; 4:12-19; 5:9-10

248

7. Knowledge. – II Pet. 1:2, 8; 2:20; 3:18

8. Grace. – I Pet. 1:2, 13; 3:7; 4:10; 5:5, 10, 12; II Pet. 1:2; 3:18

9. Virtues. – II Pet. 1:5-11

C. The meaning and significance of suffering.
   1. Christ sufferings.
      a. Christ's sufferings were predicted. – I Pet. 1:11
      b. Christ suffered for those who would follow His steps. – I Pet. 2:21
      c. Christ did not retaliate during his sufferings. – I Pet. 2:23
      d. Christ became our sin bearer by suffering for sin. – I Pet. 2:24
      e. Christ suffered death "once for all." – I Pet. 3:18; 4:1
      f. Christ's sufferings are to be shared by His followers. – I Pet. 4:13
      g. Christ's sufferings are confirmed by eyewitnesses. – I Pet. 5:1
   2. Christian's sufferings.
      a. Christian suffering is just "for a little while." – I Pet. 1:6; 5:10
      b. Christian suffering is designed for testing faith. – I Pet. 1:7; 4:12
      c. Christian suffering can be accepted even when it is unjust. – I Pet. 2:19-20
      d. Christian suffering is cause for happiness. – I Pet. 3:14; 4:13-14; (cf. Matt. 5:11; Acts 5:41)
      e. Christian suffering is within the will of God. – I Pet. 3:17
      f. Christian suffering proves one belongs to Christ. – I Pet. 4:1
      g. Christian suffering is to be expected. – I Pet. 4:12
      h. Christian suffering is nothing to be ashamed of. – I Pet. 4:15-16, 19
      i. Christian suffering is universal. – I Pet. 5:9
      j. Christian suffering gives God opportunity to make one stronger. – I Pet. 5:10

D. False teachers. – II Pet. 2:1-22
   1. False teachers are described. – II Pet. 2:1-3
   2. False teachers are headed for destruction. – II Pet. 2: 4-12

3. False teachers are deceptive. – II Pet. 2:13-19

4. False teachers face a grave danger. – II Pet. 2:20-22

E. Christ's second coming.

1. Christ's revelation. I Pet. 1:7

2. Christ's Glory. – I Pet. 4:13; 5:1

3. The day of the Lord is both certain and uncertain. – II Pet. 3:3-10

4. The way man should live in view of Christ's second coming: - II Pet. 3:11-18; (cf. I Pet. 4:7-11)

   a. Holy in conduct. – II Pet. 3:11

   b. Eager in anticipation. – II Pet. 3:12-13

   c. Diligent in spirit. – II Pet. 3:14

   d. Steadfast in truth. – II Pet. 17-18

Christ Revealed

I Peter

1. Jesus Christ. – I Pet. 1:1, 2, 3, 7, 13; 2:5; 3:21; 4:11

2. Lord Jesus Christ. – I Pet. 1:3

3. Christ. – I Pet. 1:11, 19; 3:15, 16, 18; 4:1, 13, 14; 5:1, 10, 14

4. Holy One. – I Pet. 1:15

5. Sacrificial Lamb. – I Pet. 1:19; (cf. John 1:29; Heb. 9:13-14)

6. Lord. – I Pet. 1:25; 2:3, 13; 3:12, 15

7. Stone. – I Pet. 2:4-8

   a. Living Stone. – vs. 4

   b. Choice Stone. – vs. 6

   c. Precious Corner Stone. – vs. 6; (cf. Isa. 28:16)

   d. Rejected Stone. – vs. 7; (cf. Ps. 118:22)

   e. Stumbling Stone. – vs. 8; (cf. Isa. 8:14)

8. Suffering Savior. – I Pet.2:21-23; (cf. I Pet. 4:1, 13; 5:1; Isa. 53:9)

9. Sinless sin bearer. – I Pet. 2:24; 3:18; (cf. Isa. 53:4)

10. Shepherd of souls. – I Pet. 2:25; (cf. Isa. 53:6; John 10:11)

11. Guardian of your souls (Bishop or Overseer). – I Pet. 2:25

12. Threefold description of Christ. – I Pet. 3:21-22
    a. His proof: the resurrection. – I Pet. 3:21; 1:3; rom. 1:4
    b. His position: right hand of God…heaven. – I Pet. 3:22a; Mark 16:19; Heb. 1:3
    c. His power: angels and authorities subject to Him. – I Pet. 3:22b; Eph. 1:20-23

13. Faithful Creator. – I Pet. 4:19; John 1:3; Col. 1:16

14. Chief Shepherd. – I Pet. 5:4

II Peter

1. Jesus Christ. – II Pet. 1:1

2. God and Savior, Jesus Christ. – II Pet. 1:1

3. Jesus our Lord. – II Pet. 1:2

4. Lord Jesus Christ. – II Pet. 1:8, 14, 16

5. Lord and Savior Jesus Christ. – II Pet. 1:11; 2:20; 3:18

6. My beloved Son. – II Pet. 1:17; (cf. Matt. 17:5; Mark 9:7; Luke 9:35)

7. Morning Star. – II Pet. 1:19; (cf. Matt. 2:2; Rev. 2:28; 22:16)

8. Master. – II Pet. 2:1

9. Lord. – II Pet. 2:9, 11; 3:8, 9, 10, 15

10. Lord and Savior. – II Pet. 3:2

11. The One who is coming. – II Pet. 3:4ff

I, II, and III John

The letters of I, II and III John were probably written from Ephesus to other churches in Asia Minor similar to the book of Revelation, Rev. 1:4, during the closing years of the Apostle John's life, 85-100 A.D. The letters do not claim the authorship of John but the vocabulary, style and general content are very close to the Gospel of John. From the second century onward these letters have been credited to John also known as the Apostle of love. The purpose for writing I John is clearly stated, "These things have I written unto you that believe on the name of the Son of God; that ye may know that ye have eternal life, and that ye may believe on the name of the Son of God." (I John 5:13). The Gospel of John was written to produce faith so the believer might have life in Christ, John 20:30-31, and the book of I John was written to establish assurance enabling the believer to enjoy life in Christ, I John 5:13. The book of II John is addressed to "the elect lady and her children" (the elect lady is thought to be a specific Christian woman or a specific congregation), and the purpose is to encourage Christians to walk in the truth, II John 4, 6. Third John is addressed to "beloved Gaius," apparently a friend of John and the purpose of the letter is to deal with three personalities and their attitude toward Christian missions. Both II and III John convey the desire to share more information at later times, "face to face," II John 12; III John 13-14. Toward the end of the first century a need for assurance and certainty regarding the Christian faith was needed due to the various philosophies that were perverting the truth of the gospel and deceiving the brethren, I John 2:26; II John 7. There were four typical heresies that were making appearances in the church of John's day and they were: (1) Gnosticism, a belief that knowledge is superior to faith; spirit is good, matter is evil. (2) Docetism, a belief that Jesus was a ghost or phantom; He only seemed to be real. (3) Cerinthianism, a belief that the human Jesus was inhabited by deity only in the period of time from His baptism to just before His death on the cross. (4) Nicolaitanism, a heretical sect that was known for its immorality, idolatry, and indulgence of the flesh, (cf. Rev. 2:6, 15, 20-24). These four heresies posed real threats to the church because they attacked the person of Jesus denying both His humanity and His deity. They were also a danger to the moral purity of the church because they encouraged worldliness.

Breakdown

I John

A. That you may know the Gospel. – I John 1:1-10

B. That you may know the promise. – I John 2:1-29

C. That you may know love. – I John 3:1-24

D. That you may know truth. – I John 4:1-21

E. That you may know assurance. – I John 5:1-21

II John

A. The purpose of Christian fellowship. – II John 1-3

B. The joy of Christian fellowship. – II John 4

C. The nature of Christian fellowship. – II John 5-6

D. The corruption of Christian fellowship. – II John 7-9

E. The preservation of Christian fellowship. – II John 10-13

III John

A. Commendation of Gaius, a hospitable soul. – II John 1-8

B. Confrontation of Diothrephes, a haughty spirit. – II John 9-11

C. Confirmation of Demetrius, a humble servant. – III John 12-14

I John

In I John the pivotal word appears to be "know" And it is used 36 times. There are two words from the original Greek that have been translated to the English word "know" and they are: (1) Ginosko – "to know, recognize, understand." This word implies the inception of, or progress in knowledge, and it is used 22 times, I John 2:3, 4, 5, 13, 14, 18, 29: 3:1, 6, 19, 20, 24; 4:2, 6, 7, 8, 13, 16; 5:2, 20. (2) Oida – "to see, have seen, known, perceived." This word suggests fullness of knowledge and understanding, and it is used 14 times, I John 2:11, 20, 21, 29; 3:2, 5, 14, 15; 5:13, 15, 18, 19, 20. It appears as though John desires for those reading his letter to have not only factual knowledge, but knowledge derived from experience as well.

II and III John

For II and III John the word "truth" occurs five times, II John 1, 2, 3, 4 and six times, III John 1, 3, 4, 8, 12. John speaks of loving truth, knowing truth, walking in truth, and working with the truth.

Important Verses

I John 1:7-10 – The powerful, continual cleansing blood of Jesus.

I John 2:1-2 – Jesus Christ is the righteous advocate.

I John 2:15-17 – "Love not the world…"

I John 3:1-2 – "… when he shall appear, we shall be like him, for we shall see him as he is."

I John 4:4 – "Ye are of God, little children, and have overcome them: because greater is he that is in you, than he that is in the world."

I John 4:10 – "Herein is love, not that we loved God, but that he loved us, and sent his son to be the propitiation for our sins."

I John 5:4 – "For whatsoever is born of God overcometh the world and this is the victory that overcometh the world, even our faith."

I John 5:13 – "These things have I written unto you that believe on the name of the Son of God, that ye may know that ye have eternal life, and that ye may believe on the name of the Son of God."

II John 7 – "For many deceivers are entered into the world, who confess not that Jesus Christ is come in the flesh. This is a deceiver and an antichrist."

II John 9-11 – Warnings against false teachers.

III John 2 – The prospering soul and the healthy body.

III John 4 – "I have no greater joy than to hear that my children walk in truth."

III John 11 – Good and evil.

Major Themes

A. John states his purpose.
    1. Our joy may be made complete. – I John 1:4
    2. That you may not sin. – I John 2:1
    3. Our sins are forgiven. – I John 2:12-14
    4. Because we know the truth. – I John 2:21
    5. There are some who are trying to deceive us. – I John 2:26
    6. So that we may know that we have eternal life. – I John 5:13

B. John's vivid contrast.
    1. Light – darkness. – I John 1:5-7
    2. Love – hate. – I John 2:9-11; 4:20
    3. Love of father – love of the world. – I John 2:15-17
    4. Christ – anti-Christ. – I John 2:18, 22; 4:3; II John 7
    5. Children of God – children of the Devil. – I John 3:10

6. Righteousness – lawlessness. – I John 3:4-7

7. Life – death. – I John 3:14

8. Truth – error. – I John 4:6

9. Sin not leading to death – sin leading to death. – I John 5:16

C. Theology of the Godhead.

   1. God the Father:

      a. God is Light. – I John 1:5

      b. God is Righteous. – I John 2:29; 3:7

      c. God is Love. – I John 4:8, 16

      d. God is Truth. – II John 9

      e. God is Good. – III John 11

   2. God the Son:

      a. Jesus is really human. – I John 1:1 (audible, visible, tangible)

      b. Jesus is really divine. – I John 2:22; 4:3, 15; 5:1, 5, 6-8; II John 7

      c. Jesus is really the solution for sin:

         1. Cleanser. – I John 1:7-10

         2. Advocate. – I John 2:1

         3. Propitiation. – I John 2:2; 4:10

         4. Sinless sin-bearer. – I John 3:5

         5. Savior. – I John 4:14

         6. Giver of eternal life. – I John 4:9; 5:11-13

   3. Holy Spirit:

      a. Anoints the Christian at baptism. – I John 2:20, 27; (cf. II Cor. 1:21-22; Acts 2:38)

      b. Given to abide or dwell in Christians. – I John 3:24; 4:13; (cf. Rom. 8:9-11)

      c. Greater than the one who is in the world. – I John 4:4

      d. He is the Spirit of truth. – I John 4:1-6; 5:7; (cf. John 14:17, 26; 15:26; 16:13)

D. The Christian concept.

   1. The titles of the Christian.

      a. Little children. – I John 2:1, 12, 28; 3:7, 18; 4:4; 5:21

      b. Children of God. – I John 3:1-2; 5:2

c. Born of God. – I John 2:29; 3:9; 4:7; 5:1, 4, 18

d. Brethren. – II John 3, 5, 10

e. Friends. – III John 14

2. Our confidence in Christ.

    a. His coming. – I John 2:28

    b. Before God. – I John 3:21

    c. In the Day of Judgment. – I John 4:17

    d. In our prayers. – I John 5:14-15

3. Victory in Jesus.

    a. Over the evil one. – I John 2:13; 5:18-19

    b. Over false prophets. – I John 4:4

    c. Over the world. – I John 5:4-5

Christ Revealed

I John

1. Word of Life. – I John 1:1; (cf. John 1:1, 4)

2. His son Jesus Christ. – I John 1:3; 3:23; 5:20

3. Jesus His Son. – I John 1: 7

4. Advocate (paracletos- one called alongside to help). – I John 2:1

5. Jesus Christ the righteous. – I John 2:1

6. Propitiation for our sins (satisfaction). – I John 2:2; 4:10

7. Jesus is the Christ (Messiah). – I John 2:22; 5:1

8. Son. – I John 2:22, 23, 24; 4:14; 5:12

9. His coming. – I John 2:28; 3:2

10. He is righteous. – I John 2:29; 3:7

11. The Son of God. – I John 3:8; 5:10, 12, 13, 20

12. He laid down His life for us. – I John 3:16

13. Jesus Christ. – I John 4:2; 5:6

14. Jesus. – I John 4:3, 15

15. His only begotten Son (unique, only one of His kind), - I John 4:9; (cf. John 3:16)

16. Savior of the world. – I John 4:14

17. Jesus is the Son of God. – I John 4:15; 5:5

18. The true God and eternal life. – I John 5:20; (cf. John 17:3)

II John

1. Jesus Christ, the Son of the Father. – II John 3

2. Jesus Christ as coming in the flesh (incarnate). II John 7; (cf. John 1:14)

3. Christ. – II John 9

4. Son. – II John 9

III John

1. The Name. – III John 7
    a. This may refer to the name Christian. Acts 11:26; 26:28; I Pet. 4:16; James 2:7
    b. More than likely "the name" refers to Jesus Christ.
       1. KJV- "his name's sake"
       2. Literally – "in behalf of his name"
       3. John 15:21; Acts 5:41; Phil. 2:9-11

2. The church – the body of Christ as represented by a local assembly or congregation of believers. – III John 9, 10

Jude

Summation

This small book has very aptly been referred to by some as "The Acts of the Apostates." The author of Jude is the half-brother of Jesus, Matt. 13:55; Gal. 1:19, and is identified in verse 1 as "Jude, a bondservant of Jesus Christ, and brother of James." Jude's intent in writing the letter changed from developing the theme of salvation to dealing with the pressing problems caused by false teachers and Jude made an urgent appeal for the brethren to "… earnestly contend for the faith…" (Jude 3). The problem faced by the early church was a grave one as evidenced in verse 4 by Jude where he lets it be known the false teachers were distorting the grace of God and denying the Lord Jesus Christ. These same problems were addressed by John and Peter. The book of Jude is very similar to II Peter 2, (cf. also Jude 17-18 and II Peter 3:2-3). Jude is usually dated sometime after II Peter and close to the time of John's writings around 70-85 A.D. Jude makes an emphasis on the judgment and punishment of God against those who are unfaithful and ungodly and in so doing makes reference to Enoch and other uninspired writings though this does not mean he considered them to be inspired for Paul also quoted uninspired writer, Acts 17:28; I Cor. 15:33; Tit. 1:12.

Breakdown

A. The Faith delivered. (exhortation) – Jude 1-3

B. Faith corrupted. (illustration) – Jude 4-16

C. Faith maintained. (admonition) – Jude 17-25

Pivotal Word – Keep

Five different times Jude uses some form of the word "keep," Jude 1, 6, 21, and 24. Keep or kept means, "to watch over, to guard, to preserve or maintain." Christians are "… (kept) preserved in Jesus

Christ." (Jude 1). Disobedient angels who "kept not their first estate" are "reserved, or kept" for judgment, Jude 6. Christians are to "keep" themselves in the love of God, Jude 21 and God is able to "keep" Christians from stumbling, Jude 24.

Important Verses

Jude 3 – "… common salvation, it was needful for me to write unto you, and exhort you that ye should earnestly contend for the faith which was once delivered unto the saints."

Jude 14-15 – God's judgment against the ungodly.

Jude 18 – "… should be mockers in the last time, who should walk after their own ungodly lusts."

Jude 21 – "Keep yourselves in the love of God…"

Jude 23 – "And others save with fear, pulling them out of the fire…"

Major Themes

A. Faith once delivered to the Saints. – Jude 1-3
   1. "The faith" refers to a body of doctrine, a body of recognized truth, that which is believed. – Acts 2:42; 6:7; Rom. 6:17; Gal. 1:23; 6:10; Jude 20
   2. The "common salvation" is the result of a common faith. – Tit. 1:4
   3. The faith is final and complete – "once for all." – Heb. 2:1-4; II John 9
   4. The faith is to be earnestly contended for, which means to agonize, suffer, and struggle for, not to argue and quarrel over. I Tim. 6:3-5; II Tim. 2:23-26.

B. Corruption of faith by false teachers. – Jude 4-16
   1. Nature of corruption. – Jude 4
      a. Deceptive people. – I John 4:1-3
      b. Distorted message. – Gal. 1:9-10

2. Examples of corruption. – Jude 5-11
   a. Israel in the wilderness (unbelief). – Heb. 3:16-19
   b. Rebellious angels (disobedience). – II Pet. 2:4
   c. Sodom and Gomorrah (immorality). – Gen. 19:1-5, 24-25
   d. The Devil (blasphemy). – Rev. 12:7-9
   e. Cain (self-will). – Gen. 4:19
   f. Balaam (love of money). – Num. 22-24
   g. Korah (presumption). – Num. 16:1-35
3. Descriptions of corruption. – Jude 12-16
   a. Hidden reefs – dangerous. – Jude 12
   b. Waterless clouds – deceptive. – Jude 12
   c. Fruitless trees unproductive. – Jude 12
   d. Wild waves – shameless. – Jude 13
   e. Wandering stars – unreliable. – Jude 13
   f. Ungodly – reserved for judgment. – 14-15
   g. Arrogant grumblers – selfish. – Jude 16

C. How to maintain the faith. – Jude 17-25
    1. Remember the word. – Jude 17-19; II Pet. 3:2-3
    2. Build yourselves up in the faith. – Jude 20; Col. 2:7
    3. Pray in the Holy Spirit. – Jude 20; Eph. 6:18
    4. Keep yourselves in the love of God. – Jude 21; Rom. 8:35-39
    5. Wait for the Lord to return. – Jude 21; Phil. 3:20
    6. Save souls. – Jude 22-23
    7. Hate sin. – Jude 23; Rev. 3:4
    8. Stand blameless. – Jude 24-25

Christ Revealed

1. Jesus Christ. – Jude 1

2. Master and Lord, Jesus Christ. – Jude 4

3. Lord. – Jude 5, 9, 14

4. Lord Jesus Christ. – Jude 17, 21

5. A description of Christ. – Jude 25
    1. God our Savior. – Luke 1:47; I Tim. 1:1; 2:3; 4:10; Titus 1:3; 2:10, 13; 3:4
    2. Jesus Christ our Lord. – Phil. 2:9-11
    3. The one who blesses god. Four attributes belong to God our Savior, through Jesus Christ our Lord. – Jude 25
        a. Glory- radiance and splendor.
        b. Majesty – royal greatness.
        c. Dominion – sovereignty.
        d. Authority – power and rule.
    4. The One who never changes. "… both now and forever." (cf. Heb. 13:8)

Revelation

The book of Revelation is God's final word to mankind and the church, Jude 1:3. The book furnishes insights on the consummation of all things similar to Genesis that furnishes information on the beginning of all things. Genesis tells of the origin of sin, suffering and death. Revelation tells man of an eternal existence free from sin, suffering, and death, Rev. 21:4, 27. Genesis tells of man losing the right to the Tree of Life and in Revelation man is told of free access to the Tree of Life being restored, Rev. 2:7; 22:2, 14, 19. Genesis tells man of redemption in Christ to come, Gen. 3:15, and in Revelation eternal redemption in Christ is finally possessed, Rev. 1:5-6; 5:9-10. Revelation brings together the culmination of God's recorded will for man and illustrates the closing of providential efforts of writing and collecting God's Book.

Revelation has been ignored, neglected and most certainly abused by those wishing to further their own theology. There are some who call it the most difficult book in the Bible to understand while others have said it is the easiest. Some have confessed that Revelation cannot be understood while others have used it as a detailed timepiece calculated to describe every source of evil and every major event from the time of Jesus' ascension to the time of His Second Coming. All such extremes need to be avoided.

The Greek word for Revelation is Apokalupsis which means an uncovering or revealing, thus the title "Revelation." God intended for Revelation to uncover and reveal not hide and conceal or even to be a puzzle. It must be remembered that Revelation is apocalyptic literature similar to Ezekiel, Daniel, and parts of Zechariah. Literature written in the apocalyptic style uses numbers, colors, symbols, signs, visions, figurative language, etc., but it does not lend itself to literal interpretations as some have attempted to do with some parts of Revelation. A very simple key to the interpretation of revelation is not a detailed interpretation of all the numbers, colors, signs, etc., but to have a clear grasp of Jesus Christ as the risen, glorified, triumphant Lamb of God.

The book is written by the Apostle John while he was in exile on the Island of Patmos in approximately 95 A.D., Rev. 1:1, 4, 9-11; 22:8. John wrote what he saw in a book or scroll and sent it to the seven churches of Asia to be read and circulated among them, Rev. 1:3, 4, 11; 22:16. The seven churches and others of the day were experiencing difficult days of persecution and suffering at the hands of the Roman Emperor Domitian, 81-96 A.D. To a persecuted church John presented a victorious vision of Jesus Christ to cheer the faint and encourage the weary. Those reading the letter understood all of what John wrote, he did not send a mysterious message forecasting future events which had to be deciphered and decoded to be understood. It should be noted here that any message that John did not understand and the first century Christians could not understand is most certainly not the right view but the wrong view. Revelation contained a vital message to the first century church, and that same message is relevant to the church today, and will continue to be one until the Lord returns: The church shall be victorious! God's people will win!

<u>Breakdown</u>

Two outlines are offered. One outline is based on Rev. 1:19 and divides the book in to three time frames – past, present, and future. The other outline divides the book into four major visions based on the key phrase "in the Spirit," Rev. 1:10; 4:2; 17:3; 21:10.

Outline One – Rev. 1:19

A. The things which you have seen. – Rev. 1:1-20

B. The things which are. – Rev. 2:1-3:22

C. The thing which shall take place after these things. – Rev. 4:1-22:21

Outline Two, "in the Spirit."

A. First vision: Christ the Living One. – Rev. 1:1-3:22
    1. The Son of Man. – Rev. 1:1-20
    2. The seven letters. – Rev. 2:1-3:22

B. Second vision: Christ the Redeemer. – Rev. 4:1-16:21
    1. Divine throne room. – Rev. 4:1-5:14
    2. Divine judgments. – Rev. 6:1-16:21

C. Third vision: Christ the Warrior-King. – Rev. 17:1-21:8
    1. The judgment of the Great Harlot (Rome). – Rev. 17:1-19:4
    2. The marriage supper of the Lamb. – Rev. 19:5-10
    3. The downfall of Babylon (Rome). – Rev. 19:11-21:8
        a. The war between Christ and the Beast. – Rev. 19:11-21
        b. The thousand – year reign. – Rev. 20:1-10
        c. The final judgment. – Rev. 20:11-15
        d. The new heaven and new earth. – Rev. 21:1-8

D. Fourth vision: Christ the Lamb. – Rev. 21:9-22:5
    1. The heavenly Jerusalem's appearance. – Rev. 21:9-21
    2. The heavenly Jerusalem's inhabitants. – Rev. 21:22-27
    3. The heavenly Jerusalem's provisions. – Rev. 22:1-5

E. Final testimony and solemn warnings:" Christ the Alpha and
    Omega. – Rev. 22:6-21
    1. Do not disobey these words. – Rev. 22:6-9
    2. Do not seal up these words. – Rev. 22:10-17
    3. Do not tamper with these words. – Rev. 22:18-21

Pivotal Word

Some variation of the word "overcomes" is found 15 times in
Revelation: overcomes, Rev. 2:7, 11, 17, 26; 3:5, 12, 21; 21:7,
overcome, Rev. 5:5; 11:7; 13:7; 17:14, overcame, Rev. 3:21; 12:11,
victorious, Rev. 15:2. All of these words are derived from the Greek
word "nike" which means "victory, to conquer or prevail." Revelation

reveals that those that overcome will have a right to the tree of life, Rev. 2:7, shall not be hurt by the second death, Rev. 2:11, will receive a new name from God, Rev. 2:17; 3:12, will have authority over the nations, 2:26, shall be clothed in white and have their name in the Book of Life, Rev. 3:5, will sit on the throne with Jesus, Rev. 3:21, and will inherit all things, Rev. 21:7. The Christian can overcome because Christ overcame, Rev. 3:21; 12; 11; 17:14. Ultimate victory is assured to those who belong to Christ.

Important Verses

Rev. 1:1-3 – Introduction to the book.

Rev. 1:9-11 – The author, occasion, and audience of the book.

Rev. 2 and 3 – Letters to the seven churches of Asia.

Rev. 3:20 – "Behold, I stand at the door, and knock: if any man hear my voice, and open the door, I will come in to him, and will sup with him, and he with me."

Rev. 5:9-13 – The new song, "Worthy art Thou."

Rev. 6:10 – "… How long, O Lord, holy and true, dost thou not judge and avenge our blood on them that dwell on the earth?"

Rev. 12:7-11 – Satan cast out of heaven to the earth.

Rev. 15:3-4 – The song of Moses and the Lamb.

Rev. 17:14 – "… for he is Lord of lords, and King of kings, and they that are with him are called, and chosen, and faithful."

Rev. 20:1-10 – The so-called 1,000 year reign or millennial.

Rev. 11-15 – The Great White Throne of Judgment.

Rev. 21 –The heavenly Jerusalem described.

<u>Rev. 22:18-19</u> – Do not add to or take away from the words of this prophecy.

<u>Major Themes</u>

A. Seven basic principles for interpreting Revelation. – Rev. 1:1-3
    1. It is the Revelation of (from-by-about) Jesus Christ. (source, Author, Object) – Rev. 1:1a
    2. It was given by God to Christ. (divine origin) – Rev. 1:1b
    3. It is addressed to Christ's bondservants, the seven churches of Asia. (Audience) – Rev. 1:1e-2; 22:8
    4. It is primarily concerned with "the things which must shortly take place." (context) – Rev. 1:1d, 3, 19; 22:6
    5. It was communicated or signified (by signs) to John. (method and writer) – Rev. 1:1e, 11
    6. It was sent by Christ's messenger through visions. (Agent and medium) – Rev. 1:1e-2; 22:8
    7. It is designed to be a blessing to those who read, hear, and heed its message. (purpose) – Rev. 1:3

B. Seven letters
    1. What Christ thinks of the church: consistent pattern in each letter.
        a. Christ is revealed among the churches.
        b. Commendation: "I know thy works…" – Rev. 2:2
        c. Condemnation: "I have somewhat against thee…." – Rev. 2:4
        d. Command: "He that hath and ear, let him hear…" – Rev. 2:7
        e. Commitment and Reward: "To him who overcometh…" – Rev. 2:7
    2. What is expected of the church: Marks of a true church.
        a. Ephesus: The church with a forgotten purpose. – Rev. 2:1-7 (love)
        b. Smyrna: The church with a fearless perseverance. – Rev. 2:8-11 (suffering)
        c. Pergamum: The church with a foolish paganism. – Rev. 2:12-17 (truth)

d. Thyatira: the church with a faithless prophet.
　　　　　– Rev. 2:18-29 (holiness)
　　　e. Sardis: the church with a famous past.
　　　　　– Rev. 3:1-6 (reality)
　　　f. Philadelphia: The church with a faithful passion.
　　　　　– Rev. 3:7-13 (opportunity)
　　　g. Laodicea: The church with a false prosperity.
　　　　　– Rev. 3:14-22 (wholeheartedness)

C.　A relationship of the church to Christ.
　　1. The church's vision of Christ. – Rev. 1
　　2. The church's life in Christ. – Rev. 2-3
　　3. The church's redemption through Christ. – Rev. 4-7
　　4. The church's witness to Christ. – Rev. 8-11
　　5. The church's conflict for Christ. – Rev. 12-14
　　6. The church's vindication by Christ. – Rev. 15-20
　　7. The church's eternal union with Christ. – Rev. 21-22

D.　Beatitudes in Revelation.
　　1. "Blessed is he that readeth, and they that hear the words of this
　　　　prophecy, and keep those things which are written therein for
　　　　the time is at hand." – Rev. 1:3
　　2. "… Blessed are the dead which die in the Lord from
　　　　henceforth…"- Rev. 14:13
　　3. "… Blessed is he that watcheth, and keepeth his garments, lest
　　　　he walk naked, and they see his shame." – Rev. 16:15
　　4. "…Blessed are they which are called unto the marriage supper
　　　　of the Lamb…." – Rev. 19:9
　　5. "Blessed and holy is he that hath part in the first resurrection
　　　　on such the second death hath no power…" – Rev. 20:6
　　6. "… blessed is he that keepeth the sayings of the prophecy of this
　　　　book." – Rev. 22:7
　　7. "Blessed are they that do his commandments, that they may
　　　　have right to the tree of life, and may enter in through the gates
　　　　into the city." – Rev. 22:14

E. Seven new things.
   1. New name. – Rev. 2:17; 3:12; 22:4
   2. New song. – Rev. 5:9; 14:3
   3. New heaven. – Rev. 21:1; (cf. Isa. 65:17; 66:22)
   4. New earth. – Rev. 21:1; (cf. II Pet. 3:3)
   5. New Jerusalem. – Rev. 21:2, 10; 3:12
   6. New conditions. – Rev. 21:3-5
   7. New heavenly home. – Rev. 21:10-22:5

F. Eternal principles of Revelation.
   1. The guaranteed presence of Christ in the church.
      – Rev. 1:12-13, 20
   2. Faithfulness to Christ regardless of tribulation.
      – Rev. 2:10; 12:11
   3. God is in control of the universe. All true government proceeds from God and is upheld by God. – Rev. 11:15-18; 15:3-4
   4. The church's unavoidable conflicts, assured safety, and ultimate triumph. Victory is a foregone conclusion. Faith triumphs over might. Death is not defeat! – Rev. 13:10; 14:12-13; 17:14
   5. The ultimate defeat of evil and Satan. – Rev. 20:10
   6. Eternal punishment for the wicked in Hell. – Rev. 21:8
   7. Eternal reward for the righteous in Heaven. – Rev. 22:14

Christ Revealed

The entire book of Revelation is "The Revelation of Jesus Christ."
– Rev. 1:1

1. Jesus Christ. – Rev. 1:1, 2, 5

2. A six point description of Christ. – Rev. 1:5-6
   a. The faithful witness. – Rev. 3:14
   b. The first-born of the dead. – I Cor. 15:20
   c. The ruler of the Kings of the earth. – Rev. 17:14; 19:16; I Tim. 6:15
   d. Him who loves us. – Rom. 8:37

e. Him who released us from our sins by His blood. – Eph. 1:7

f. Him who made us to be a kingdom of priests. – I Pet. 2:5, 9

3. Coming One. – Rev. 1:7; (cf. Dan. 7:13; Matt. 24:30)

4. Pierced One. – Rev. 1:7; (cf. Zech. 12:10; John 18:37)

5. Jesus. – Rev. 1:9; 12:17; 14:12; 19:10; 20:4; 22:16

6. Son of Man. – Rev. 1:13-20; 14:14; (cf. Ezek. 1:26-28; Daniel. 7:13-14)

    a. His robe. – Rev. 1:13

    b. His breasts. – Rev. 1:13

    c. His head. – Rev. 1:14

    d. His hair. – Rev. 1:14

    e. His eyes. – Rev. 1:14

    f. His feet. – Rev. 1:15

    g. His voice. – Rev. 1:15

    h. His right hand. – Rev. 1:16

    i. His mouth. – Rev. 1:16

    j. His face. – Rev. 1: 16

    k. His words of comfort. – Rev. 1:17a

    l. His claims. – Rev. 1:17b-18

        1. I am the first and the last. (eternal) – Rev. 2:8; 22:13

        2. I am the living one. (Immortal) – Luke 24:5

        3. I was dead. (sacrificial) – Heb. 2:9

        4. I am alive forevermore. (triumphant) – Rev. 4:9

        5. I have the keys of death and of Hades. (sovereign) – Rev. 3:7; Matt. 16:19

    m. His command. – Rev. 1:19

    n. His explanation. – Rev. 1:20

7. Christ walks among the churches as the Divine Overseer or Shepherd.

    a. The One who holds the seven stars. – Rev. 2:1; (cf. 1:20)

    b. The first and the last, who was dead, and has come to life. – Rev. 2:8

c. The One who has the sharp two-edged sword. – Rev. 2:12

d. The Son of God. – Rev. 2:18

e. He who has the seven Spirits of God. – Rev. 3:1

f. He who is holy, true, and has the key of David. – Rev. 3:7

g. The Amen, the faithful and true witness, the beginning of the creation of God. – Rev. 3:14

8. He who searches the minds and hearts. – Rev. 2:23; (cf. Acts 1:24)

9. The Lion that is from the tribe of Judah. – Rev. 5:5; (cf. Gen. 49:9; Heb. 7:14)

10. The root of David. – Rev. 5:5; 22:16; (cf. Isa. 11:1, 10; Rom.15:12)

11. Lamb. (used 28 times) Christ as the Lamb recalls the Passover Lamb of the Old Testament (Ex. 12) and the redemption available through Him, John 1:29, 36; I Cor. 5:7, I Pet. 1:18-19.

a. The slain Lamb worthy of praise. – Rev. 5:6, 8, 12

b. The reign of the Lamb. – Rev. 5:13; 6:1; 7:9, 10; 14:1; 21:22-23; 22:1, 3

c. The wrath of the Lamb. – Rev. 6:16; 14:10

d. The blood of the Lamb. – Rev. 7:14; 12:11; 13:8

e. The leadership of the Lamb. – Rev. 7:17; 14:4; 21:14

f. The song of the Lamb. – Rev. 15:3-4

g. The victorious Lamb. – Rev. 17:14

h. The marriage of the Lamb. – Rev. 19:7, 9; 21:9

i. The Lamb's book of life. – Rev. 21:27; (cf. Rev. 3:5; 13:8; 17:8; 20:12, 15)

12. Lord (Master). – Rev. 6:10; 11:8, 15

13. The Judge and Avenger of those who killed the martyrs. – Rev. 6:10; 19:2

14. Shepherd. – Rev. 7:17; (cf. John 10:11; Heb. 13:20; I Pet. 2:25; 5:4)

15. Christ (Messiah). – Rev. 11:15; 12:10; 20:4, 6

16. He will reign forever and ever. – Rev. 11:15; (cf. Dan. 2:44; 7:14, 27)

17. Son, male child, Child. – Rev. 12:4-5, 13

18. He who sat on the cloud. – Rev. 14:15-16; (cf. I Thess. 4:17)

19. Lord of lords and King of kings. – Rev. 17:14; 19:16; I Tim. 6:15

20. Bridegroom or Husband. – Rev. 19:7; 21:2, 9; 22:17; (cf. Rom. 7:1-4)

21. Multiple description of Christ. – Rev. 19:11-16; cf. 1:13-20
    a. He is called faithful and true. – Rev. 19:11
    b. He judges and wages war in righteousness. – Rev. 19:11
    c. His eyes. – Rev. 19:12
    d. His head. – Rev. 19:12
    e. His robe. – Rev. 19:13
    f. His name is called the Word of God. – Rev. 19:13; (cf. John 1:1)
    h. His armies. – Rev. 19:14
    i. His mouth. – Rev. 19:15
    j. His rule and wrath. – Rev. 19:15
    k. His title: King of kings, and Lord of lords. – Rev. 19:16

22. The Judge on the Great White Throne. – Rev. 20:11-15; 22:12; cf. Matt. 16:27; John 5:22, 27; Acts 10:42; 17:31; Rom. 2:16; II Cor. 5:10

23. The Temple or Sanctuary of Heaven. – Rev. 21:22

24. The alpha and the Omega, the first and the last, the beginning and the end. – Rev. 22:13; 1:17; use of God in Rev. 1:8 and 21:6. Alpha and Omega are the first and last letters of the Greek alphabet, similar to saying, "Jesus is the A and Z."

25. The Bright Morning Star. – Rev. 22:16; (cf. Rev. 2:28; Matt. 2:2; Num. 24:17)

26. The Lord Jesus who promises, "I am coming quickly." – Rev. 22:7, 12, 20; 3:11; (cf. I Cor. 16:22)

Author's Note

It is hoped by this author that all who use this study guide to the Bible will find it helpful and informative. In the opinion of the author the Bible is the inspired word of God, 2 Tim. 3:16, and must be respected as such. Man has no right to alter, manipulate or corrupt the word of God in any way. When man changes the word of God in some fashion he no longer has the word of God but a contrivance of man, Deut. 12:32, Deut. 4:2. So often men attempt to make the word of God more palatable or more acceptable for a majority of people so much so that they make the word of God of none effect in their lives and the lives of those they teach, Mark 7:13. The Bible is not up for private interpretation, II Pet. 1:20. If man truly believes that the Bible is inspired by God he will respectfully leave it alone and accept it as God has given it to man. When man changes the Bible in some fashion he essentially is making the point that God in all His infinite wisdom did not give man what man needed but instead made some grave errors that man has attempted to correct by making changes to the Bible. This line of thought is incorrect and will lead man to his final doom. The author believes and so do many more Christians that God, because He is God cannot make mistakes. To think even for a moment that God is capable of a mistake makes Him no longer God. Psalms 18:30 clearly tells us that God's way is perfect, therefore God is perfect. God gave man the Bible to direct his steps, Psalms 119:105, and contained therein is all the knowledge and wisdom man will ever need to have life and fulfill the will of God, II Pet. 1:3.

The Bible is well able to explain itself and man need not bother trying to create allegories and hidden messages from the pages of the Bible. God does not hold respect of persons, Acts 10:34, and He would not reveal knowledge to some and withhold it from others. God desires for all men to come to a knowledge of Him, II Pet. 3:9, and in order for that to occur He would need to give all mankind a word that they could all be able to understand and He has in the form of what we call the Bible.

Bibliography

A Glimpse at the Bible

Baxter, J. Sidlow. 1966. *Explore the Book*. (6vols. In 1) Grand Rapids, Michigan: Zondervan Publishing House.

Beers, V. Gilbert. 2007. *What everyone should know about the Bible*. Carol Stream, Illinois. Tyndale House Publishers, Inc.

Collett, Sideny. *All About The Bible*. Old Tappan, New Jersey: Fleming H. Revell Company, n.d.

Dowling, W.W. 1887. *The Bible Hand book*. Joplin, Missouri: College Press.

Geisler, Norman L. 1968. *Christ: The Key to Interpreting the Bible*. Chicago: Moody Press.

Henry, Carl F. H. ed. 1960. *The Biblical Expositor*. New York: A.J. Holman Company.

Keller, Werner. 1956. *The Bible as History*. New York: William Morrow and Company.

Lee, Robert. 1982. *The Outlined Bible*. Grand Rapids, Michigan: Zondervan Publishing House.

Lockyer, Herbert. 1966. *All the Books and Chapters of the Bible*. Grand Rapids, Michigan: Zondervan Publishing House.

Morgan, G. Campbell.1959. *An Exposition of the Whole Bible*. Old Tappan, New Jersey: Fleming H. Revell Company.

Morgan, G. Campbell. 1982. *Living Messages of the Books of the Bible*. Grand Rapids, Michigan: Baker book House.

Morgan, G. Campbell. 1964. *The Analyzed Bible.* Old Tappan, New Jersey: Fleming H. Revell Company.

Sawyer, Wyatt. 1955. *Panoramic Views of the Bible.* (3 vols.) Fort Worth, Texas: Sawyer Publications.

Scroggie, W. Graham. 1953. *Know Your Bible.* Old Tappan, New Jersey: Fleming H. Revell Company.

Morgan, G. Campbell. 1970. *The unfolding Drama of Redemption.* Grand Rapids, Michigan: Zondervan Publishing House.

Stringfellow, Alan B. 1978. *Through the Bible in One Year.* Tulsa, Oklahoma: Virgil W. Hensley, Inc.

Tidwell, J.B. 1966. *The Bible Book by Book.* Grand Rapids, Michigan: William B. Eerdmans Publishing Co.

Wegener G.S. 1963. *6000 Years of the Bible.* New York: Harper & Row Publishers.

Old Testament

Anderson, Bernard W. 1957. *Understanding the Old Testament.* Englewood Cliffs, New Jersey: Prentice-Hall, Inc.

Archer, Gleason L. 1964. *A Survey of Old Testament Introduction.* Chicago: Moody Press.

Beers, V. Gilbert. 2007. *What everyone should know about the Bible.* Carol Stream, Illinois. Tyndale House Publishers, Inc.

Bullinger, E.W. 2005. *The Companion Bible.* Grand Rapids Michigan: Kregel Publications.

Elkins, Garland and Thomas B. Warren, Eds. 1977.*The Living Messages of the Books of the Old Testament.* Jonesboro, Arkansas: National Christian Press.

Hailey, Homer. 1972. *UA Commentary on the Minor Prophets*. Grand Rapids, Michigan: Baker Book House.

Halley, Henry H. 2007. *Halley's Bible Handbook 25th Edition*. Grand Rapids, Michigan: Zondervan.

Harrison, Roland Kenneth.1969. *Introduction to the Old Testament*. Grand Rapids, Michigan: William B. Eerdmans Publishing Co.

House, Paul R. 1998. *Old Testament Theology*. Downers Grove, Illinois. Inter Varsity Press.

Lewis, Jack P. 1966. *The Minor Prophets*. Grand Rapids, Michigan: Baker Book House.

Schultz, Samuel J. 1960. *The Old Testament Speaks*. New York: Harper and Row Publishers.

Shelly, Rubel. 1982. *A Book-By-Book Study of the Old Testament*. Nashville: Twentieth Century Christian.

Stevenson, Dwight E. 1961. *Preaching on the Books of the Old Testament*. New York: Harper and Brothers Publishers.

Wood, Leon J. 1970. *A Survey of Israel's history*. Grand Rapids, Michigan: Zondervan Publishing House.

Wood, Leon J. 1979. *The Prophets of Israel*. Grand rapids, Michigan: Baker Book House.

Yates, Kyle M. 1942. *Preaching form the Prophets*. Nashville: Broadman Press.

New Testament

Carson, D.A., Douglas J. Moo, and Leon Morris. 1992. *An Introduction to the New Testament*. Grand Rapids, Michigan: Zondervan.

Beers, V. Gilbert. 2007. *What everyone should know about the Bible.* Carol Stream, Illinois. Tyndale House Publishers, Inc.

Bullinger, E.W. 2005. *The Companion Bible.* Grand Rapids, Michigan: Kregel Publications.

Dunnet, Walter. 1960. *An Outline of New Testament survey.* Chicago: Moody Press.

Elkins, Garland and Thomas B. Warren, Eds. 1976. *The Living Messages of the Books of the New Testament.* Jonesboro, Arkansas: National Christian Press.

Guthrie, Donald. 1971. *New Testament Introduction. 3vols. In 1.* Downers Grove, Illinois: Inter-Varsity Press.

Halley, Henry H.2007. *Halley's Bible Handbook 25th Edition.* Grand Rapids, Michigan, Zondervan, 2007.

Howard, V.E. and Hines J.L. 1976. *Howard-Hines Study of Revelation.* West Monroe, Louisiana: Central Printers & Publishers.

McRay, John. 1962. *A Survey Outline of the New Testament.* Searcy, Arkansas: Harding University Press.

Morris, Leon. 1991. *The First and Second Epistles to the Thessalonians.* Grand Rapids, Michigan: William B. Eerdmans Publishing Co.

Newman, Barclay M. 1966. *The Meaning of the New Testament.* Nashville: Broadman Press.

Shelly, Rubel. 1982. *A Book-By-Book Study of the New Testament.* Nashville: Twentieth Century Christian.

Stevenson, Dwight E. 1956. *Preaching on the Books of the New Testament.* New York: Harper and Row Publishers.

Stott, John R.W. 1964. *Basic Introduction to the New Testament.* Downers Grove, Illinois: Inter-Varsity Press.

Tenny, Merrill C. 1961. *New Testament Survey.* Grand Rapids, Michigan: William b. Eerdmans Publishing Co.

Thiessen, Henry Clarence. 1950. *Introduction to the New Testament.* Grand Rapids, Michigan: William b. Eerdmans.

Vos, Howard F. 1973. *Beginnings in the New Testament.* Chicago: Moody Press.

If you have any questions or desire more information the author can be contacted at kerusso.of.truth@gmail.com.

Churches desiring to use this book in a class setting contact the publisher/author for special pricing by quantity.